KENYA

Publisher: Aileen Lau
Editor: Irene Khng
Assisting Editor: Aileen Lau
Design/DTP: Sares Kanapathy
Karen Leong
Brian Wyreweden
Sarina Afandie
Illustrations: Soon Chieu Gwat
Cover Artwork: Susan Harmer
Maps: Hong Li

Published in the United States by
PRENTICE HALL GENERAL REFERENCE
15 Columbus Circle
New York, New York, 10023

ISBN 0-671-87901-4

Titles in the series:
Alaska - American Southwest - Australia - Bali - California - Canada - Caribbean - China - England - Florida - France - Germany - Greece - Hawaii - India - Indonesia - Italy - Ireland - Japan - Kenya - Malaysia - Mexico - Nepal - New England - New York - Pacific Northwest USA - Singapore - Spain - Thailand - Turkey - Vietnam

USA MAINLAND SPECIAL SALES
Bulk purchases (10+copies) of the Travel Bugs series are available at special discounts for corporate use. The publishers can produce custom publications for corporate clients to be used as premiums or for sales promotion. Copies can be produced with custom cover imprints. For more information write to Special Sales, Prentice Hall Travel, Paramount Communications Building, 15th floor, 15 Columbus Circle, New York, NY 10023.

Printed in Singapore

A DISCLAMER
Readers are advised that prices fluctuate in the course of time and travel information changes under the impact of the varied and volatile factors that affect the travel industry. Neither the author nor the publisher can be held responsible for the experiences of readers while traveling. Readers are invited to write to the publisher with ideas, comments, and suggestions for future editions. The publisher and the author expressly disclaim any responsibility for any liability, loss or risk, personal or otherwise which is incurred as a consequence, directly or indirectly, in the use of this book.

SAFETY ADVISORY
Whenever you're traveling in an unfamiliar city or country, stay alert. Be aware of your immediate surroundings. Wear a moneybelt and keep a close eye on your possessions. Be particularly careful with cameras, purses, and wallets, all favorite targets of thieves and pickpockets.

KENYA

Text by Christine Pemberton

Project Editor
Irene Khng

Prentice Hall Travel

New York London Toronto Sydney Tokyo Singapore

C O N T E N T S

INTRODUCTION

HISTORY, GOVERNMENT & ECONOMY

PHYSICAL PROFILE

MEET THE PEOPLE

C O N T E N T S

C O N T E N T S

WHAT TO DO

C O N T E N T S

The Kenyans possess a strong sense

of tribal identity underneath the

cloak of modernity.

The waterfront has been a symbolic door keeping the country

open to the outside

world ever since the 1st century AD.

Endowed with an abundance of nature dominated principally

by wildlife, Kenya's flora also mark the landscape, particularly after a good shower.

Introduction

"J*ambo Bwana*". Hello, sir, and "*Karibu*" - welcome to Kenya, a country which demands superlatives to describe it, and still leaves you searching for yet more expressive ways of describing the space, the raw beauty of the landscape and the breathtaking spectacle of the wildlife.

For many visitors, Kenya is their first experience of going on safari, their first exposure to the wealth of wildlife roaming the endless, acacia-studded grasslands. Kenya rarely disappoints, for no one can remain unmoved by the sheer size and grandeur of the vast open plains, nor the thrill of seeing herds of zebra, wildebeest and giraffe wandering together in search of food. No one can remain indifferent, when, in the early morning light, your safari driver points

The shy smile of a Kamba woman whose tribe forms the fourth largest ethnic group in Kenya.

A water hole at a quiet time of the day and the Chyulu Hills in Tsavo West.

Cheetah leitmotif.

quietly and you see your first pride of lions spending a quiet moment together.

The first time visitor may well arrive in Kenya with certain preconceived notions. He or she will have seen ***Out of Africa***, and possibly the Gregory Peck classic, ***The Snows of Kilimanjaro***. They may have read Karen Blixen, Beryl Markham and Robert Ruark and they think they know what to expect.

Yet however much preparation you may have done, nothing will detract from the visual impact of this beautiful country: the snowy peak of Mount Kilimanjaro glimpsed in the early morning; drifting over the Maasai Mara in a hot air balloon; Maasai shepherds striding down a dusty track, their vivid red cloaks a splash of color against the dry tones of the landscape; the surface of Lake Bogoria completely hidden by thousands upon thousands of dazzling pink flamingoes; the "Big Five" – rhino, elephant, giraffe, cheetah and lion; the spectacular annual wildebeest migration. And, wherever you go, the friendliest people on earth, everyone ready with a smile and a happy "*Jambo*" – hello.

Hard Facts

The land where civilization began and which today is dedicated to wildlife and the ecology, Kenya is a study in contrasts, both geographic and climatic. To the north lie Ethiopia and Sudan and

A splendid vision of the crowned crane.

the parched, arid desert around Lake Turkana while Mount Kenya is snow-capped, its fertile lower slopes devoted to farming. The north-eastern plains, as arid as Turkana, give way to the hot and humid coastal belt.

More than 40 different ethnic groups compose the mosaic that is Kenya, ranging from tribes whose way of life has changed little over centuries to Muslim boat-builders in the Lamu archipelago, from white Kenyan farmers settled in the highlands for generations to the prosperous Indian traders. There are Christians and Muslims, animists and Hindus, sophisticated town dwellers and timeless villagers.

Although Kenya has a strong agricultural base with large sisal, coffee and tea plantations, the country's priority is tourism, particularly wildlife tourism. Safaris are the lifeblood of Kenya and the country is efficiently geared towards providing the highest standards of infrastructure in the most dramatically remote locations.

Part of the magic of a Kenyan safari is knowing that you are miles and miles from the nearest town, that your tented camp is remote and surrounded by the bush, and knowing with equal certainty that there are lions out there, and that the dry martini that the barman is preparing will be perfectly mixed. You arrive back in camp after a bumpy, dusty drive, miles from even the nearest village, and find a huge buffet lunch waiting. Surrounded by endless plains and

The bright bougainvillea contribute generously to the dusty color of Kenya.

thorn trees and the occasional wildlife at the very least, there is a chilled Tusker beer ready for you when you have finished your hot shower. Unspoilt nature and pampered luxury, small wonder that a Kenyan safari is an experience that always lives up to expectations.

You do not need to be especially knowledgeable in advance about flora and fauna in order to enjoy your safari,

Fast Facts

Geography : The Republic of Kenya is situated in East Africa, and covering 582,646 sq km (224,901 sq miles), including 13,600 sq km (5,250 sq miles) of inland water, it consists of a small coastal strip on the Indian Ocean and a much larger interior. The Equator passes through the country. Its neighbors to the north are Sudan and Ethiopia, Somalia is to the northeast, Tanzania to the south and Uganda is to the west, part of the boundary running through Lake Victoria, the largest lake in Africa.

There are six mountains in Kenya which are over 3,000 m (9,900 ft), the highest being Mount Kenya at 5,199 m (17,058 ft).

Population : about 23 million, but with one of the highest birth rates in the world. This figure is expected to increase substantially in the closing years of the century. The population is overwhelmingly African though there are Asian and European minorities who wield an economic importance much greater than one would expect of their small numbers.

Capital : Nairobi is less than a hundred years old but has grown into a large, busy city with top class hotels, tower blocks, office complexes and an efficient infrastructure.

Government : President Daniel arap Moi is only the second President in the country's 30 years of independence, and he governs over a one-party state. There is a legislative assembly, the majority of whose members are elected. Kenya is a member of the Commonwealth.

Flag : The country's flag is a black, red and green striped background with a shield and two crossed spears. The national motto is the one word *Harambee* which means "Let's all pull together", an emotive word which was used during the long struggle for independence and which Kenyans take very seriously today, aware of the need for the country's otherwise diverse tribal groupings to work together to preserve their identity.

Economy : The mainstay of Kenya's economy is agriculture which employs nearly 80 percent of the population and accounts for more than half of the country's export earnings, yet tourism remains the single biggest earner of foreign currency. The tourist industry is well organized, highly efficient and the country is at pains to protect its wildlife which remain the biggest draw for the one million visitors who arrive annually in Kenya.

Religion : Along the coast, most people are Muslims while inland, the majority of people are Christians. The major Christian sects are represented in Kenya, from Roman Catholicism to the Seventh Day Adventist church, as well as many African Christian sects unique to the country which incorporate both Christian and African beliefs.

Language : Among the 40 major tribes represented in Kenya, there is naturally a wide variety of languages spoken but the official languages of the country remain English and Kiswahili and in many parts of the country, you will find people who speak excellent English.

Currency : The Kenyan unit of currency is the shilling which is subdivided into 100 cents.

though clearly, a little pre-safari homework will come in useful. Even if you are a complete novice in the wildlife department, within a day or so, you will find yourself able to identify a Thomson's gazelle from a Grant's gazelle, convincingly and effortlessly.

Even if you think you are not particularly "into" wildlife, the panorama is so dramatic, the sheer numbers of animals you can see in one day is so great, that you cannot fail to be enthused. And then, one day, you will realize that you have just spent five enthralled minutes watching a gorgeously colored Lilac-breasted Roller through your binoculars, you, who thought you cared little for birds and knew even less. The safari magic has taken hold.

Maasai children in front of their dung and twig hut.

Wildlife Aside

Even though the emphasis on a Kenyan holiday is definitely on viewing the country's rich and varied fauna, there is more to Kenya than just early morning game drives. For the historian, the coastal belt has a particularly fascinating culture complete with ruined forts and mosques for it was formerly a series of warring Muslim city states. Mombasa is a study in contrasts, the timeless Swahili way of life offsetting the relaxed

holiday lifestyle of the beach-front hotels. The coast offers an excellent range of watersports, and around the northern Lamu archipelago, you can fish, dive, learn wind sailing or charter a dhow for a long trip to the remoter islands.

For the ethnologist, Kenya offers rich rewards for the country is home to a wide range of tribes, each with its own culture, language and way of life. Although you will see tribesmen and women as you travel the country, it is not always easy to go into their villages and meet the people on their home territory. Follow the advice of your Kenyan guides when it comes to photographing villagers in particular. Some, like the Maasai, do not like being photographed, whereas children, like their counterparts the world over, are usually happy to pose for you.

Kenya is a country that is still young, politically speaking, for it only obtained its independence from Britain in December 1963, yet in those 30 years, much progress has been made. Kenya is a country that has been mercifully free from military "coups d'état" in a continent that sadly has too many. Land redistribution, improved education, medical care and housing have given the country a degree of economic and political stability lacking in many of its neighbors. However, with improvement in the quality of life and political and economic stability Kenya is facing a new problem. The country currently has an exceptionally high birth rate and unless this is curbed, problems are bound to follow in its wake. Although tribal differences still simmer below the surface, often centering on land rights and occasionally erupting into violence, the visitor will see or feel virtually no tension or unease. Kenya remains one of the world's ultimate destinations. "*Karibu*" and welcome.

History

Historical information about Kenya is divided between two basic sources, written records and archeological evidence. The earliest written records we have all concern the outward-looking coastal region, which, for centuries, traded with the southern Arab nations whereas written information about the vast Kenyan interior is scant. Prior to the 19th century, there is little reliable information about the interior which remained largely undocumented until the arrival of the Europeans in the second half of the 19th century. For clues to the development of civilization in the Kenyan heartland, we have to rely on archeology.

The simple elegance of the National Monument in the incongruous setting of Kenyan wildlife.

The Rift Valley, which runs through the center of Kenya, is now regarded as being the **cradle of civilization** and of mankind itself. Although theories and coun-

Olorgesailie, site of human habitation 400,000 years ago.

ter theories still abound, the East African Rift Valley may well have been the place where man first stood upright and started a life-time of wandering in search of food and water.

The pioneering work carried out by **Mary** and **Louis Leakey** from the 1930s onwards established many facts although much still remains to be discovered. The excavations carried out by the Leakeys in Kenya and in neighboring Tanzania uncovered **fossil remains** of *Zinjanthropus Boisei* or *Zinj*, the Nutcracker Man, regarded as an early ape man, and, later, of *Homo habilis* or Handy Man, a 10,000 to 12,000-year-old ancestor of modern man. The area around Lake Turkana is still yielding up its secrets with further fossilized clues to the origins of man.

When dealing with pre-history, firm dates are not easy to ascertain but what is clear is that over the centuries, Kenya became a major migratory route, a theory which is borne out by the fact that the country today is home to many of the major African tribes. The first migrants to arrive were tall, **Cushitic**-speaking pastoral nomads from Ethiopia who moved south to Kenya some 2,000 years BC in search of fertile land to graze their flocks. As the Kenyan climate changed over the centuries, and the lakes dried up, the southern Cushites moved on eventually going as far south as central Tanzania.

A thousand years later, a second wave of nomads, the **Eastern Cushitics**

Stone tools on the Olorgesailie site are displayed as they had been found.

Frescos at Nairobi Museum depicting the country's national interest – wildlife.

or Yaaku, moved into Kenya settling in the central part of the country. The thousand years from around 500 BC, to AD 500 saw the constant arrival of different tribes from all over the African continent-Cushitic, Nilotic and Bantu — all drawn by the region's fertile land. Even up until the turn of this century, there was still much movement within the country including competition for land rights which was always of vital importance in what was then a totally agrarian society.

The Coast's Open Doors

All the early tribal migrations took place in the interior of the country, whereas the **coastal strip** had a very different history. Virtually cut off by natural barriers from the interior, the coast had a distinctly more outward-looking development. One of the earliest descriptions of the Kenyan coastal strip is from the log of a Greek explorer, **Diogenes**, who lived in Egypt and who visited the coast around AD 110. Diogenes noted the various types of merchandise at the Mombasa docks which even then included ivory and rhinoceros horn. Some 40 years later, another Egypt-based Greek, the geographer **Ptolemy**, incorporated some of his compatriot's details into his "map of the world".

From the 8th century onwards, Arabs and Persians began to visit the East African coast to trade, importing glass,

The Lunatic Express

Mombasa Railway Station.

There is a little poem written about the Mombasa-Uganda railway which was penned by Henry Labouchere, one of its fiercest opponents back in Victorian England :

> What it will cost no words can express,
> What is its object no brain can suppose,
> Where it will start from no one can guess,
> Where it is going to nobody knows.
> What is the use of it none can conjecture,
> What it will carry there's none can define,
> And in spite of George Curzon's superior lecture,
> It clearly is naught but a lunatic line.

And thereafter, the "Lunatic Express" it was to remain.

When George Whitehouse, a young English man, arrived in Mombasa on 11 December 1895, he had an impressive title, Chief Engineer of the planned Mombasa-Lake Victoria Railway, which rather masked the reality of the job for his brief was both very specific and totally vague at the same time. He had been ordered, quite simply, to build a railway across East Africa, but the authorities in London had been unable to give him any proper maps and plans. Three years earlier, an admittedly sketchy preliminary survey had been carried out and this was the sum total of Whitehouse's information. The only thing he knew for sure was that London expected him to complete the railway well within the four-year time frame they had naively imposed.

The cost of constructing this 1,058-kilometer (657-mile) railway was conservatively estimated at £3 million which the British tax-payer was expected to underwrite. The proposed railway had already aroused much political passion back in London. The government, led by Lord Salisbury, had declared that in one fell swoop, the railway would increase commerce, open up East Africa to development and settlement and wipe out the then flourishing slave trade to which Britain was implacably opposed.

The opposition party in Parliament refused to accept these arguments maintaining that the railway was nothing but a British bid to expand her imperial possessions. According to their argument, the railway would enable Britain to control the strategically important River Nile because through the Nile, Britain would effectively control Egypt, and through Egypt, the Suez Canal – which had to be protected at all costs to safeguard the route to the jewel in the Britannic imperial crown, India.

And it was George Whitehouse who had to handle this thorny issue.

textiles and wine and exporting ivory, rhinoceros horn and slaves. Many of the local people were converted to Islam and some of the visitors settled down, laying the foundation for the distinctive **Swahili** character of the Kenyan coast

The Reality

The building of this railway was to become one of East Africa's classic sagas for with a cocktail of politics, business, tribal warfare, man-eating lions and slave traders, how could the result be anything but colorful?

For the Chief Engineer, however, most of his problems were logistic rather than political considerations. He had no workers, no equipment, a sketch map and a pressing deadline to meet. First of all, workers to build the railway tracks were needed and so laborers were brought over to East Africa from India including thousands of coolies, craftsmen and clerks. After completing their contract, many returned to India but many more settled down in East Africa, laying the foundations for today's prosperous and substantial Indian community in Kenya.

The logistics of not only building the railway itself but also of providing suitable living conditions for the thousands of workers was mind-boggling. For example, huge quantities of drinking water were required but Mombasa, from where the whole project begun, could not hope to supply a fraction of the daily requirement. Huge quantities of material had to be shipped to Mombasa – for nothing was available locally – but before anything could even be off-loaded, docks had to be built. Wharves, warehouses, accommodation, repair shops, work-shops – all these had to be built from scratch before the construction of the first railway track could even be contemplated.

The land also had to be cleared of the tenacious creepers and thorn bushes proliferating the region. The inhospitable climate took a huge toll on the coolies who suffered from malaria, dysentery and tropical ulcers. Deserts had to be crossed, and rivers had to be spanned. The immensity of the Rift Valley had to be tamed, with its steep escarpments. Man-eating lions terrorized the workers at Tsavo (see box story p.178).

And then there were the Nandi tribesmen. They took quite a fancy to the steel and copper used in the construction of the railway which they coveted for making jewelry and weapons. They helped themselves liberally to all the goodies that the toiling coolies kindly spread out for them every day, but, as the remarkably reasonable Sir Charles Eliot, a former East African Commissioner, wrote, "One can imagine what thefts would be committed on a European railway if the telegraph wires were pearl necklaces and the rails first-rate sporting guns, and it is not surprising that the Nandi yielded to the temptation."

The Price was Steep

Already costs were escalating and by June 1896, only six months after Whitehouse had landed in Mombasa, Parliament was being asked to approve an outlay of £5 million. Before Mrs Florence Preston would drive home the last nail in the last sleeper, on the shores of Lake Victoria on 21 December 1901, there had been accidents, derailments, attacks and harassment by tribes all the length of the railway. Hundreds of coolies fled the terror of the man-eating lions. Hundreds of pack animals had died. The huge workforce had had to endure the searing heat of the deserts as well as the Arctic temperatures in the mountainous highlands. And somewhere en route a town called Nairobi had come into existence.

The Lunatic Express still exists though now it runs through two countries, Kenya and Uganda. It is one of the most popular ways of traveling between Nairobi, unrecognizable from its earlier swampy origins, to Mombasa. Henry Labouchere would not be able to believe his eyes – an overnight trip on his much reviled Lunatic Express, one of the high spots of everyone's visit to Kenya? Pure lunacy.

(see chapter The Coast). Over the centuries, the trading links extended across to India, and even as far afield as China, and the string of coastal city states grew affluent on trade.

It was into this atmosphere of Islam

Lamu waterfront on the Kenyan coast.

and relative prosperity that the **Portuguese** sailed in 1498, rounding the Cape of Good Hope in search of the sea route to India. Under the command of Vasco da Gama, they sailed into Mombasa harbor to an unsympathetic welcome from the Arabs, but they received a royal welcome a little further north in Malindi. After a series of punitive raids over the next century, the Portuguese finally occupied Mombasa and set about building **Fort Jesus** from 1593-98 with admirable determination.

The coastal Arabs did not cede

Mombasa without a struggle, however, even with the help of the Turkish pirate **Ali Bey**, they were unable to dislodge the tenacious Portuguese who survived siege and sickness, living off supplies shipped in from their Indian stronghold, Goa. Portuguese rule was harsh, economically crippling for the local people and unpopular. The demise of the

Painful reminder of the Portuguese presence in Fort Jesus, Mombasa.

Portuguese finally took place after a siege of Fort Jesus which began in 1696 and lasted almost three years. When the fort surrendered, there were only 13 survivors out of 3,000, and the Arabs immediately slaughtered them all. By 1720, the last remaining Portuguese had left the coast for good. Other than a cross overlooking the sea at Malindi and Fort Jesus, virtually no other trace of the hated Portuguese rule remains today: unlike in Goa, for example, there are no religious or linguistic reminders of 200 years of European rule over the coast.

During the 18th century, the **Omanis** established themselves along the coastal belt, nominally, but ineffectively, under the control of the Sultan of Oman. Domestic intrigues, however, oc-

The narrow white-washed streets of Lamu are solid reminders of her Arabic heritage.

cupied most of their energies. When **Sultan Seyyid Said** came to the Omani throne in 1805, after assassinating the ruler, he decided to get the East African city states into some kind of order, but first he had to secure his own position in Oman. In 1822, with his throne safe and his income ensured through the highly lucrative slave trade (see box story on p.21), the Sultan sent an army to subdue the troublesome islands of Paté, Pemba and Mombasa. Mombasa was at the time ruled by the **Mazruis**, a very violent, local aristocratic Mombasa family who were reluctant to bow to the authority of Muscat.

At this stage, one of the more bizarre incidents in the coast's history occurred. Desperate in the face of the Omani build-up, the Mazruis asked the captain of a British ship, Captain Vidal, for protection against the Omanis, who, unfortunately for the Mazruis, were at that time British allies. When the offer was politely declined, the Mazruis went ahead anyway and ran up their own homemade version of the Union Jack over Fort Jesus. A few weeks later another British ship, under the command of a deeply religious anti-slaver by the name of Captain Owen, sailed into Mombasa harbor, and the Mazruis promptly petitioned Captain Owen for protection against the Omanis. On 7 February 1824, having extracted a promise from the Mazruis that they would abolish slavery, Owen proclaimed Mombasa a **British protectorate**, raised the

Ivory used to be a lucrative business in the region as far back as the 2nd century.

Union Jack, appointed his first officer, Lieutenant Reitz as proconsul and sailed off, after asking London for post-fact ratification of his treaty. The Mazruis, of course, promptly continued their trade in slaves, and within two months Reitz died of malaria. The end of this little saga came three years later, when the tardy response from London finally arrived, but it was not the expected reply. Owen's treaty was totally repudiated, the Union Jack was lowered, and the first British involvement in East Africa was over.

Johanne Rebmann, a German explorer, was the first European to see Mount Kilimanjaro though his report was initially refuted.

The Sultan of Oman regained his economic and political supremacy over the coast, dreaming of a larger African empire, and the slave trade continued to flourish, its wretched victims setting sail from his ports. In 1832, Seyyid Said moved his court to the island of **Zanzibar**, and the British, who were actively and vocally anti-slavery, established a consulate at his court and set about pressurizing the Sultan to ban slavery, which he finally did in 1847.

Explorers with a Mission

The **Germans**, who were also as keen as the British to abolish slavery and to convert Africa to Christianity, arrived in Kenya in 1844, and in pursuit of their religious and humanitarian aims, traveled far into the Kenyan interior. Two of the earliest German explorers were missionaries, **Johan Krapf** and **Johanne Rebmann**, whose motivation was the abolition of the slave trade and the conversion of Africa to Christianity. On 11 May 1848, the devout Rebmann became the first European to see Mount Kilimanjaro, but his subsequent report provoked much outrage in London where he was all but accused of perpetrating a hoax. Eighteen months later, in December 1849, the equally devout Krapf was the first European to see Mount Kenya.

Intrepid **British explorers** also began to push further and further into the

The Slave Trade

One of the earliest commodities to be shipped onto the dhows leaving *Zinj*, or "the land of the black people", and sailing to Arabia and the Far East was human. Along with the rhinoceros horn and the elephant tusks, slaves were regarded as another highly profitable African export.

The slave trade existed for centuries, but when it came to the notice of the European nations in the 19th century, the degree of outrage it caused was to have far-reaching effects not only along the coast, but on East Africa as a whole. Committed to the eradication of the trade in human beings, the early missionaries and explorers set out to try and convert, wheedle, persuade or force the Arabs and Swahilis to outlaw the practice. The anti-slavery movement was to become one of the main wedges used to "open up" the African interior.

But first, how did the slave trade work? In the 19th century, when Seyyid Said, the Sultan of Zanzibar, ruled over coastal East Africa, caravans of several hundred men, led by Arab and Swahili traders, would leave the coast for the interior, a world which was still unmapped and virtually unknown to the outside world. They would trek into the interior, in search of ivory and slaves, and, abhorrent as both trades now appear, there is one thing positive to be said for these slavers. They were the first real explorers of East Africa who opened up the trails which later European explorers would follow.

A Profitable Business

Slaves of all ages were bought for beads, pieces of cloth or grain, and were bought cheaply, though they would later be sold in the coastal slave markets for large profits. After being captured, the slaves were yoked and were forced to transport the ivory tusks which formed the other half of the caravan's merchandise.

Victorian literature about the "Dark Continent" is rife with the horrors of the slave trade, of the bestiality of the traders, of the enormous loss of life, and of the shaming indignity inflicted on human beings. The depopulation of the East African interior during the 19th century was massive, with estimates ranging from a quarter to half a million people each year.

Both ivory and slaves were hugely profitable, and Zanzibar, where the Sultan lived, grew rich on the trade, while thousands of miles away in Europe, the tide of public opinion became more vociferously anti-slavery. Slavery had been abolished in Great Britain by the late 18th century and in 1807 it was outlawed in the British Empire, despite the powerful West Indian sugar lobby. The anti-slavery movement quickly spread across the channel to France, Spain and Portugal.

Anti-slavery Initiatives

Although Zanzibar was by no means the only country dealing in slaves, because of the Anglo-Omani alliance, the Omani Sultan of Zanzibar came under British pressure to outlaw the trade. Since the Sultan also ran a highly efficient and enormous slave operation, the British felt that it was vital to crush it. Initially, gentle overtures were made by the British to Seyyid Said, who just as gently ignored them, but over the years the language of the courtly exchanges between the two countries became tougher. Oman was regarded as an important defence outpost on the vital route to India, and, ever sensitive to anything which might rock the India boat, especially with the hated Napoleon in the wings, the British had to handle Seyyid Said carefully.

Nevertheless, slavery had to go, and by 1847, the export of slaves from Zanzibar to the Persian Gulf was banned. Banning the trade was one thing, ensuring that the ban was enforced was quite a different matter. With only a handful of ships available to patrol the East African coast and with a host of procedures and exceptions to the treaty, the British were initially unable to enforce their rules with any degree of success.

In 1873, a British mission, armed with a new, much stricter anti-slavery treaty arrived in Zanzibar, by then ruled by Barghash bin Said. Barghash did all he could to avoid the issue, for abolishing slavery spelt economic ruin for him, but within a few months he was forced to agree.

...The Slave Trade

By 1876, he had outlawed slave caravans in the interior, and though the number of slaves inevitably dropped, there were always abuses.

What remained was to outlaw the actual status of slavery, for only trading in slaves had been banned. Many European missionaries set up freed-slave settlements along the coast, especially around Mombasa, where they harbored those slaves who managed to escape. This was highly laudable, but, paradoxically, illegal since slavery itself had still not been banned. Amazingly, the institution of slavery remained legal until 1907.

Back in London, a body of opinion felt that a severe blow to the slave trade would be dealt by the opening up of the country. And in true Victorian thinking, the children of the British Industrial Revolution could think of no better way of opening up East Africa than by building a railway line across it. The "Lunatic Express" was to be the final nail in the coffin of the hated slave trade.

heart of Africa, driven by a variety of motives. There was the firmly rooted Victorian conviction that it was the virtual duty of any good 19th-century explorer to propagate Christianity and stamp out slavery as he hacked his way across the "Dark Continent". Then there was the strong driving scientific curiosity. And there was also a healthy dose of political rivalry which viewed with distrust any moves by the Germans to expand into Africa.

When the Germans produced a rough map of the East African interior showing a large inland sea or lake, the quest began in earnest to find out if this was indeed the source of the River Nile. In 1856, Richard Burton and John

Hanning Speke set out from Zanzibar, to try and discover whether this lake was indeed the head of the Nile.

One of the most colorful and epic expeditions was the one to Maasai land, led by an irrepressibly confident 26-year-old-Scot called **Joseph Thomson**. Thomson set off in March 1883 with a small party, hardly any of whom could

Thomson Falls was discovered by the young explorer Joseph Thomson on one of his epic expeditions.

even fire a rifle, and proceeded to map most of modern day Kenya, with the exception of the northern desert region. He was constantly troubled by the Maasai whom he alternately scared or amazed with a variety of tricks including removing his false teeth and making Eno's salts froth in a glass, all the while beating a trail across Kenya.

Thomson marched from the base of Kilimanjaro north to Lake Naivasha, and continued further north to the Aberdare mountain range where he saw Mount Kenya as Krapf had indeed re-

London cabs queueing outside Norfolk Hotel in Nairobi, remnants of the colonial presence in the country.

ported. He pushed further north to Lake Baringo, crossed the western plains, and returned to the coast via Lake Victoria. As he traveled, he named the Aberdares after the President of the Royal Geographical Society and a waterfall after himself, Thomson's Falls.

Thomson's adventures inspired other explorers to set out to fill in the few blanks in his charts and maps. An expedition led by the rich Austro-Hungarian Count Teleki von Szek crossed the Kikuyu heartland and discovered **Lake Turkana** in the extreme north of the country, which was named Lake Rudolf, in honor of the Austrian Crown Prince. An American expedition, led by Donaldson Smith and William Chanler, mapped the course of the **Tana River** and the plains of the northeast.

And concurrently with all these expeditions, the Germans continued with their aggressive push into East Africa. One particularly enterprising mercenary, **Carl Peters**, would persuade illiterate tribal chieftains to sign grandly titled "Treaties of Eternal Friendship" with Germany which trans-

The railway, a painful and impossible task, as realized today.

ferred vast tracts of land at the same time in her favor.

In 1886, with the prevailing 19th-century European disregard for indigenous rights, the British and the Germans drew up an agreement and coolly partitioned their historic "spheres of interest": what is today Tanzania went to the Germans and Kenya and Uganda went to the British. The Sultan of Zanzibar was allowed to retain a 16-kilometer (10-mile) wide strip of land along the coast, as a British Protectorate. This situation remained until 1963 when the last Sultan of Zanzibar handed the territory over to the new Kenyan government.

In 1888, with capital of just under a quarter of a million pounds and a Royal Charter, the **Imperial British East Africa Company (IBEA)** came into existence, the brainchild of a Scot, Sir William Mackinnon. Despite its distinctly unimpressive headquarters in Mombasa, the IBEA soon set about coining its own money, printing its own postage stamps, and dispatching young officers to plant the IBEA flag deep in the heart of the Kenyan interior.

The British were still driven by their anti-slavery crusade and felt that one of the ways of stamping it out was to open up the country, and what better way of doing this than by building a railway — a railway which would run inland from Mombasa to Lake Victoria, a mere but very hostile 1,000 km away. The seeds of the **Lunatic Express** had been sown (see box story p.14).

Government

In 1899, when the Lunatic Express reached a flat, swampy stretch of land, the last level land before the steep, eastern escarpment of the Great Rift Valley, the project engineer, George Whitehouse, decided that this disease-ridden area would have to be his main upcountry railhead. The Maasai called the unprepossessing place *Nyrobi*, meaning "place of the cool waters", and from this decidedly unhealthy start, **Nairobi** began. (See chapter on Nairobi.)

Parliament House in Nairobi saw the country through to Uhuru.

As Nairobi progressed from a shanty-town to a semblance of a town, the colonial administration moved there from Mombasa and **white settlers** began to trickle into the country, lured by the prospect of land. They moved into the fertile highlands north of Nairobi, later to be known as the "White Highlands", beginning a saga of conflict and resentment with the Africans that would not be resolved until independence. The Maasai and the Kikuyu tribes both lost vast amounts of land to the ever increasing numbers of white set-

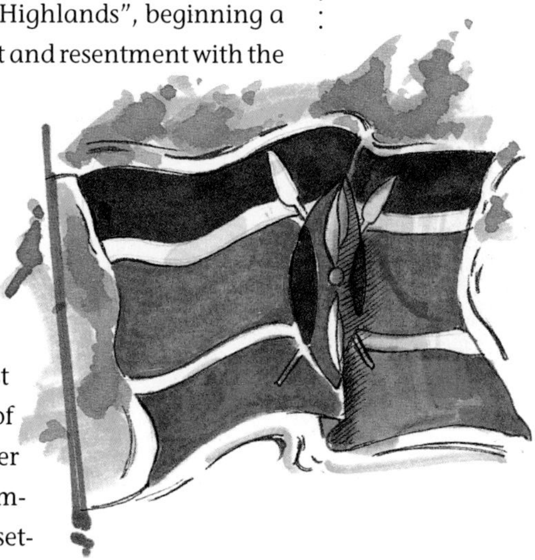

The Kenyan flag flies proudly for the African nation, the struggle for independence and the fertile land of the country.

tlers and the Kikuyu in particular harbored deep resentment as they saw the fertile land around their sacred Mount Kenya being taken away from them and given quite blatantly to the Europeans.

The leader of the white settlers in the early days of the 20th century was the colorful Lord Delamere, whose early agricultural experiments in Kenya were expensive failures. However, by the time **World War I** broke out, the settlers had begun to put the colony on a sounder economic footing with their mixed agricultural farms and extensive plantations. At the same time the war brought a temporary halt to white settlement as the British left the farms to the management of their wives and set off to fight the Germans in Tanganyika (today's Tanzania). Under the treaty of Versailles, Germany lost Tanganyika which was given to the British to control.

The war had another effect for the British Government offered land in the Kenyan highlands to war veterans at rock-bottom prices — but only to white veterans, not African veterans. White settlers flooded in and African resentment increased accordingly. Totally overlooked in the land distribution process, they suspected that the whole exercise was to create a permanent white man's Kenya. Poor and disappointed, increasing numbers of Kenyans, especially the bitter Kikuyu, formed political associations whose principal aim was the return of their land.

Statue of Jomo Kenyatta, the first President of Kenya who led the country to independence in 1964.

Awakening

An early leader of this Kikuyu political movement was **Harry Thuku** whose East African Association was the first pan-Kenyan nationalist movement. He was also supported by several influential Asians. Thuku's arrest by the colonial authorities in 1922 led to the massacre of at least 23 Africans, who had gathered in protest outside Nairobi Central Police Station. Thuku was exiled for seven years, being released only after he had agreed to co-operate with the colonial authorities, a stance which was to cost him the leadership of the Kikuyus.

Thuku's mantle passed to Johnstone Kamau who later changed his name to **Jomo Kenyatta** and became first the propaganda secretary of the East African Association, and then later the secretary-general of the Kikuyu Central Association (see box story p.32). In 1929, Kenyatta sailed to London to plead the Kikuyu cause, in which he failed, but he did tie up with the League Against Imperialism with which he traveled to Moscow, Berlin, and briefly back to Nairobi, before returning to 15 years of self-imposed exile in London.

Back in Kenya, the findings of the **Carter Land Commission**, convened to judge on land interests, only served to harden the differences between Africans and Europeans for it marked out permanent barriers between the white-owned farms and the African "reserves", barriers which were later confirmed by law. Inevitably political groups demanding greater African participation increased. It was hardly surprising therefore that the colonial government banned all African political associations in 1940.

World War II increased African discontent, for Africans fought in large numbers alongside their colonial masters, acquiring not only skills in the use of firearms, but also an awareness that the white man was far from invincible. When the demobbed soldiers returned to Kenya, there was no way they would accept a return to the old order. The status quo had changed irrevocably.

In 1946, Jomo Kenyatta returned from his years in exile to Kenya and quickly assumed the leadership of the **Kenya African Union** (KAU) for he was widely perceived to be the only person capable of uniting the various Kenyan political factions. As the KAU grew rapidly in size and as its demands became increasingly vocal, the attitude of the colonial authorities hardened. **Oath-taking ceremonies**, for long a traditional part of Kikuyu life, bound the participants to kill Europeans and Africans who were thought to be "collaborators", and by the early 1950s, the Kikuyu dominated **Mau Mau organization** had been formed, an organization pledged to violent resistance to European domination in Kenya.

Confrontation

By late 1952, the battle lines had been drawn. The Governor, Sir Evelyn Baring, refusing to compromise the interests of Kenya's white minority in any way at all, declared a state of emergency, imposed martial law and imprisoned Kenyatta and five colleagues.

The Mau Mau took to the hills, and in early 1953 the **Mau Mau rebellion** began. As their reign of terror got under way with the Mau Mau murdering whites and those "loyal" Kikuyu who continued to work for the Europeans, Kenyatta was put on trial charged with organizing the Mau Mau, a charge he always denied. He was sentenced to seven years' hard labor in the harsh, remote Turkana region.

The Mau Mau rebellion lasted until 1956 when they were defeated but during the three years of civil war, 13,500 Africans and a little over 100 Europeans were killed, and another 30,00 Kenyans had been imprisoned.

Although some political demands were finally conceded to by the colonial government and there was limited Afri-

The National Monument, a symbol of the people's struggle for independence.

can and Asian representation on the Legislative Council, there were still whites who demanded the partition of the country. White settlers began to leave the country. Kenyatta was sentenced to a further two years' imprisonment, but nevertheless was elected president "in absentia" of the political successor to KAU, a new party called the **Kenya African National Union**, generally referred to by its initials, KANU.

Growth of Local Parties

KANU advocated a firm central government while yet another party, the **Kenya African Democratic Union** or KADU, favored a decentralized federal form of government, principally in order to avoid Kikuyu domination. Leaders of both KANU and KADU, with the exception of the still imprisoned Kenyatta, attended the talks at Lancaster House in London to discuss the political future of a free Kenya. Following on these talks, general elections were held in February 1961 in which KANU fared better than KADU. But KANU, along with the Asian Kenya Freedom Party and a number of independent candidates refused to participate in government unless Kenyatta was released, and, as political pressure built up, he was finally released in August 1961.

Although KANU and KADU continued to be at loggerheads over the eventual form the government of an

Mzee Jomo Kenyatta

At his death in 1978, all of Kenya mourned the passing of *Mzee*, the respected elder, who led his country from colonial status to a successful independence. Destiny had transformed a poor Kikuyu peasant boy called Kamau Ngengi into a world leader and statesman.

Kamau Ngengi was probably born in 1894 in the highlands to the southwest of Mount Kenya, in what was then British East Africa. For the first ten years of his life, he lived the traditional life of a young Kikuyu peasant and from his grandfather, a diviner with a knowledge of magic and medicine, he learned a healthy respect for tribal spiritual knowledge. When he was ten years old, Kamau fell ill and was cured at a Church of Scotland mission hospital. This early and successful contact with Europeans was to be the first of many turning points in his life for the young boy ran away from home to join the mission where he attended school, learned English and, naturally, the Bible, and was baptized Johnstone Kamau.

The bright lights of Nairobi beckoned and within a few years, he had a job with the Nairobi Town Council, took the name Kenyatta and got married. In 1921, Harry Thuku, a Kikuyu, founded the East African Association (EAA) to protest against the white-settler dominance in the government. Kenyatta joined the Association in 1922 and after Thuku's arrest and deportation, continued to work for the EAA as their propaganda secretary. When the EAA was disbanded in 1925, its members regrouped as the Kikuyu Central Association (KCA), and three years later, Kenyatta resigned from his municipal job to become the secretary-general of the KCA.

In 1929, a proposal for a closer political union between the East African territories of Kenya, Uganda and Tanganyika was recommended to the agreement of the white settlers and the disapproval of the KCA and Kenyatta went to London to testify against the scheme. Although the British government refused to meet him, Kenyatta made contact with several groups which were critical of British colonial policy, and under the aegis of these groups, he spent the next few years traveling within Europe and then spent the next decade in England.

During this period Kenyatta studied anthropology at the London School of Economics, and in 1938 he published his thesis, "Facing Mount Kenya", a study of the traditional Kikuyu way of life. Another stage in his life was reached when Kenyatta again changed his name from

independent Kenya should take, Kenyatta agreed to a **coalition government** until independence. The first universal elections in the country held in the country took place in May 1963, with a landslide victory for Kenyatta and KANU.

On 1 June 1963, Jomo Kenyatta became the first Prime Minister of Kenya. In his inaugural speech, he spoke eloquently of ***Harambee*** or "pulling together", inviting Africans, Asians and Europeans to work together to build the nation.

Uhuru

The date for independence was fixed as 12 December 1963 and after decades of bloodshed and bitterness, ***Uhuru*** or independence, was finally a reality for Kenya. Over the ensuing months, a program of land purchase, funded by the British government, settled landless Africans on former European-owned farms.

By November 1964, when KADU crossed the floor of Parliament to join forces with KANU, Kenya became in

Johnstone to Jomo, meaning "burning spear".

Kenyatta remained in England during World War II while back in Kenya, the KCA was banned as being a potentially subversive organization. In September 1946, Kenyatta at last returned to Kenya to lead the newly formed Kenya African Union in a country still dominated politically by the white settlers. The country's discontent with the unyielding stance of the Europeans erupted in the 1952 Mau Mau rebellion. Kenyatta was arrested, put on trial and in April 1953, sentenced to seven years' imprisonment on charges of organizing the Mau Mau, an allegation he always refuted.

As the colonial government moved slowly towards African majority rule, Kenyatta was freed in 1961, and in early 1962, at the London conference, he negotiated the terms of his country's independence. On 12 December 1963, Jomo Kenyatta became Prime Minister of the newly independent Kenya, and a year later became the country's first President.

Despite his years of imprisonment at the hands of the British, Kenyatta remained one of the more pro-British leaders of Africa, and Kenya quickly became one of the most stable African countries, a legacy which survives today.

effect **a one-party state**. The bi-cameral Legislature became the single chambered National Assembly. A year to the day after Uhuru, on 12 December 1964, Kenya became a **republic** with Kenyatta as the first President. Under his leadership, the newly independent country avoided the upheavals of military coups and dictatorship that so plagued other newly independent African countries.

By 1965, **foreign investors** had begun to invest in Kenya. In 1967, Daniel Toroitich arap Moi, the current President, became Vice-President, and a year later in 1968, the still young country saw its athletes triumph in the Mexican Olympic Games, coming second only to the USA in the medal tally.

In the years before Kenyatta's death, the country progressed steadily along the road to **prosperity**: ten years after independence, the national income had doubled, the all-important tea and coffee production had increased and education was becoming increasingly widespread. When Kenyatta died on 22 August 1978, he was succeeded by **Vice-President Moi** in a seamless transition of authority.

The new President cracked down on corruption and nepotism and **dissolved all tribal organizations** in the wider interests of national unity. The unexpectedly dramatic year 1982 saw an abortive coup by the Kenyan Air Force which led to the disbanding of the entire air force and its replacement by a new unit, '82 Air Force.

Although achievements and developments continue, as does President Moi's rule, sadly the country's economy is far from strong. By 1980, Kenya had to import half of its grain, today the country has a huge budget deficit, and, potentially the most worrying statistic of all, Kenya has the highest rate of population growth in the world. Yet, on the positive side, Kenya's economic outlook is far healthier than any of its neighbors, with notably a solid tourist industry, and a stable society: no wars, no civil unrest, and a strong belief in democracy.

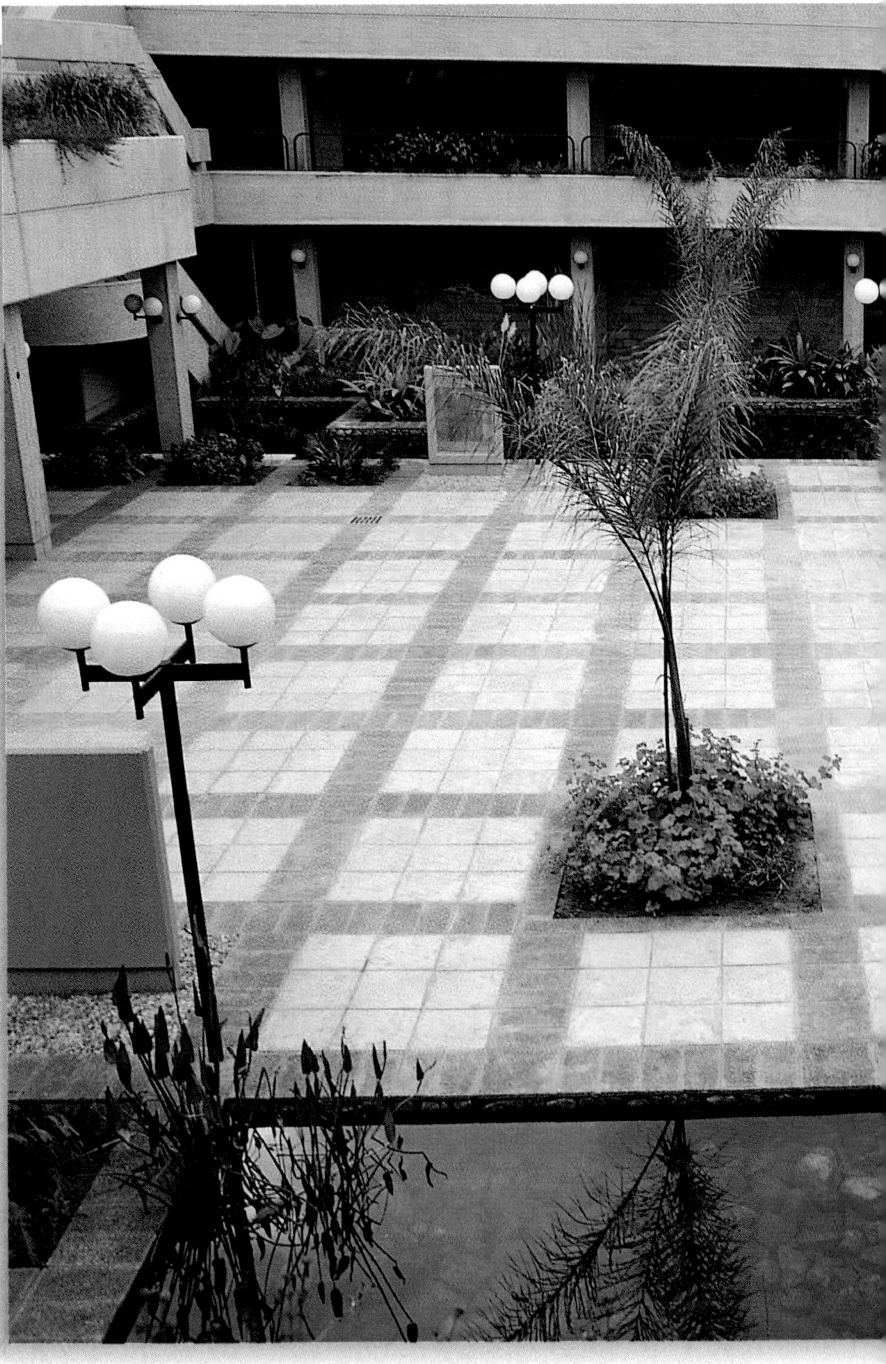

The cool interior of the UNEP (United Nations Environment Program) Building reflects Kenya's place in the international scene.

Economy

In November 1993, a group of international donors met in Paris and decided on a **support package** of US$850 million for Kenya. This was an especially welcome move in view of the country's recent cold-shouldering by Western donors. Economic pressure had been discreetly put on the country during the previous two years because the people who hold the international purse strings had not been happy with some aspects of the way Kenya was run.

Preparing for the balloon safari, a sport as well as a way to tour the terrain.

On 29 December 1992, the country's first pluralist **elections** in 26 years were held. Various import and export licences were abolished easing the path towards a freer trade movement. Inflation was beginning to slow down after reaching dizzying heights, and the Kenyan shilling was floated. Moves were made to abolish foreign exchange controls and four banks that had been involved in a financial scandal in early 1993 were

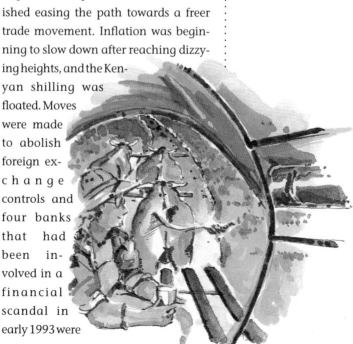

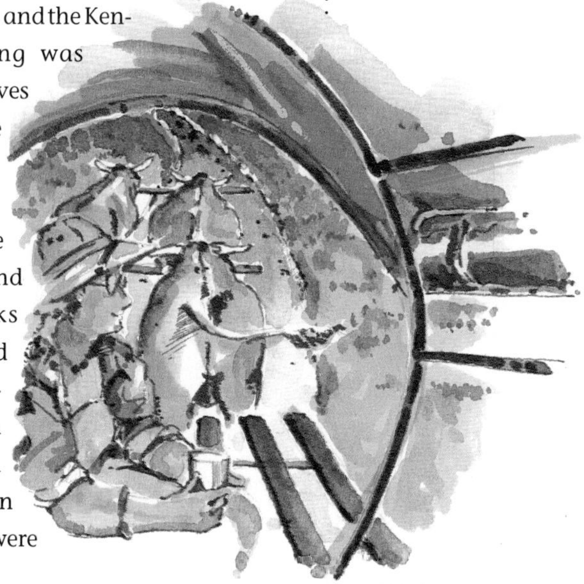

Nairobi has all the profiles of a modern city.

closed down.

Mixed Economy

Thirty years ago when Kenya gained its **independence**, the national economy was based on subsistence agriculture and the barter of goods, with a heavy reliance on foreign exchange which was earned through agricultural exports such as tea and coffee. After independence, the government tried to steer the country towards a **mixed economy** comprising both privately-owned and state-run businesses. Much of the Kenyan economy is today in private hands, including a substantial amount of foreign investment, but the government also shapes the country's development through "**parastatals**" or enterprises that it either fully or partly owns.

The aims of the mixed economy, namely economic growth, stability, employment and the maximization of foreign exchange earnings, were by and large successful for the first ten years after independence. The oil crisis of 1973, which saw oil prices rise dramatically, brought problems to Kenya as it did for many countries. This, combined with the periodic droughts from which the country suffers as well as an uncomfortably high rate of population growth have all proved to be major setbacks for Kenya. In the face of these problems, the country has been unable to maintain a favorable balance of trade, unemploy-

Grain drying in subsistence farming.

ment and poverty persist and the population continues to grow at far too fast a rate – a very worrying statistic for the 21st century.

Agriculture

Coffee is one of the country's principal cash crops.

In common with many of its East African neighbors, Kenya's economy is closely linked to its natural resources. In the case of Kenya, this means that **agriculture** is still one of the fundamental elements in the country's economy, employing nearly 80 percent of the population, with primary agricultural products accounting for more than 50 percent of export earnings. Agriculture not only supplies the manufacturing sector

Pineapple plantations are gaining in importance as Kenya steps up her export of fruit.

with raw material, but it also provides tax revenue and foreign exchange earnings to support the rest of the economy.

The principal **food crops** grown are maize, potatoes, cassava, beans, sorghum and fruit, and these are mainly cultivated as **subsistence farming**, in other words, just enough food is grown to feed the farmer and his family with no planned surplus left over for trading purposes. The principal **cash crops** grown are coffee, tea, tobacco, cotton, sisal and pyrethrum, cashew nuts and fruit. By and large, these crops are grown on large, privately owned plantations which employ contract labor. Of all of these agricultural products, **coffee** and **tea** are very important foreign exchange earners. Increasingly, the export of fruit, flowers and vegetables is bringing in large foreign exchange earnings, and in 1992, these products, for the first time, overtook coffee as a foreign exchange earner. Tea is still the highest agricultural earner.

In the absence of **irrigation**, rainfall is one of the dominant influences on agricultural output, and, as a result, on **population density**. It has been calculated that, without irrigation, arable agriculture requires a reliable annual rainfall of over 750 mm (30 in). Unfortunately for a country with such a heavy reliance on agriculture, in four years out of five, only 15 percent of Kenya can expect to receive this required amount of rainfall.

Around Lake Victoria, where rain-

Alkaline deposits from the hot springs have been mined for soda ash.

fall is higher, there is not only intensive agriculture but a high population density, and similarly along the coast, where there is good rainfall and settlement and trading links go back for centuries, there is a higher population density than in the vast, arid interior where life is, at best, lived at the subsistence level.

Some 70 percent of Kenya receives insufficient rainfall for crop cultivation since less than 500 mm (20 in) may fall in four years out of five. In such cases, the only feasible use for the land is **pastoral farming**. In the driest area of Kenya, in the deserts of the north and northeast, the camel is the principal animal and where precipitation is not quite so sparse, farmers may also own cattle, sheep, goats and a few donkeys. These animals form a **multi-purpose basis** for the livelihood and survival of their human owners providing milk, meat, blood, hides, wool or hair and transport. However, since all of these animals are dependent on land for grazing and browsing, which is often woefully inadequate, they must be kept on the move. Thus, a **nomadic way of life** has evolved which by its very nature places a limit on the accumulation of goods and physical possessions, as well as the provision of essential social and welfare services such as schools and hospitals.

Something of a social vicious circle has evolved from this pastoral, nomadic lifestyle. Although the inoculation of livestock has enabled people to enlarge

Lake Naivasha Hotel Gardens, one of the many hotels in a booming tourist industry.

their herds, this has had its downside since it has led to **overgrazing**. In a nomadic society, wealth is vested in the ownership of animals rather than in the ownership of land, so there is little incentive to conserve grazing land since it will only be used by someone else's herd. This **conflict** between traditional views and the urgent need to conserve the land is still far from being resolved.

The irrigation of arid areas such as Kenya's north-eastern deserts is limited by the amount of water that can be brought in from outside the region, and

in a drought prone country, this is extremely difficult to implement. The 70 percent of Kenya which needs irrigation in order to be cultivated is therefore dependent on water from outside: yet, tragically, only 3 percent of the country receives more than 1,250 mm (50 in) of rainfall per year, which is the minimal amount from which any considerable run-off can be expected. Only two of Kenya's rivers, the Tana and the Athi-Galana, manage to reach the sea from the highlands.

Where the land is less arid, as in the coffee plantations, irrigation is more promising and is used during the dry season or as a supplement during fluctuations in the rainy season. **Fish** and other marine products represent a small but locally important part of the country's natural resources.

Mineral Resources

Kenya's **mineral resources** are limited to the volcanic lava that covers much of the land, which provides only building stone, although the associated hot springs have formed alkaline deposits. These deposits can be mined for soda ash which is used in glass-making, but there is only one large-scale extraction of this, at Lake Magadi, in the south of the country.

Some limestone deposits along the coast and in the interior are mined for use in cement manufacture. Fluorite, which is used in metallurgy, is mined along the Kerio River in the north of the country. Although the ancient crystalline rocks have, through natural processes, formed good geological specimens, these are of little serious commercial value. They are only of retail value for tourism and little else.

Kenya has a very limited production of **coal**, just enough to run several

Diani Beach provides one of the perks to Kenya's coastal tourist industry.

The Tourist Dollar

Tourism has long been a key revenue source for Kenya.

Tourism in Kenya is a vital foreign exchange earner. The country knows this and has encouraged tourism in a big way. Kenya has superb wildlife and an impressive range of national parks, national game reserves and national game sanctuaries, all of which have been developed in the best possible way – protecting the game while providing creature comforts for the large number of visitors.

The country is geared to tourism and tourists in an efficient and organized way which, combined with the wildlife and the natural friendliness of the Kenyans, means that a stay in the country is a pleasure. Having said that, the country operates a two-tier system for just about everything concerned with the tourist industry whereby visitors pay vastly more than Kenyan residents for everything. In late 1993, entrance to any national park for Kenyan residents was 65 shillings, whereas non-residents paid 900 shillings – a cool 14 times as much. The same is true in hotels: one rate for residents and a much higher rate for non-residents.

small steel-rolling mills. Petroleum products, including jet fuel and diesel, are manufactured from imported crude at government-owned refineries near Mombasa. Engineering industries assemble machinery and motor vehicles from imported parts and components which are manufactured from imported raw materials.

Fifteen percent of the country's GDP is accounted for by **industry** which is relatively well developed and is centered around Nairobi and Mombasa. Most of this manufacturing activity is based on the processing of the country's agricultural output and agriculturally based industries account for about two-thirds of production.

Kenya has a meat and meat products industry, as well as dairy industries. Sugar, textiles, leather and paper are also produced. **Export agricultural products** include processed fruit, extract of pyrethrum for use in insecticides and wattle bark which is used to tan leather.

Kenya and the neighboring countries of Tanzania and Uganda are able to meet most of their commercial energy requirements through **hydro-electric**

Domestic flights facilitate travel within the region.

power. There is a major hydro-electric scheme on the upper reaches of the Tana River and the Owen Falls Dam in next-door Uganda also supplies some of the country's needs.

Tourist Industry

Tourism is currently Kenya's largest single export earner and it is of vital importance to the country's economy. Kenya's tourism is based essentially on two features, the wildlife and the beaches, and thanks to a determined effort in infrastructural planning, Kenya is able to exploit its tourism potential more fully than any of its neighbors and with a great deal of success.

Kenya is not unique in East Africa for its rich wildlife, its good beaches and coral reefs, but it is at the forefront in the regional tourist industry. Kenya is politically stable and the government has steadfastly supported the tourist industry building good roads, hotels and airports, as well as being highly vocal in its support for wildlife conservation – one of the country's economic lifelines.

Yet Kenya still faces economic problems ahead. The two years without foreign aid, from late 1991 to late 1993, forced the country into debt arrears of some US$700 million on its foreign debt. Yet the first economic and political reforms and the promise of more to come have at least brought the country out of the economic cold.

Geography & Climate

Kenya's 582,646 sq km (224,901 sq miles) contain, within their boundaries, a virtual mini-continent of geographic conditions since most of the world's major climates and features are represented. There are deserts and snow-capped mountains, freshwater lakes and a sandy coastline, savannah grasslands and fertile tea plantations, extinct volcanoes and coral reefs.

The Maasai Mara, Kenya's landscape in the interior.

Kenya is bisected horizontally by the Equator while the 38th meridian divides the country vertically. The country's northern neighbors are Sudan and Ethiopia; Uganda and Lake Victoria lie to the west; Tanzania and Mount Kilimanjaro are to the south; Somalia is to the northeast, and the Indian Ocean is to the east with the scattered islands of the Lamu archipelago lying off-shore.

Mount Kenya, Kenya's highest peak.

Kenya has 20 **mountains** whose peaks top 2,000 m (6,560 ft), and six of these rise to more than 3,000 m (9,900 ft). The **Tana River** is the largest in the country, rising in the Aberdares before heading off towards the east. It is the only river in the country which is suitable for river traffic, and even so, is navigable only in its lower reaches. Other than the Tana River, most of Kenya's rivers dry up during the dry season and many of the smaller lakes also suffer from large fluctuations, according to the season. Perennial water shortages

Naro Po Pong Mountain oversees the semi-arid terrain.

remain one of the country's most serious problems.

The **topography** of the country is extremely varied rising from sea-level to the snowy summit of Mount Kenya at 5,199 m (17,058 ft). The eastern half of the country slopes gently down to sea-level while to the west, the land pattern is dominated by a series of hills and plateaux which rise gradually in height, giving an impression of an oversized flight of stairs as they lead up towards the Rift Valley.

West of the Rift Valley, the land again slopes down towards Lake Victoria. The country has four main geographic areas, each with its own climate and vegetation, and taken together, they offer a study in **contrasts**.

The North and Northeast

The largest of these geographical zones is the vast, empty **arid and semi-arid area** to the north and northeast of Kenya, a huge tract of land which comprises about two-thirds of the country, but which is sparsely populated and is agriculturally unproductive. This part of Kenya is very hot with scanty tree and grass cover and a very severe shortage of water. Water is the single most dominating factor of the geography of this arid land, and, since both rainfall and ground water are sparse, the acute lack of water means that only pastoral nomads can live here.

These nomads are constantly on

The luxuriant tropical vegetation along the coast is a pleasant change from the sparse savannah and scrubland of the interior.

the move, searching for water for themselves and their herds of cattle, goats and camels which are their only means of subsistence. Although this region does have a large expanse of water in the form of **Lake Turkana** (formerly Lake Rudolf) which is the largest of the lakes along the path of the Rift Valley, the lake is alkaline. Though it supports some wildlife particularly birds, it is of very limited use to man.

The climate of these northern and north-eastern areas is the most extreme in the country, for the temperature can

vary from around 40° C during the day to 20° C at night. A glance at a map will illustrate the emptiness of these arid plains for there are only a few roads, a smattering of small towns and villages, and huge unmarked tracts. This is Kenya at its most remote, a far cry from the world of organized safaris and beach holidays.

The Coast

The **coastal belt** runs for some 480 km (298 miles) along the shores of the Indian Ocean, from the Somalian border down to the Tanzanian frontier. Close to Somalia is a scattering of islands and coral reefs and at several places along the coast, marine national reserves have been formed, to protect the life of the coral reefs.

When the Arabs and later the Portuguese came to Kenya, they arrived by sea and settled along this coastline which was rich and fertile and cut off from the interior by the plains running parallel to it. This area developed at a different pace to the rest of the country (see chapter on The Coast). Today, the narrow, coastal strip is low-lying and fertile, benefiting as it does from two monsoons and there are coconut groves, sisal and sugar cane plantations. The coastal region also has several excellent natural harbors, and Mombasa, notably, has the best harbor along the entire East African coast.

The coastal climate is hot and humid all year round with abundant rainfall and there is little variation in annual temperature.

The Interior

Inland from the coast, the land rises towards the central plateau, and the **Rift Valley and Central Highlands.**

A solitary spectacular splendor over the horizon of Maasai Mara.

This area offers some of the country's most spectacular scenery, is the most fertile, and, naturally, the most densely populated. The volcanic plateau has been split along a north-south divide by the Great Rift Valley, which runs virtually the length of Kenya from Lake Turkana in the north, south to Lake Magadi. The width of the valley varies from 48 to 128 km (30-80 miles), and its floor rises from 450 m (1,476 ft) in the north around Lake Turkana, to over 2,000 m (6,560 ft) at Lake Naivasha, while dropping again to 600 m (1,968 ft) at the Tanzanian border.

The Rift Valley floor is dotted with a chain of shallow alkaline and freshwater lakes and the eroded cones of long extinct volcanoes. The largest of these lakes is **Lake Naivasha**, while the saline **Lake Nakuru** and **Lake Bogoria** and the freshwater **Lake Baringo** are home to some of the most spectacular bird life in the country.

To the west of the Rift Valley is the **Mau Escarpment** while to the east are the **Aberdare Mountains** and **Mount Kenya**, the country's highest peak and

A volcanic lake in the Rift Valley, one of the most fertile regions in Kenya.

the second highest mountain in Africa. When the easterly winds blowing in from the coast meet the mass of the Aberdares, they deposit their precious moisture as rain, and this, combined with the rich volcanic soil, has made this part of Kenya very fertile.

The eastern highlands have long been intensively cultivated, initially by the Europeans, the so-called white settlers who arrived in the 19th century to develop the area. At the southern end of these highlands is the national capital, **Nairobi**, which was founded on swampy

The Equator

Douglas and the Equator.

Ever wondered what to do if you are lost and do not know whether you are in the northern or the southern hemisphere? There is a young man called Douglas who spends his days on the Equator and he has the answer to this potential dilemma. You can always find Douglas next to the sign marked "Equator" on the Nairobi to Nanyuki road.

Douglas says there are two ways to tell which of the two hemispheres you are in. The first way is to find some trees and then check in which direction the vines and creepers twist themselves around the trees. If they twist clockwise, you are in the northern hemisphere, anti-clockwise, and you are in the southern hemisphere. The other method requires a little more equipment, which, of course, Douglas has ready. He has a funnel, a jug of water and a handful of matchsticks, and with these, he demonstrates the difference between the northern and southern hemispheres.

First, you all walk with Douglas 20 m (66 ft) or so north of the Equator line where Douglas then pours the water from the jug into the funnel, blocking the hole with his finger. He places the matchsticks in the funnel, releases his finger, and sure enough, as the water flows through into the jug underneath, the matchsticks spin clockwise.

Everyone then troops with Douglas 20 m (66 ft) south of the Equator where the whole process is repeated. The matchsticks duly spin anti-clockwise. Now onto the Equator itself, and as Douglas repeats the demonstration for the third time, huddled under a signboard marked "Equator", everyone watches attentively. The water turns neither clockwise nor anti-clockwise, but goes straight down through the funnel. Apparently, for some 5 to 6 m (16-20 ft) either side of the Equator this phenomena takes place.

Satisfied customers then shell out a few shillings for one of Douglas's own certificates, proving that you have indeed been to the Equator. Everyone then heads off to the souvenir shops lining both sides of the Equator while Douglas settles down to wait for the next group of seekers after scientific explanation.

land known as the place of cool waters.

Generalizing somewhat, these Central Highlands and the Rift Valley have the most pleasant climate in the country though there is, naturally, a big difference between the floor of the valley and the summit of Mount Kenya. There are two rainy seasons, the "long rains" which fall between March to May, and the "short rains" which fall between October and December. The country's highest rainfall is recorded over the Aberdares and Mount Kenya. Temperatures are, overall, lower in this part of

Scrubland, a less fertile feature of south Kenya.

Kenya, ranging from between 22°- 26°C to 10°C.

The last geographic zone is **Western Kenya**, a gentle plateau running the length of the country and touching the shores of Lake Victoria. Here, the land is especially fertile and there is intensive cultivation. To the north of the lake and close to the Ugandan frontier is the second highest mountain in Kenya, **Mount Elgon**, another extinct volcano which rises to a height of 4,321 m (14,173 ft). South of Mount Elgon, the land becomes progressively less fertile and agriculture gives way to scrubland and finally to big game country. It is in this southern stretch of the country that some of Kenya's major sanctuaries are found including **Maasai Mara, Amboseli** and **Tsavo**.

Western Kenya is generally hot with rainfall throughout most of the year, and is quite humid. Annual temperatures range from the low-mid 30°C to 14°-18°C. Lake Victoria provides most of the water for irrigation in this area, rather than rainfall.

Kenya has some extremely fertile **soil** as well as some very poor soil. The former, the result of lava deposits and volcanic action, is found around Lake Victoria and in the highlands. Unfortunately, the poorer, sandy soil is far more widespread and is found in all the semi-arid and arid areas. Kenya faces an increasing problem from soil erosion which is caused by the lack of forest cover, overgrazing and over-cultivation.

Wildlife

One of Kenya's most important assets is its spectacular wildlife for with more than 80 major species of animal, plus some 1054 species of bird, visitors come to the country principally to view this superb and extensive panorama of fauna. Kenya recognizes the vital importance of its visitors who bring with them, among other things, much-needed foreign exchange. Kenya is at the forefront of wildlife and environmental protection, not through posturing or a feeling that ecology is a fashionable pursuit, but through a deep-seated awareness that much of the fabric of Kenyan society is inextricably linked with the wild. Tribal society lived alongside the animals for centuries and the natural balance of nature ensured that both sides survived. It is only recently that Man has started to encroach upon na-

Found in the grasslands and open savannah, the cheetah is the fastest animal in the world.

Not only is the lion native and distinctive in the African landscape but it has also contributed to its history.

ture to such an extent that the balance of nature is disturbed. Kenya is at great pains to protect the natural balance wherever it can. Serious measures against poaching are being undertaken, and one of the most frequently seen bumper stickers on cars in Nairobi says "Only elephants should wear ivory."

Formerly the big game hunters came to Kenya to bag the "Big Five", which are elephant, rhinoceros, buffalo, lion and leopard. Today's visitors also shoot them but through the telephoto lens of a camera. Although the sight of any animal in the wild against the sweeping backdrop of Kenya's vast, open plains is a wonderful moment, spotting the "Big Five" remains especially thrilling.

The wildlife profiles which follow are not exhaustive but will help identify the major species and those most likely to be seen on safari. The Latin name as well as the Swahili name is given. The term "length" refers to the total length of the animal, from the tip of its nose to the end of its tail. Height is very often to the shoulder, and measurements are given in both kilograms/pounds and meters/inches. See box story for Birds on p.68.

Mammals

Sable antelope
Latin name : *Hippotragus niger*
Swahili name : *Palahala or mbarapi*

The **sable antelope** stands about

127-137 cm (50-54 in) at the shoulder. It is one of the most beautiful of the antelopes but it can only be seen in one part of Kenya, in the Shimba Hills, near Mombasa. The male's coat looks like black satin, while the female's is of a dark reddish-brown color, and both sexes have very long scimitar-curved horns.

Roan antelope

Latin name : *Hippotragus equinus*
Swahili name : *Korongo*

The **roan antelope** is the third largest of the antelope species found in Kenya, and is an aggressive animal. The average height at the shoulder is 140-145 cm (55-57 in). Both sexes have thick, heavily ridged scimitar-curved horns though those of the female are shorter; those of the male measure on average 70 cm (just over 24 in). The life span is around 15 years and they live mainly on the shores of Lake Victoria and in the trans-Mara area.

Bongo

Latin name : *Boocercus euryceros*
Swahili name : *Bongo*

The **bongo** is a thick-set antelope and an adult male stands 112-127 cm (44-50 in) at the shoulder. The female is shorter. It is a beautiful red, chestnut color with 12-14 vertical white stripes down its flanks, and both sexes have spiral horns. Bongos live in pairs, in herds of around 30 animals, and have a life span of some 12 years.

The bongo is rarely seen because it is an extremely shy, nocturnal animal and also because of its mountain habitat. It occurs on Mount Kenya, the Aberdares, the Mau Forest and the Cherangani Hills. Visitors to The Ark lodge in the Aberdares stand a good chance of seeing it, and at the Mount Kenya Safari Club, in the attached orphanage, there are several bongo, allowing visitors the rare opportunity of seeing them at very close quarters.

Buffalo

Latin name : *Syncerus caffer*
Swahili name : *Nyati or mbogo*

As you drive past a large herd of **African buffalo** grazing and browsing in the hot sun, they may well look docile but this animal is probably the most dangerous out there on the Kenyan plains. It has a quick, unpredictable temper which makes it a very dangerous animal. Buffalo are widely distributed and large herds live in Amboseli, Maasai Mara, Meru National Park, the mountain national parks, Samburu and Tsavo.

The height at the shoulder averages 145-153 cm (57-60 in) and they have widely curved horns which turn downwards. The buffalo has a life span of 15 to 20 years.

The buffalo moves around in large herds, anything from 500 to 2,000 animals, and they are found all over the country, anywhere where water and copious amounts of fodder are available, from sea-level to high-level forests in the mountains.

Bushbuck

Latin name : *Tragelaphus scriptus*
Swahili name : *Mbawala or pongo*

The **bushbuck** is a shy, mainly nocturnal creature which lives principally in forested area. It stands 76-92 cm at the shoulder (30-36 in) and has dappled white markings. It has a short, bushy tail which is white underneath, and it raises as a danger signal to others. Its principal enemy is the leopard.

Blue duiker

Latin name : *Cephalophus monticola*
Swahili name : *Paa*

This little nocturnal creature is approximately the size of a hare as it is only about 33 cm (or 13 in) at shoulder height. It is gray in color with a brown tinge on its back, its face and its limbs. It has small horns which are set well back on its head and which are almost hidden by a tuft of hair.

Bush or gray duiker

Latin name : *Sylvicapra grimmia*
Swahili name : *Nsua*

The **bush duiker** is a medium-sized antelope, standing about 56-63 cm from hoof to shoulder (22-25 in). It is a fawnish color with a dark stripe down the center of its face. Only the males have horns. It either lives alone or in pairs, and is mainly nocturnal.

Harvey's or red duiker

Latin name : *Cephalophus harveyi*
Swahili name : *Funo*

This thick-set antelope is between 41-43 cm (16-17 in) at the shoulder. It is a bright, dark-red color, with a black stripe down the center of its face and on its hind legs. Its fore legs are dark brown. Both males and females have short horns. They either live in pairs or alone, and are mainly nocturnal.

Yellow-backed duiker

Latin name : *Cephalophus sylvicultor*
Swahili name : *Paa*

The largest of the duikers, the **yellow-backed duiker** is very large, with an average height at its shoulder of 86 cm (34 in), and it is heavy and thick-set. True to its name, it has a yellow stripe from the middle of its back which broadens out over the rump into a triangle. The rest of the body is a blackish-brown color. Both males and females have horns.

This unusual looking, nocturnal animal is, however, elusive, and can only be seen, and even then with great difficulty, in the Mau Forest in the western highlands.

Kirk's dikdik

Latin name : *Rhynchotragus kirkii*
Swahili name : *Dikidiki or suguya*

The dikdik is a gentle, shy animal

The dikdik is so called because of its cry of alarm which sounds like "zic-zic".

living in thickets, usually in pairs and sometimes in family groups. **Kirk's dikdik** is between 36-41 cm (14-16 in) at the shoulder, and is a gray-brown colored antelope. Its hindquarters are higher than its front shoulders and with its sloping back and thin legs, it looks permanently frightened. It has an elongated, trunk-like nose and only the male has horns. They usually live in pairs or in family groups.

Guenther's dikdik

Latin name : *Rhynchotragus guentheri*
Swahili name : *Dikdik or suguya*

With a height at the shoulder of 36 cm (14 in), **Guenther's dikdik** is slightly smaller than Kirk's dikdik. It is more uniformly gray in color and has a more elongated nose. They occur singly or in pairs, and are found only in northern Kenya, north of Lake Baringo.

Eland

Latin name : *Taurotragus oryx*
Swahili name : *Pofu or mbunja*

Despite its massive weight, which can reach anything up to a ton, the **eland** is a nimble animal able to leap to a height of 2 m (about 7 ft) from a standing position. It is the largest of Kenya's antelopes, measuring between 175-183 cm (69-72 in). Both sexes have thick, spiralled horns and they have a very distinctive tufted dewlap which hangs down below the neck. They are found over much of the country, usually living in small herds.

Thomson's gazelles are gregarious and always move around in herds.

Elephant
Latin name : *Loxodonta africana*
Swahili name : *Tembo or Ndovu*

The **African elephant** can weigh anything from $3^1/_2$ - $6^1/_2$ tons and is the biggest of all land animals. A male can measure between 2.80-3.56 m (9-11.5 ft) at the shoulder, with the female slightly smaller. Unlike the Indian elephant, both male and female African elephants have tusks which are used almost as tools to clear, to lift and to carry. An average tusk weight is between 22-45 kg (50-100 lbs), although much larger tusks have been recorded.

The average life span is from 50 to 70 years. The elephant, which lives in a herd, is widely distributed throughout Kenya and can be found in Amboseli, the Aberdares, Maasai Mara, Meru National Park, Mount Kenya, Samburu and Tsavo. Some of the largest tuskers have been sighted in northern Kenya, on the Marsabit Mountain.

Grant's gazelle
Latin name : *Gazelle granti*
Swahili name : *Swara granti*

Grant's gazelles are both grazers and browsers and are capable of enduring extreme heat and a lack of water for long periods. They are constantly on the move during the day, not bothering to seek shade, in herds that range in size from 6 to 30 animals.

The average height at the shoulder of a male animal is between 81-99 cm (32-35 in), while the female is smaller.

They are a sandy or fawn color, with the white markings on the buttocks extending above the tail to the rump - the only definite way of distinguishing them from the Thomson's gazelles, in fact. The average life span is from 10 to 12 years.

Thomson's gazelle
Latin name : *Gazella thomsoni*
Swahili name : *Swara tomi*

This is a smaller animal than the Grant's gazelle, with a shoulder height of 64-69 cm (25-27 in). It has less extensive white markings on its buttocks, for, unlike the Grant's, these markings end below its black tail which it moves constantly. Both males and females have horns, those of the female are slender and straight while those of the male curve upwards and outwards.

It is seen in abundance in central, southern and south-western Kenya, living on grassy plains and grasslands. Thomson's gazelles move around in herds often with other plains animals including the Grant's gazelle.

Gerenuk
Latin name : *Litocranius walleri*
Swahili name : *Swara twiga*

In the Somali language, **gerenuk** means "giraffe-necked", an accurate description of this unique looking animal. Its height to the shoulder, and therefore excluding its neck, is 91-104 cm (36-41 in). Only the male has horns which are massive and heavily ringed.

Its exceptionally long neck enables it to reach higher up into the acacia thorn bushes for food, and it has also learned how to stand on its back legs when eating. Seeing a gerenuk standing on its hind legs, nibbling away on a thorn bush, is a fascinating sight. When it moves, the gerenuk can run very fast. They inhabit arid grasslands and bush and semi-desert scrub in the eastern half of the country.

Masai giraffe
Latin name : *Giraffa camelopardalis tippelskirchi*
Swahili name : *Twiga*

The giraffe, world's tallest animal, is a fairly common sight in many of Kenya's national parks and is absolutely unmistakable, wandering along nibbling at the juiciest leaves, its head at tree level, or moving with its own distinctive loping run.

There are three races of giraffe in the country, the Masai, the reticulated and the Rothschild. The **Masai giraffe** is found, as its name implies, around the Maasai Mara, to the southwest of the Athi river. The male stands a massive 4.56-5.48 m (15-18 ft), and the female is a little smaller. The Masai has two, sometimes three, horns on its head, and they have jagged-edged markings.

Reticulated giraffe
Latin name : *Giraffa camelopardalis reticulata*
Swahili name : *Twiga*

The **reticulated giraffe** is far less common than the Masai giraffe and is found north of the Tana River. The male

The gerenuk feeding on its hind legs is not an uncommon sight.

is between 4.56-5.18 m (15-17 ft) tall, and the female is a little smaller. Its white markings form a neat network design on its darker red skin.

Rothschild's giraffe

Latin name : *Giraffa camelopardalis rothschildi*

Swahili name : *Twiga*

The **Rothschild's giraffe** is usually the same height as the Masai giraffe, but is paler and more thickset. Its markings are less jagged and it has distinctive legs, for they are unmarked below the knees, giving it the appearance of wearing white "stockings". It has either three or five horns.

It is only found in the wild in Lake Nakuru National Park and at the small Langata Giraffe center, a short distance outside Nairobi.

Coke's hartebeest

Latin name : *Alcelaphus buselaphus cokii*

Swahili name : *Kongoni*

This is the most common of the hartebeest species and stands around 122 cm (48 in) at the shoulder and weighs between 62-90 kg (132-198 lbs). It has a long face, and is fawn colored, with a whitish rump. It has a hump-shouldered appearance and both males and females have short bracket-shaped horns.

The life span is between 12-15 years, and for much of this, the males are celibate, often moving around in "bachelor" herds. The victors of courtship battles move in a herd with many females. They are widespread in the south of Kenya.

Hunter's hartebeest or hirola

Latin name : *Damaliscus hunteri*

Swahili name : *Kongoni*

Hunter's hartebeest are smaller than the Coke's, with an average shoulder height of between 107-117 cm (42-46 in). They have a very distinctive white chevron between their eyes and are of a pale fawn color, with a white tail tuft.

They are rarely seen in the wild since they are only found east of the Tana River, heading towards Somalia. Recently, a few animals have been introduced into the Tsavo National Park which is south of their usual range.

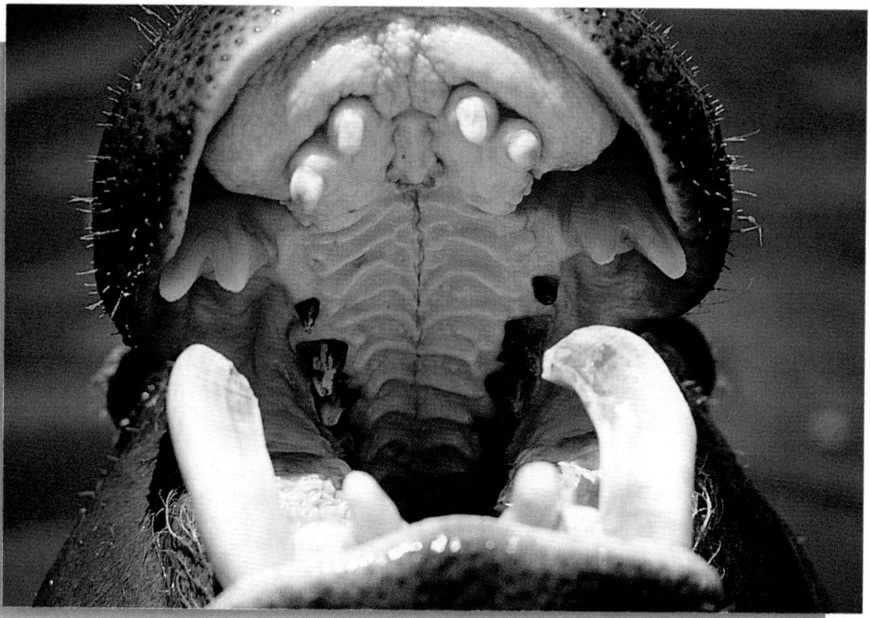

The hippo has an insatiable appetite.

Jackson's hartebeest
Latin name : *Alcelaphus buselaphus jacksoni*
Swahili name : *Kongoni*

Larger than the more common Coke's hartebeest, the height of a **Jackson's hartebeest** at the shoulder averages 132 cm (52 in). It is more tawny-red in color. They are found around Lake Victoria.

Lelwel hartebeest
Latin name : *Alcelaphus buselaphus lelwel*
Swahili name : *Kongoni*

This is closely related to the Jackson's hartebeest but has dark markings on the lower part of the legs. It is rare and is only found in the extreme northwest of the country, living amid arid bush and grassland.

Hippopotamus
Latin name : *Hippopotamus amphibius*
Swahili name : *Kiboko*

The huge, pig-like amphibian **hippopotamus** divides its life between water and land. It eats and gives birth under water, spends most of its day lazing around in the water but goes onto dry land each evening to go to sleep. Its height at the shoulder is 140 cm (58 in) and its average length is 4.26 m (14 ft).

Not surprisingly, given its size, the hippopotamus eats a lot. Since a full grown male can weigh anything up to 4 tons, making it the third largest land mammal, each animal eats something

Birding in Kenya – by Morten Strange

Kenya is officially the best place in the world to watch birds. Other countries have longer species lists, e.g. Indonesia and Columbia, but Kenya's birds are more accessible and more varieties have been seen here in one day than anywhere else. Over 1,100 species occur in total, the great majority being residents that can be found all year round – that is far more than in all of North America including Mexico together. On a well arranged four-week tour with a good guide, it is possible to see 600 of these! So study your field guide well before you go, so as not to lose track of all the new names. Many a general visitor going to the national parks, looking for big mammals, have been so impressed by the spectacular birdlife that he has come back a converted birdwatcher. Out of the enormous variety some East African bird species and families that you find in Kenya stand out as special, watch out for them.

Unique Species

We all know the **Ostrich** which is really unique being the largest and heaviest of all living birds; males stand up to 2.75 m (9 ft) tall and weigh up to 150 kg (330 lbs). Although there are several subspecies, the Ostrich is the only member of its family and even forms its own suborder. There are many flightless birds in the world, some are well known like the kiwis, cassowaries and penguins but there are also some flightless rails and ducks, a cormorant and even a flightless parrot, however, none are more popularly known than the Ostrich.

Though it does not fly, the Ostrich can easily outrun the fastest human being. It cruises along at 50 kmh (30 mph) on its massive legs reaching 70 kmh (40 mph) in short bursts. And yes, it does hide on occasions by sticking its head close to the ground while keeping a sharp eye on the intruder but it does not bury its head in the sand as is popularly believed. The Ostrich is confined to Africa where it lives in some desert areas but is found especially in the East African savannah which is its prime habitat, sometimes forming flocks of up to 50 individuals; no visit to Kenya is complete without seeing a few of these peculiar birds.

The Secretary Bird.

Few birds are so unique that they have no close relatives, however they form their own family. Even fewer form their own suborder (no single bird forms its own order). In Kenya there are several such birds – the **Hammercop** is one, the Secretary Bird another. The Hammercop is related to storks and herons and found near a variety of wetlands like marshes and rivers. There must be open woodlands nearby with larger trees where it can build its enormous nest, the largest nest of all birds. It is distributed widespread across all of sub-sahara Africa. It is common in places although usually just one or a few birds are seen as the Hammercop does not form large flocks like many other waterbirds do.

Another East African waterbird is the **Shoebill** which also constitutes it own family but within the stork/ibis suborder. It is unmistakable in the field with its massive bill, usually seen solitarily and rather lethargically standing out in the reedbeds. The **Secretary Bird** is a long-legged bird of prey related to hawks and falcons. It is another savannah specialist feeding on reptiles and small mammals in the long grass areas. Like the Ostrich and the Hammercop it can be seen right outside Nairobi so do not leave Kenya without having seen one!

Characteristic Birds

And then you have the larger bird families where several, sometimes dozens, of species occur in the Kenyan landscape. Some of these birds are large and conspicuous, others are small and difficult to tell apart. Your guide may not know them all so if you see a species you do not recognize consult somebody in your group

Flamingoes congregate in a Rift Valley lake.

who is more knowledgeable on African birds, most birdwatchers love to share their wisdom! Or better still, make a quick sketch of the bird on the spot and consult your field guide book that evening at the lodge or in the tent when you digest the experiences of the day and update your notes and records.

You will see a lot of birds of prey or **raptors** as they are called among birders: vultures, eagles and hawks especially. There are usually many at mammal carcasses and raptors are often more approachable here than on other continents. The **weavers** of East Africa are legendary, their woven nests hang in clutches from acacia trees. In some years species like the Red-billed Quelea multiply into millions and become pests for the farmers. Not everybody realizes, however, the complexity of these families. During one holiday in Kenya you should be able to see 15-20 different weavers plus many other seed-eaters like the finches, widow-birds, waxbills, bishops, sparrows and so forth – the diversity is staggering.

Around hotels, lodges and camping grounds birds are often attracted by the food available or the ornamental vegetation. Many good African birds are easy to view here like the starlings, hornbills, barbets, thrushes and sunbirds. The open savannah and scattered woodlands provide ideal living conditions for many members of the shrike, roller, flycatcher, bee-eater, warbler, kingfisher, woodpecker and pigeon families. Swifts and swallows patrol the airspace for flying insects.

To some people the wetlands in Kenya are the most impressive of all bird habitats. The sight of maybe one million Lesser Flamingoes in one of the Rift Valley lakes, just 150 km (90 miles) from Nairobi, is unforgettable. Lake Nakuru used to be the place to go but fishes introduced and other human intrusions have altered the ecological balance of the habitat and some of the birds have moved to other nearby locations. Some fish-eating species like pelicans and herons have in the meantime increased in numbers and the national park is always a great place to go to watch birds and mammals. Other waterbirds include ducks and storks and during the northern winter there are also many migratory shorebirds from the Palearctic region.

Favored Bird Habitats

In Kenya tourism is a synonym for ecotourism, even business visitors are tempted to go out on a safari if nothing else at least for a day in the Nairobi National Park which lies within sight of the big city – surprisingly it is even one of the better parks! But there are over 50 national parks and nature reserves across the nation, and although they all have wildlife for the traveler especially interested in birds some places are more interesting than others.

First of all, as a keen birder it is nice if you have your own transport and can set your own pace. Also you do not always want to go into the

...Birding in Kenya

Despite its size and bulk, the Ostrich is one of the fastest birds.

core of the major national parks; they are often crowded and most importantly you are not allowed to leave your vehicle. By staying at sites just outside the park perimeters you can walk around as you please; you see so much more this way and you are free to take your time and sneak up close to the birds for a better view or for a photograph. Also some of the lesser known parks in the mountains or at the coast may not be so famous for large mammals but they will have new bird species that you cannot find at the savannah environs.

Lake Naivasha including **Crescent Island** is a great place to stay and to birdwatch and is even closer to Nairobi than **Lake Nakuru**. Do not, however, miss this latter destination, it will undoubtedly be one of your birding highlights in Kenya. There are countless flamingoes and waterbirds in and around the lake and landbirds as well, especially close to the lake shores.

Southwest of these lakes near the Tanzanian border the **Maasai Mara National Reserve** is probably the best known park in Kenya for large mammals, "big game" as the term goes. It is however also a busy place with a lot of pressure from visitors traveling in anything from buses to hot air balloons. Farmers outside are encroaching on the marginal areas. It all threatens to diminish the natural value of the place, some birders touring Kenya simply give Maasai Mara a miss. The same goes for the famous Amboseli National Park further south. There are so many other beautiful places in Kenya where you can go and see good birds without having to endure the zoo-atmosphere!

The **Tsavo National Park** is one of those places. Covering 21,000 sq km (8,190 sq miles) it is vast and by far the largest park in Kenya, so visitors are easily absorbed. It is a bit dry but splendid for the arid type of savannah birds and is generally a great expanse of wilderness comprising the best of East African nature.

Mountains, Rainforests and the Seashore

Kenya, however, is much more than savannah and that is precisely what makes this particular country so rich and interesting. Savannahs in the south, endless deserts in the far north and northeast, and just three hours' drive north of Nairobi is the **Mount Kenya National Park** providing a totally different habitat again. The summit is at 5,199 m (17,058 ft) but do not go near it if you want to see birds. In fact the best elevation is anywhere between 2,000 and 3,500

in the order of 60 kg (132 lbs) of fodder per day. One of the best places to see the hippo is in the clear waters of the Mzima Springs in Tsavo National Park, where an observatory has been constructed below water level allowing you to watch hippos swimming enviably effortlessly past you.

m (6,560 and 11,480 ft) above sea-level for montane species; above that conditions are just not favorable for birds, nor for birders either, for it is cold, damp and exhausting to walk. The local checklist includes about 150 species, almost all of which will be new for somebody coming from the savannah so you will have to get your field guide book out of the bag and start all over again trying to tell them apart.

The **Aberdare National Park** just southwest of Mount Kenya is another well-known montane destination with visitor's facilities. It is not quite as high but has a good rainforest cover with turaco, francolin, babbler and parrot species that you will never find in the lowlands.

Further to the west not far from Uganda there are patches of tropical rainforest typical of central and west Africa. At **Kakamega National Reserve** there are provisions for you to stay and capable guides available. The elevation is around 1,500-1,800 m (5,000-5,900 ft) which is perfect for tropical submontane birds. Birding here is so different from the savannah, there are fewer birds but an exciting variety of rare and shy species. They often move through the forest in mixed species flocks, so-called birdwaves typical of tropical rainforest avifauna. A guide is recommended in the forest; the birds and also the animals are simply so much harder to spot, let alone see well and a knowledge of the calls can give you many more opportunities. It is doubtful if you will ever find the Blue Flycatcher or the Blue-shouldered Robin-Chat unless some expert calls it out for you!

Along the Kenyan coast the climate is hot and steamy but there are some incredible spots for birding or general vacationing or a combination of both. South of Mombasa the **Kisite-Mpunguti National Park** includes some beautiful marine environment and north of the city at **Malindi-Watamu National Park** there are sandy beaches as well as the sheltered estuaries which most coastal birds prefer. At the mangrove forests and on the mudbanks of deposited silt that develop these places thousands of migratory shorebirds congregate during migration, especially in the spring period from March to May. Resident coastal birds occur as well, including the enigmatic Crab Plover – another one of those African birds which is the only one in its family! This scene is a far cry from the savannahs of the interior but it is an enchanting part of Kenya that should not be missed.

More Information

The most important book to bring with you to Kenya is ***A Field Guide to the Birds of East Africa*** by J. G. Williams, 1980. It is an invaluable identification aid covering all the birds you will ever see there. The same author published in the same year ***A Field Guide to the National Parks of East Africa*** which is a great help if you are driving yourself around looking for the best places to birdwatch.

While you are there you will probably want to enjoy watching the mammals as well. Knowing exactly what you are looking at makes the experience so much more enjoyable so get ***A Field Guide to the Mammals of Africa*** by Haltenorth & Diller. Apart from these very useful titles there are many coffee-table type of books featuring African wildlife including birds available. They are of varying quality and you can always pick them up on location when you get there.

The more serious student of Kenyan avifauna would do well to contact the International Council for Bird Preservation in Nairobi. Together with the Department of Ornithology at the National Museum of Kenya they produce a newsletter called "Kenya Birds" containing details on the latest news regarding species, sites, bird events, research and so on. The address is PO Box 40658, Nairobi, Kenya.

Giant forest hog

Latin name: *Hylochoerus meinertzhageni*

The **giant forest hog** is a very large, thickset pig, with coarse black hair and tusks. Males have a distinctive wart-like swelling below the eyes. It is a bulky animal measuring 81 cm (32 in) at the shoulder, and its length is 122-127 cm

Though the antithesis of "beauty", the wart hog is an unusual creature with its tusks, warts and little "mane".

(48-50 in).

The giant forest hog is mainly nocturnal, and is only found in small numbers in the forests on Mount Kenya and in the Aberdares, and in the forests to the west of the country.

Wart hog

Latin name : *Phacochoerus aethiopicus*
Swahili name : *Ngiri*

The unlovely looking **wart hog** is a grayish colored wild pig with bristles down its back and shoulders and large warts on both sides of its face. Its length is 91-102 cm (36-40 in) and its shoulder height is 76 cm (30 in). It has tusks and when it runs, it holds its tail up straight looking rather comical. It is commonly seen on open plains, grasslands, savannah and semi-arid bush.

Tree hyrax

Latin name : *Dendrohyrax arboreous*
Swahili name : *Perere*

Hyraxes are rabbit-sized animals without tails, and they are dark brown or gray in color. It is often difficult to distinguish between the two species of hyrax in the field, and habitat, either trees or rocks, is probably the best guide to identification.

The **tree hyrax** is a nocturnal animal found in forests at virtually any altitude, from sea-level up to 4,000 m (13,125 ft). It is 41 cm long (16 in), and its color varies from gray to deep brown, with a pale cream colored streak down the center of its back. The tree hyrax has

The male impala is capable of having a harem of up to 100 females.

longer and much softer fur than the rock hyrax. Its cry, which can be eerie when heard in the middle of the night, acts as a territorial call, much like the lion's roar. To help the tree hyrax climb trees, the animal continuously secretes a substance which keeps the soles of its feet sticky.

Rock hyrax

Latin name : *Heterohyrax brucei*

Swahili name : *Pimbi*

The **rock hyrax** is lighter in color than the tree hyrax, with coarser, stiffer and shorter hair. It also has a cream colored streak along its back. It measures 38-46 cm (15-18 in). To enable it to keep its grip when climbing steep precipices, the soles of its feet have semi-elastic pads.

Impala

Latin name : *Aepyceros melampus*

Swahili name : *Swara pala*

The beautiful, graceful **impala** is a species of antelope standing 92-107 cm (36-42 in) at the shoulder. It is fawn-colored, dark fawn above with a well-defined mark, below which it is a paler color. Its rump is white, with a black streak on either side. The male has distinctive, lyre-shaped horns.

The impala is common in the south-western part of Kenya, living in herds. It is capable of very high leaps when danger threatens, and can jump over obstacles that are 3 m high (10 ft) and clear ditches up to 10 m wide (33 ft). Each

Kenya's Flora

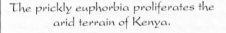

The prickly euphorbia proliferates the arid terrain of Kenya.

Scadoxus Multiflora or Fireball Lily.

Desert Rose.

If you drive across Kenya's savannah grasslands and endless plains during the dry season, you could be forgiven for thinking that flora and any variety of colorful vegetation were in distinctly short supply. The predominant tone is a bleached yellow color and even the acacia trees that dot the plains look parched. In the semi-arid deserts of the north and the north-east, the vista is one of endless thorn bushes. If you were to travel that same route after the rains, the scene would be totally different for then there are scores of brightly colored flowers and juicy looking green grass. Even the parched, arid deserts have a sprinkling of color from the short-lived flowers that appear with the rains.

Yet the lasting impression you take away with you is still of the dry grass rippling, the thorn bushes, the brilliant splashes of gaudy color from the bougainvillea which grow in profusion around the lodges and the prickly euphorbia, for all the world an overgrown cactus tree. The euphorbia can be trained to grow into hedges and since it grows to a thorny 2 m (7 ft), it forms an effective barrier. The acacia

time the animal lands, it changes course in an attempt to trick predators.

Klipspringer

Latin name : *Oreotragus oreotragus*

Swahili name : *Mbusi mawe*

The **klipspringer**, a member of the antelope family, measures 51-56 cm to the shoulder (20-22 in) and weighs between 11-18 kg (25-40 lbs). It is capable of extraordinary jumps and even as it walks, it bounces along on its hooves. Its

The frangipani exudes a singular beauty and fragrance.

two, giving the tree a very organized profile.

One of the more intriguing trees in Kenya is the baobab tree, a swollen looking tree resembling a large bottle. Try and locate a particularly huge, old, fine looking specimen outside Mombasa on the Diani road which has been placed under presidential protection.

If you are in Nairobi from late September to November, you will be lucky enough to see the city at its prettiest for that is when the jacaranda blossoms and the streets are carpeted by the delicate pale purple colored petals.

Some species of trees and flowers are indigenous such as the Nandi flame tree, the Cape chestnut and the red-hot poker tree while others have been introduced. The flamboyant flame tree originally came from Madagascar, and bottlebrush came from Australia. The camel's foot tree, whose flowers resemble orchids, is actually a native of Asia. Along the coast and in the hills, the beautifully scented frangipani has come to Kenya via the West Indies and its perfume, on a cool up-country evening, is one of Kenya's lingering memories.

tree is ubiquitous in Kenya, with its distinctive flat top, and, if you are lucky, you may see a hungry gerenuk standing on its back legs to reach up for the higher leaves.

Wherever there is any source of water, however sparse, the vegetation is inevitably lusher and if you climb any of Kenya's mountains, you will be climbing through thickly forested land. As you climb, the vegetation changes until at 3,000 m (9,840 ft) and above, the characteristic plants are the giant lobelia and the groundsel tree which has flowers that resemble nothing so much as cabbages.

Along the coast, there are mangrove swamps and in Lamu particularly, the wood from these swamps is used in the construction industry mainly for scaffolding. Along the coast there are a variety of palm trees – coconut, date and doum. You can recognize the doum palm, which is indigenous to Kenya, by the very fact that unlike other palm trees, it has branches. Each branch divides, regularly and neatly into

yellowish olive-brown fur is stiff and brittle and acts as a cushion, protecting it from shocks when hitting rocks as it jumps. It lives in rocky hills, and marks its territory with a secretion from its scent glands.

Greater kudu

Latin name : *Strepsiceros strepsiceros*

Swahili name : *Tandala mkubwa*

The **greater kudu** is one of the most impressive looking of the antelopes, especially the male with his superb, long, spiralling antlers, and a heavy fringe of hair from the throat down to the chest. An adult weighs between 280-320 kg (600-700 lbs), yet can jump more than 2 m ($6^1/_2$ ft). Despite its weight, the pale gray animal is elegant with a shoulder height of 140-153 cm (55-60 in). It has between six and eight narrow, vertical, white stripes on each flank. It has large, rounded ears which they can turn in almost any direction. It is not frequently seen and is only found in any significant numbers in the Marsabit National Reserve.

Lesser kudu

Latin name : *Strepsiceros imberbis*

Swahili name : *Tandala ndogo*

The **lesser kudu**, as its name implies, is smaller than the greater kudu, measuring 99-102 cm (39-40 in) at the shoulder. It is dark or light gray in color, and has more stripes than the greater kudu – between 10 and 15. It does not have the neck fringe that the greater kudu has.

Oribi

Latin name : *Ourebia ourebia*

Swahili name : *Taya*

This is a beautiful, small antelope with a relatively long neck and a silky coat which can range in color from fawn to a bright reddish-brown. The male has horns. Its shoulder height is 61 cm (24 in).

Beisa oryx

Latin name : *Oryx beisa*

Swahili name : *Choroa*

The oryx measures 122 cm (48 in) at the shoulder, and is a thickset, pale gray antelope. It has black and white markings on the face, and both sexes have straight, rapier-like horns. These long horns of the oryx are used defensively and aggressively by the animal which will often impale its victim, the horns passing right through the body. An average length of an oryx's horns is 70 cm (over 2 ft) long.

There are two races of oryx in Kenya, the Beisa and the Fringe-eared. The **Beisa oryx** has pointed ears, without a tuft of hair at the tips, and is found north of the Tana River.

Fringe-eared oryx

Latin name : *Oryx beisa callotis*

Swahili name : *Choroa*

The **fringe-eared oryx** has a distinctive fringe of black hair at the tips of its ears, and is found south of the Tana River.

Bush pig

Latin name : *Potamochoerus porcus*

Swahili name : *Nguruwemwitu*

Although the **bush pig** is found over much of Kenya in large numbers, it is a nocturnal animal and so rarely seen. It measures between 71-76 cm (28-

30 in) at the shoulder and is 86-92 cm (34-36 in) long. It has short, knife-like tusks; its color varies from bright to dark brown and it has a white dorsal mane.

Bohor reedbuck
Latin name : *Redunca redunca*
Swahili name : *Tohe*

This elusive antelope is shy and is easily frightened. It is usually only seen at sunrise and sunset and spends the day resting in reeds or tall grasses. It measures between 71-76 cm (28-30 in) at the shoulder, and is a sandy color, with a white belly and a bushy white tail. Only the male has horns, but both sexes have a strange, bare patch immediately below their ears. It is common in the south of the country, west of the Tana River.

Chanler's mountain reedbuck
Latin name : *Redunca fulvorufula chanleri*
Swahili name : *Tohe*

This animal is slightly larger than the bohor reedbuck, but is grayer in color, with sandy-colored thighs and legs. Only the males have horns. It is found on open, grassy slopes, up to an altitude of 4,000 m (13,125 ft) in central and western Kenya.

Black rhinoceros
Latin name : *Diceros bicornis*
Swahili name : *Kifaru*

Two species of rhinoceros are found in Kenya, the black and the white, and both are seriously endangered. Uncontrolled poaching over many years has reduced their numbers to dangerous levels, and they are therefore much more difficult to see than many other animal, which makes the thrill of seeing one in the wild that much more exciting.

The **black rhino** is smaller than the white, weighing between 1,000-2,540 kg (1-$1^1/_2$ tons) and it is not as tall as the white. It has two horns, the front horn measures on average 50-89 cm (20-35 in) and the rear up to 53 cm (21 in), although longer lengths have been recorded. It has a prehensile, pointed upper lip.

The black rhinoceros can be seen in Amboseli, the Aberdares, Maasai Mara, Mount Kenya, Nairobi National Park, Samburu and Tsavo.

White or square-lipped rhinoceros
Latin name : *Diceros simus*
Swahili name : *Kifaru*

The **white rhino** is not white at all: its name is a corruption of an Afrikaaner word *weit*, meaning "wide-mouthed". The white rhino weighs around 3,550 kg ($3^1/_2$ tons), and is the second biggest land animal after the African elephant. It differs from the black rhino in the shape of its square-mouthed muzzle

Smaller even than the dikdik, the suni is one of the more solitary antelopes.

which does not have a prehensile upper lip. It is a more docile animal than the black rhino, less likely to charge and moves around in small family groups. It was originally only found in north-western Uganda but has been introduced into Meru National Park.

Sitatunga or marshbuck
Latin name : *Limnotragus spekei*
Swahili name : *Nzohe*

The aquatic **sitatunga** has a unique characteristic among antelopes for it has two-toed, elongated hooves, giving it the ability to move about in boggy swamps or on a mass of floating weeds, that are its natural habitat. A strong swimmer, whenever the animal is frightened, it barks and sinks into the water until only its nostrils show.

Its height to the shoulder is 109-117 cm (43-46 in), the males are a dark grayish-brown, with long, twisted horns while the female is redder in color, and without horns. The sitatunga is rare for it can only be seen in one place in Kenya, in the tiny Saiwa Swamp National Park, in the northwest of the country.

Steinbok
Latin name : *Raphicerus camestris*
Swahili name : *Dondoro*

Standing 56 cm (22 in) at the shoulder, the **steinbok** is a pretty antelope. It is a bright reddish-fawn color, with very large ears, and the male has slender, vertical horns.

The wildebeest in its dramatic annual migration in search of food.

Suni

Latin name : *Nesotragus moschatus*

Swahili name : *Paa*

A tiny, graceful antelope, it measures 30-33 cm (12-13 in) at the shoulder. It is brownish-gray in color with a white belly, and the male has ringed horns which slope backwards. It is mainly nocturnal and lives either alone or in pairs.

Topi

Latin name : *Damaliscus korrigum jimela*

Swahili name : *Nyamera*

The **topi** is a large animal with its shoulders noticeably higher than its rump, giving it a resemblance to the hartebeest. Its shoulder height is 122-127 cm (48-50 in). It is of a reddish-brown to purple-red color, and with distinctive dark patches which look just like stains on its face, forehead, legs, thighs and hips. They have ridged horns which curve backwards and upwards.

The males are territorial, marking out their territory and guarding it against other males. When two males fight, they drop down to their knees and clash horns. Topi are very common in the Maasai Mara and also north of the Tana River and to the east of Lake Turkana. A closely related species, the **tiang**, is found only on the northwest shores of Lake Turkana.

Common waterbuck

Latin name : *Kobus ellipsiprymnus*

Swahili name : *Kuro*

The **common waterbuck** is a thick-

The unmistakable stripes of the zebra make their mark on the African wildlife.

set antelope, measuring 122-137 cm (48-54 in) up to the shoulder. It has a shaggy, grayish-brown coat with a white ring around the buttocks. The males have impressive, heavily ringed horns which reach an average length of 70 cm (roughly 2 ft). Waterbuck tend to live in small family herds,usually a polygamous setting comprising a bull, few cows and calves.

As their name implies, waterbuck are water orientated: they swim very well and live close to the water which provide them with a means of protec-

tion when predators are around. As an ambivalent plus point, they also give off a strong, rather unpleasant, musky smell that lingers long after them. This odor does not appeal to predators.

Defassa waterbuck
Latin name : *Kobus defassa*
Swahili name : *Kuro*

The **Defassa waterbuck** can only be distinguished from the common by one trait : it has a pure white rump.

Wildebeest or white-bearded gnu
Latin name : *Connochaetes taurinus*
Swahili name : *Nyumbu*

The strange, ungainly-looking **wildebeest** may not be the most beautiful animal out on the Kenyan plains but it is the undisputed star of one of the most spectacular wildlife events in the world – the annual wildebeest migration across the Serengeti plains and into the Maasai Mara, when more than a million animals set off to find fresh pasture, and then, several months later, retrace their steps.

The wildebeest stands 132 cm (52 in) tall up to the shoulder, and weighs between 160-220 kg (350-480 lbs). It is gray or dark brown in color, with darker vertical stripes on its body. It has an odd combination of physical features – a humped back, horns like a buffalo, a black mane and a wispy white beard on its throat.

They are common in southern Kenya and, although gregarious, when they walk, they do so in single file which is unique among plains animals.

Burchell's or common zebra
Latin name : *Equus burchelli*
Swahili name : *Punda milia*

Just as no two human beings have identical finger prints, no two zebras have identical markings. To the untrained eye, all zebras may look the same, with their distinctive black and white stripes, but in fact each animal is unique. **Burchell's zebra** resembles a pony in its shape, with short, narrow ears and a short mane. It measures 128 cm (50 in) and has broad stripes.

Zebras live in herds and are common over most of the country, inhabiting grassy plains, savannah grasslands and semi-arid bush.

Grevy's zebra
Latin name : *Equus grevi*
Swahili name : *Punda milia*

Grevy's zebra resembles a mule more than a pony, and is taller than the Burchell's standing 152 cm (5 ft) to the shoulder. It is also more beautiful with narrower, close-set stripes. The animal's body is white with either black or dark brown stripes and its belly has no stripes. It has a thick mane, and large, round, heavily fringed ears. It is found north of the Tana river, and north-westwards towards Lake Turkana. Living in herds, sometimes along with Burchell's zebra and antelopes, it can be found on open plains and in the arid bush.

Carnivores

Although one of the most thrilling moments of your safari may be when you see an animal making a kill, do remember one thing - never try and de-rail the process of nature. Disturbing a carnivorous animal when it is hunting, is tantamount to depriving it of its food for the day. Always respect the balance of nature, which means that however tempting the drama may seem, do try not to drive too close to the scene of the action.

Aardwolf
Latin name : *Proteles cristatus*
Swahili name : *Fisi ndogo*

In appearance, the **aardwolf** resembles a very small striped hyena, and certainly a more elegant version. It is 89-97 cm (35-38 in) long, and its height to the shoulder is between 46-51 cm (18-20 in). It has a sandy-brown coat with vertical dark stripes, and a mane of hair right down its back. It is found all over the country mainly in arid and semi-arid plains, but it is nocturnal and rarely seen.

Caracal
Latin name : *Felis caracal*
Swahili name : *Simba mangu*

This rarely seen cat stands 41-46 cm (16-18 in) to the shoulder, and is a long, sleek animal, red-brown in color, with long tufted ears and a short tail. The hind legs of the caracal are longer than its forelegs, giving it the ability to leap up as high as 3 m (about 10 ft) into the air to bring down a bird in flight. It can climb trees.

African wild cat
Latin name : *Felis sylvestris lybica*
Swahili name : *Paka pori*

If you should be lucky enough to spot this nocturnal, rather rare animal, you could be forgiven for thinking that

A skilful hunter, the serval cat is capable of catching a bird in mid-flight.

it was simply another domestic tabby cat. It stands 23 cm (9 in) at the shoulder, and is thickset with a broad head. Its tail is somewhat shorter than that of a domestic cat and its markings are a little less distinct, but the resemblance is really quite strong.

Serval cat

Latin name : *Leptailurus serval*

Swahili name : *Mondo*

The **serval cat**, which weighs between 12-15 kg (30-35 lbs), is found throughout Kenya. The average height to the shoulder is 46-51 cm (18-20 in). It is a large, dark yellow animal with large black spots in a linear pattern along the length of its body. It eats rodents, lizards, vegetables and even fish and small antelopes. But being a nocturnal animal it is rarely seen.

Cheetah

Latin name : *Acinonyx jubatus*

Swahili name : *Duma*

The **cheetah** is the lightest of the big "cats", weighing between 45-65 kg (95-140 lbs), but what it lacks in body weight, the cheetah makes up for in speed. It is the fastest animal in the world and speeds of over 110 kmh (70 mph) have been recorded, although the animal can only maintain such high speeds over short distances. It is unique among the cats in being able to retract its claws.

It stands 71-81 cm (28-32 in) at the shoulder, and is tawny yellow in color with black spots which are rounded and dotted all over its body. Its long tail is ringed with black and has a white tip.

Cheetah are fairly widely distributed throughout Kenya's grasslands and open savannah and live in Amboseli, Maasai Mara, Nairobi National Park and Samburu. It is probable that the cheetah is less common than the leopard but because it is a day-time or diurnal animal, it is more often seen.

African Civet

Latin name : *Civettictis civetta*

Swahili name : *Fungo*

The **civet** is a long-haired animal with a long spotted body, a dorsal crest, and a long bushy tail. The height to the shoulder is 38 cm (15 in), while its body is 107 cm long (42 in). Its color is usually gray with vertical, blackish stripes and blotchy markings although all-black specimens can also be seen.

It can weigh between 9-20 kg (20-45 lbs). It is rarely seen since it spends most of the day, even at nights, hiding in old burrows and thickets. It is a very secretive, solitary nocturnal creature. It has a low growl.

African palm civet or two-spotted civet

Latin name : *Nandinia binotata*

Swahili name : *Fungo*

The palm civet is 92 cm (36 in) long with a long tail. It is brown with a thick coat that has dark brown spots. It has an unusual white spot next to each shoulder. The **African palm civet** mews, rather than growls, and is rarely seen, since it is nocturnal, and spends much of its time in trees.

Hunting dog

Latin name : *Lycaon pictus*

Swahili name : *Mbwa mwitu*

This long-legged dog-like animal stands 61-76 cm (24-30 in) at the shoulder, and has a truly extraordinary appearance. It has massive jaws, very large, erect, rounded ears, and its color can only be described as a mixture of black, white and reddish-brown blotches. It hunts in small packs and is found wherever there is open plain or bush. It is commonly seen in the reserves.

Apart from its length, the genet resembles the domestic cat.

Bat-eared fox

Latin name : *Otocyon megalotis*

Swahili name : *Mbwela masikia*

This little creature resembles a very small jackal. It is 20-33 cm (12-13 in) at the shoulder, has enormous ears and a long body and tail. It is grayish brown in color with a black face, black legs and a black-tipped bushy tail. The **bat-eared fox** uses its outsized ears not only to pick up the sounds of possible attackers but also to locate the insects it eats. If danger threatens, it flattens its ears against its face. The animal spends much of the day sleeping and is active at night.

Neumann's or Small-spotted genet

Latin name : *Genetta genetta*

Swahili name : *Kanu*

The **Neumann's genet** is a long-bodied, spotted animal with a resemblance to a cat. It can easily be identified by its dorsal crest. It is 92 cm (36 in) long. The solitary animal is widespread throughout Kenya's savannah, but it is mainly nocturnal.

Large-spotted or Bush genet

Latin name : *Genetta tigrina*

Rarer than the Neumann's genet, it is slightly longer in the body, has shorter fur and larger body spots, hence its name. It does not have a dorsal crest. The large-spotted genet is widespread throughout Kenya's woodlands and forests and is generally nocturnal.

Spotted hyena

Latin name : *Crocuta crocuta*

Swahili name : *Fisi*

The hyena may look like a dog but it is a particularly cruel killer, following pregnant females and eating their newly-born animals. Hyenas even turn on other members of their own pack and kill them.

Hyenas hunt in packs of up to 30 animals, they can run as fast as 60 kmh, and they eat almost anything. At night, they produce an eerie wailing call which sends a chill down your spine.

The **spotted hyena** stands 69-91 cm (27-36 in) at the shoulder, and is large and long with a distinctive sloping back. It has large, rounded ears and massive jaws. Its color ranges from a reddish-brown to a dull gray with dark spots.

The hyena is often associated with its out-of-this-world wail at night.

Striped hyena

Latin name : *Hyaena hyaena*

Swahili name : *Fisi*

The **striped hyena** is of a slighter build than the spotted hyena, standing 76 cm (30 in) at the shoulder. It is long-haired, with a dorsal mane and a bushy tail. Its ears are not rounded but pointed and upright. As its name indicates, the animal is striped with vertical black stripes on a gray body. It is mainly nocturnal, producing an eerie wail at night, and is rarer than the spotted hyena.

Black-backed or silver-backed jackal

Latin name : *Canis mesomelas*

Swahili name : *Mbweha*

This is the most common of Kenya's jackals and it can be identified by its white underbelly and a broad black stripe along its back. It has a long body and a long tail, and is 41-43 cm (16-17 in) at the shoulder. Jackals are scavengers, hunting in packs of up to 30 animals. This species is both diurnal and nocturnal, and is widely found all over Kenya.

Gray or golden jackal

Latin name : *Canis aureus*

Swahili name : *Mbweha*

The **golden jackal** is 86 cm (34 in) long with a long tail, and stands 43-46 cm (17-18 in) at the shoulder. Its body color ranges from a dull yellowish color to reddish-gray, and its tail is reddish-brown with a dark tip. It is a scavenger

A sociable animal, Coke's hartebeest or kongoni is often found in the company of the zebra and the wildebeest.

that may be found very close to towns and villages where it raids the rubbish dumps at night. They have even been seen in the suburbs of Nairobi.

Side-striped jackal

Latin name : *Canis adustus*

Swahili name : *Mbweha*

As its name implies, this animal has a pale stripe along the side of its brownish-gray body. It is the same size as the much more common black-backed jackal.

Leopard

Latin name : *Panthera pardus*

Swahili name : *Chui*

The **leopard** is a graceful, beautiful creature and is much more difficult to spot than the cheetah mainly because it hunts by night, and spends much of the day dozing in the branches of a tree. It is more powerfully built and is a more thickset animal than the cheetah, with shorter legs and a relatively bigger head. Its height to its shoulder is 61-71 cm (24-28 in). Its black spots form rosettes.

A leopard weighs between 30-80 kg (65-180 lbs), and it is a fast moving agile animal, killing its prey by leaping on it from the branch of a tree. The leopard will eat some of its kill immediately, and it will drag the rest up into the high branch of a tree, out of the way of scavengers.

Although leopards are widely distributed, they are, however, rarely seen. Forests of any kind and rocky mountain areas are preferred areas for this secretive animal.

Lion

Latin name : *Panthera leo*

Swahili name : *Simba*

The sight of a pride of lions basking in the afternoon sun in the Maasai Mara is one of the most exciting ones on safari. Kenya's largest "cat" is a beautiful animal, moving around in prides of up to 30 animals. A **lion** is one animal that everyone recognizes instantly, with its tawny color, and the males with their superb manes which can range in color from sandy to black.

A male adult weighs up to 280 kg (620 lbs). When you see a full grown male dozing under a tree in the hot midmorning sun, just remember that this lazy looking animal is no pussy cat. He is a very powerful piece of hunting machinery, capable of leaping across a distance of 9 m (30 ft) in one go, and running up to 65 kmh (40 mph) when chasing its prey. Each lion or lioness kills around 20 animals a year. Lions are widely distributed and are found particularly in Amboseli, Maasai Mara, Nairobi National Park, Samburu and Tsavo West.

Dwarf mongoose

Latin name : *Helogale parvula*

Swahili name : *Nguchiro*

As its name implies, this is the smallest of Kenya's mongooses, only 31-33 cm (12-13 in) long, with a short tail and is reddish-brown in color. It is a nomadic creature, usually moving around in packs of up to 15 animals, and they attack their prey as a team. They eat a wide range of things from insects, eggs and small rodents to reptiles and young birds. They live in dry savannah woodlands, often taking over old termite hills and making homes out of them.

Large gray mongoose

Latin name : *Herpestes Ichenumon*

Swahili name : *Nguchiro*

This is the largest of Kenya's mongooses, measuring 122 cm (48 in) with a long, slender tail, terminating in a black tuft. It is grayish-brown in color, and lives on the edges of lakes and swamps and in woodlands and thick bush.

Slender or black-tipped mongoose

Latin name : *Herpestes sanguineus*

Swahili name : *Nguchiro*

As its name implies, this animal is slender in build, with a long black-tipped tail which it holds up straight like a squirrel. It is a deep red-brown color. It is a solitary animal, found over much of the country.

White-tailed mongoose

Latin name : *Ichneumia albicauda*

Swahili name : *Nguchiro*

This is a large, thickset animal, with shaggy hair and a white tail. Its body is 102 cm (40 in) long. It is fairly common and is a highly adaptable creature capable of living in forests or the open plains, or even by water where it will quite happily eat crabs and molluscs.

Banded mongoose
Latin name : *Mungos mungos*
Swahili name : *Nguchiro*

This medium-sized animal is gray-brown in color, with darker bands of a darker color along its body. It is a gregarious animal often moving around in packs of up to 50 creatures. It is found in Tsavo, Amboseli and Maasai Mara.

Clawless otter
Latin name : *Aonyx capensis*
Swahili name : *Fisi maji*

The **clawless otter** is a long animal, 152 cm (60 in) in length, with a long tail. It has short legs, its toes are not webbed and, as its name implies, they do not have claws. It is a rich brown color, with a white chin, and can be seen around rivers, streams and swamps.

Spotted-necked otter
Latin name : *Lutra maculicollis*
Swahili name : *Fisi maji*

This is a smaller, allied species of the clawless otter, with brown spots on its throat, and webbed feet. It is found in Lake Victoria.

Ratel or honey badger
Latin name : *Mellivora ratel*
Swahili name : *Mbweha*

This thickset, short-legged animal resembles a badger, but as it is nocturnal, it is rarely seen. It is 71-81 cm (28-32 in) long, with a bushy tail, and its height is 20 cm (8 in) to the shoulder. The top half of its body is pale gray while the bottom half is black.

Primates

Greater galago
Latin name : *Galago crassicaudatus*
Swahili name : *Komba*

With its thick, grayish-brown fur, its long bushy tail, large ears and large eyes, the **greater galago** is an appealing looking animal. It is 64 cm (25 in) long, with a long tail. It is nocturnal and is found in woodlands and coastal bush wherever there are trees.

Bushbaby or lesser galago
Latin name : *Galago senegalensis*
Swahili name : *Komba*

If the greater galago is appealing, the **lesser** or **bushbaby**, is even more so, looking for all the world like a soft, cuddly toy. It is smaller, 41 cm (16 in) with a long, thin tail. Its face is smaller and rounder than the greater galago, and its ears and eyes even larger. Its fur is woolly and it has a distinctive white stripe down its nose. It is widespread over Kenya, is nocturnal, but less solitary than the greater galago.

Olive baboon
Latin name : *Papio anubis*
Swahili name : *Nyani*

The two species of baboons found in Kenya both walk on all fours, they bark like dogs and they are carnivorous. They can cover long distances every day in their search for food which includes plants and flowers, insects and the occasional hare or young gazelle. They are

Belying its looks, the bushbaby is actually a primate.

very social and live in "troops" of between 40-80 animals, with a recognized dominant male as the leader. They are fierce fighters, be it for dominance over the troop or for their food.

The **olive baboon** is the larger of the two species, and is also the most common, being found all over the country except in the eastern region. It carries its long tail in a loop, upright from the base. It is a heavy, thickset animal with a long, dog-like profile. It has long facial hair and the males especially carries a mane on its shoulders.

Yellow baboon
Latin name : *Papio cynocephalus*
Swahili name : *Nyani*

The **yellow baboon** is smaller, lighter in color and slimmer in build, and is found in the eastern part of the country.

Black and white colobus
Latin name : *Colobus polykomos*
Swahili name : *Mbega*

The black and white **colobus monkeys** are divided into two groups : the *abyssinicus* with short hair on the head, and the *angolensis* with long hair. They are attractive animals, black in color, with a white "mantle" and white hair at the end of their long tail.

The male is 168-195 cm (66-76 in) in height with a long tail. Unlike other monkeys, colobus monkeys do not have a thumb. They also differ from most other monkeys, by living almost all their

The baboon often visits human habitation to look for food.

lives in trees, rarely coming down to earth. They are gregarious and are found principally in forests from sea-level up to 3,350 m (11,000 ft).

Red colobus

Latin name : *Colobus badius*

This is a smaller, much rarer monkey than the black and white, and, as its name implies, is a reddish-brown color, with white underparts. It is only found in some of the coastal forests and along the Tana River.

Blue or Sykes' monkey

Latin name : *Ceropithecus mitis*

Swahili name : *Kima*

Sykes' monkeys are members of the blue monkey race, which are a deep blue-gray color. The Sykes' monkey has a white throat and chest patch and its back has a very slight reddish-brown tinge to it. The male is 140-158 cm (55-62 in) long, and the female is a little smaller. They are found in the forests east of the Rift Valley.

Brazza monkey

Latin name : *Ceropithecus neglectus*

This is an allied species of the blue monkey and is a virtual riot of color : pale blue-gray in color with black limbs, a thick, white beard, and an orange band across its forehead. It is found in the forests of western Kenya mainly around Mount Elgon and the Cherangani mountains.

Patas monkey or Red Hussar

Latin name : *Erythrocebus patas*

This is the only primate that does not mix with other species of monkeys. It lives almost all its life on the ground, can stand fully erect and is able to walk on its hind legs. It uses trees and termite hills only as vantage points. It is 168-183 cm (66-72 in) long, and is a bright ginger color, with white underparts.

Red-tailed or white-nosed monkey

Latin name : *Ceropithecus nictitans*

True to its name, this monkey has a conspicuous white nose, and a bright chestnut colored tail. Its body, which measures 116-142 cm (46-56 in), is a dark brown color, sometimes tinged with olive. It is common in the forests of western Kenya.

The vervet monkey is often seen in the parks and reserves.

Black-faced vervet monkey
Latin name : *Ceropithecus aethiops*
Swahili name : *Tumbiri or tumbili*

This monkey is a grayish color, tinged with yellow or olive, and its underparts are white, and, as its name implies, it has a black face though the cheeks are white. It is 122-142 cm long (48-56 in), with the female being a little smaller. It is a gregarious animal and is found especially in woodlands near a water source. It has excellent vision and hearing but a poor sense of smell.

Reptiles

Crocodile
Latin name : *Crocodylus niloticus*

Just as you should never be fooled by "crocodile tears", nor should you be fooled by its impressive mouthful of teeth. The crocodile cannot chew, but unfortunately for its victims, that does not make it any the less dangerous. The crocodile simply grips onto its prey and thrashes it around in the water until a limb is finally severed. The reptile then

The Defassa waterbuck possesses an odor that discourages even the predators.

tips its head back and swallows the entire piece of flesh which it will digest at leisure over the next few hours.

Crocodiles are cold-blooded and regulate their body heat in accordance with the external temperature. They are found in rivers, lakes and swamps, but poaching has taken its toll on their numbers. They can be seen in Tsavo East, at the Lugard Falls, in the Uaso River in Samburu, as well as at Mzima Springs in Tsavo, and in the Mara and Tana rivers. Probably the last major sanctuary for them is Lake Turkana.

The teeth of the crocodile are deceptive for they cannot chew.

People

Describing a country or a city as a "**melting pot**" has become something of an overworked cliché, but in the case of Kenya, it is, for once, an accurate description and not a hyperbole. Kenya's 23 million citizens originate principally from many different parts of the African continent, and generations of migrations have resulted in a diverse ethnic and linguistic mix. There are more than 70 tribal groupings, and though some distinctions have inevitably become blurred over the years, as modern life imposes itself on traditional ways of life, the country still has a very strong tribal framework. Urban Kenyans may well have left their tribal village long ago, but they still possess a pronounced awareness of their tribal identity.

Kenya's population is almost entirely African, although there are small and influential minorities of **Asians**, some 80,000, and **Europeans**, numbering 40,000. Although Indian traders

A Samburu dancer.

The Kenyans today still possess a strong sense of tribal identity.

had been coming to East Africa for centuries with the monsoons, it was the British project to build a railway across East Africa, the much maligned "Lunatic Express", that led to large numbers of Indian laborers arriving.

Mainly from Gujerat and the Punjab, they were brought to East Africa by the British as indentured labor. Many chose to stay on laying the foundations for the present day affluent business and trading community of Kenyan Asians and adding a particular flavor to the Kenyan culture.

Migrations into what is today Kenya took place over thousands of years, but before the arrival of the Europeans in the 19th century, the three main migratory movements can be identified as those of the agricultural **Bantu**, of the pastoral **Cushitics** and the **Nilotic** speaking tribes. Within these broad groupings there were many tribes, but it is convenient to classify tribes, roughly, into these three main groups.

Kenyans speak a variety of languages, hardly a surprising fact given the number of different tribes there are in the country. English is widely and fluently spoken in towns and by virtually everyone connected with the tourist industry. The major distinguishing feature between the many tribes still remains language. The three main groups of languages are a small number of Cushitic-speakers, speakers of the Nilotic languages, and, representing nearly two-thirds of the population, speakers of the Bantu languages.

The tribes of Kenya represent a cross section of African life, covering a wide spectrum from the unchanged to the assimilated. Some remote tribes lead a way of life scarcely touched by the 20th century while others have adapted to the ways of the west and now incorporate the best of both societies in their day-to-day lives. Some of the major tribes are described here and they come from different parts of the country and from different linguistic groupings.

Some of Kenya's tribal life remains untouched by the 20th century.

Tribal Groups

The **Turkana** are Eastern Nilotic and they inhabit a vast area of northwest Kenya from Lake Turkana west to the Ugandan border. Their current population is some 210,000. Traditionally the Turkana are herdsmen and fearless warriors, but, as is the case with so many tribes, the improvement in communications is taking its toll on their long unaltered lifestyle. Fishing in Lake Turkana is not a central part of their economy and is only practised during the dry season, or if there is a famine.

There are some 20 clans or *ategerin*, but the main factor in Turkana life is less the clan than the neighborhood or *adakar*. A Turkana homestead, or *awi*, is made up of a couple, their children, and later, the families of the married sons. Daughters leave their father's homes on marriage.

The staple Turkana diet consists of milk and blood. Fresh milk is boiled and dried, and crushed berries are mixed with blood to make cakes. During the rainy season, the women grow millet and gourds near water courses. Cattle and camels are an important element in Turkana life and donkeys are used as pack animals. Small children herd the flocks of goats and sheep which are killed for meat and for rituals.

The Maasai, who are largely pastoral nomads, are classified as Eastern Nilotic, and were, originally, a fusion of

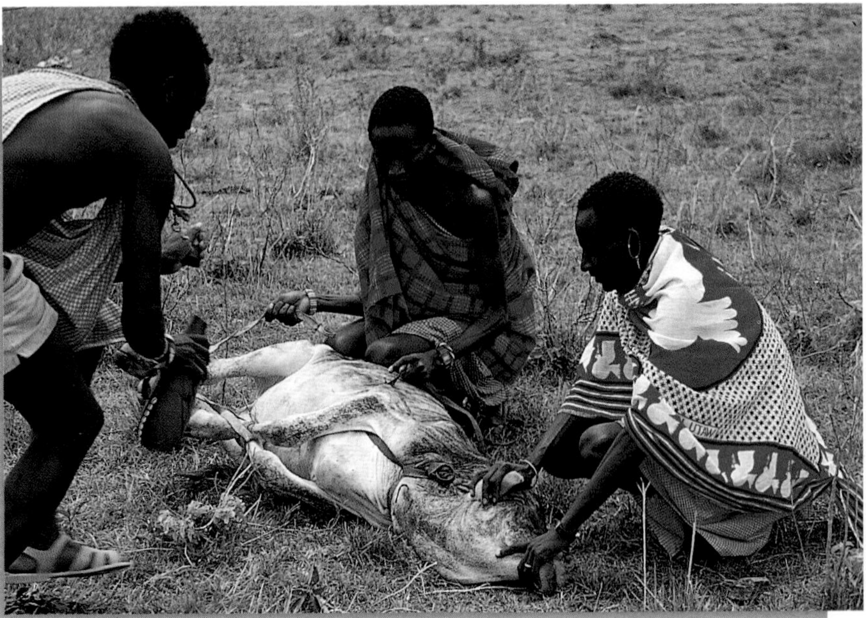

Animal blood form an ingredient in the staple food of some tribes.

Cushitic and Nilotic people. Their current population numbers around 241,500. One thousand years ago, the Maasai left their native Turkana and over the centuries, moved southwards into the fertile plains of the southern Rift Valley.

The Maasai rarely slaughter game, believing that God put them on the earth to protect wild animals. Since they also believe that God gave them responsibility over all the cattle in the world, they developed into impressive cattle rustlers, prepared to travel hundreds of miles in order to raid their neighbors' cattle, which they did with a particularly ferocious success. They were brave people, constantly on the move, in peak physical condition and always ready to

A young Maasai girl dressed for an occasion.

Number 1 Maasai wife. The Maasai have a fairly entrenched and developed social code.

A Maasai family from a Maasai Mara village.

fight. This nomadic existence remained largely unchanged for centuries, and even today, many of the Maasai are still nomads, although, inevitably, the 20th century is bringing about changes to their traditional lifestyle.

The Maasai are a tall, good-looking race, with a highly developed code of warrior behavior. The basic social unit is the *enkang*, a semi-permanent settlement of families who live together and pasture their cattle together. There are sub-divisions into clans, but authority within the tribe derives from the age-

A Samburu woman and child. The Samburu have long resisted change.

group and the age-set. Circumcision marks the passage into adulthood for young men who choose one of their number to be their *olaiguenani*, or natural leader, who will lead his particular age-group through until old age. When the warriors "retire" from their celibate, fighting life, they are permitted to marry.

Fresh milk as well as fermented milk is a staple of the Maasai diet. The blood and urine of cattle are mixed to form a stimulant.

The **Samburu** are Nilotic nomads who speak a language called Maa. There are currently about 73,000 Samburu who live in Maralal and northern Kenya between the Ewaso Nyiro River and Lake Turkana. They are thought to have migrated south from the north of Lake Turkana several centuries ago, as did the Maasai. They are pastoralists and cattle owners and wherever the land permits, they grow maize, vegetables and sorghum. Milk, often mixed with blood, is their principal food, the blood coming either from living cattle or from goats and sheep slaughtered for their meat. They also eat some roots and tree barks, added to a soup.

Like the Maasai, the Samburu also long resisted change, although, inevitably, improved education is slowly bringing about some change. Although the Samburu share their language and much of their cultural heritage with the Maasai, they differ from them in one major respect in that they are a highly tolerant people eschewing the warlike behavior of the Maasai and placing great store on *nkanyit* or a sense of respect for a fellow-man.

Samburu live in small settlements, comprising some four to ten families, which are essentially low mud huts with a separate cattle yard for each family, all of which are enclosed by a thorn fence. Like many other tribes, circumcision is practised and is performed when boys are initiated as warriors. These initiation ceremonies, or *ilayeni*, take place in specially constructed settlements, or *lorora*, according to certain lunar timings. After several days of rituals, the young men become *il-murran*, and as such, are allowed to decorate their bodies and their hair with red ochre. After five years as junior *il-murran*, there is another ceremony marking their passage to senior *il-murran*. After another six years and another ceremony, where a bull is suffocated and eaten, that particular age-set of warriors is allowed to marry. As married men, or *lpayan*, they have greater standing in a society where real power lies in the hands of the tribal elders.

The **Kamba** are Bantus, and with a population of a little over 1.7 million, they form the fourth largest ethnic group in Kenya. The Kamba are mainly concentrated in the Machakos and Kitui districts of the Eastern Province. They were originally hunters probably from the area around Mount Kilimanjaro but about four centuries ago, they began to adopt the more sedentary life of farming, and later, trading with their neighbors. The tribe's prosperity was severely affected in the 19th century by two events: the rinderpest plague, which decimated their herds, and when the Nairobi-Mombasa railway line was being constructed, a ban was placed on tribal expansion into the otherwise empty lands around Yatta and Ulu. Today, poor farming techniques and

Bright and eager children in school uniform.

Women of Maralal.

severe deforestation still impede the tribe's prosperity, and in the arid northeast around Kitui where they are based, drought and famine also take their toll. The Kamba are skilled craftsmen, particularly in the art of woodcarving which has become a major handicraft industry bringing much needed income to the region. The Kamba also use iron and copper wire to make jewelry, arrow heads and spears, while the women make clay cooking pots and baskets called *kiondo* made out of the finely plaited fibers of the baobab and wild fig trees.

The basic unit of Kamba life is the *musyi* or extended family, and, as a people, they were slow to adopt new methods of agriculture unlike the Kikuyu, for example (see box story p.106). Many Kamba served in the police and in the colonial days, in the King's African Rifles Regiment. Traditionally, the weapons of the Kamba are the bow and arrow which is usually poisoned, the throwing club and a long fighting sword, known as a *simi*.

The Luo are the largest of Kenya's non-Bantu groups numbering around 2.2 million. They are Nilotic, having moved south from the Sudan to settle around the Kavirondo Gulf of Lake Victoria. Initially the Luo were nomads but they gradually assumed a more settled lifestyle in isolated homesteads where agriculture and fishing figured alongside cattle in their economy. As well as the traditional crops of sorghum and millet, today vegetables, ground nuts,

Kikuyu

Kikuyu dancers.

In the beginning, say the Kikuyu, *Mwene Nyaga* or God created a man in his own image called Gikuyu and gave him control over all living things in the land. One day, he took Gikuyu to the highest peak of a sacred, snow-covered mountain called Kirinyaga, better known today as Mount Kenya, and showed him the whole of the surrounding countryside.

Gikuyu was to be the ruler of this beautiful land. God told Gikuyu to build his home near a cluster of fig trees, or *mikuyu*, in the center of the country. God gave him a wife called Mumbi and together they had ten daughters.

Lacking a male heir, Gikuyu prayed to God who ordered him to sacrifice a fat ram under a sacred fig tree. It had to be of only one color and without any blemish in its body. This was done and when Gikuyu returned after a few days, he found ten handsome young men waiting under the tree and they became his sons-in-law.

From these first ten couples, the tribe descended. However, since Kikuyu are superstitious about giving the exact number of living things, fearing it will bring bad luck, they will always say that there are "nine tribes plus one".

True or not, the legend of the nine plus one daughters is central to the Kikuyus and their sacred symbol, Mount Kenya, was to be at the

coffee and sugar cane are grown. Fishing is still important for the Luo who are probably the most skilled fishermen in Kenya. They use a variety of methods to catch fish from Lake Victoria including basket traps, nets, fishing lines, fish mazes and fish fences.

The Luo are an articulate and civic-heart of their later conflict with the Europeans. The Kikuyu are Bantus and are the largest of Kenya's ethnic groups numbering 3.2 million. Despite their legends, they probably moved to their homelands on the slopes of Mount Kenya around 400 years ago, and the land which was a dominant feature of Kikuyu life was to be at the root of their long-standing conflict with the white settlers.

The Kikuyu Today

Yet, despite their dislike of the usurping Europeans, paradoxically, the Kikuyu were possibly the most successful at adapting to the challenge presented by western culture and influence, and they soon became involved in politics. In 1920, they formed their own political association and the Kikuyu Central Association presented their case to the colonial government.

The Kikuyu have largely bought over the lands of the hated white settlers and are today progressive farmers who use modern methods and provide domestic supplies as well as exports of coffee, tea, vegetables, flowers, and pyrethrum. They are also active in business and commerce all over the country, and some 400,000 live in Nairobi.

The base of Kikuyu social life is the *nyumba* or family which, as it expands, divides into subclans or *mbari*, which can number from a hundred to a thousand families. Each *mbari* knows from which nine plus one daughter it is descended.

Like many tribes, youths are divided into "age groups" called *riika*, and each age-group chooses its own leader who is their delegate to the tribal elders or *kiama*. A Kikuyu proverb says that "The youth is a gift of God", and young people are highly regarded while the elders are considered to be the authority of God.

minded community who played a prominent part in their country's struggle for independence. Many leading politicians and trade union leaders were Luo including the late Tom Mboya who was assassinated in 1969 and Oginga Odinga, a former Vice President of Kenya. Today, many Luo have migrated to the towns in search of work.

Serene portrait of a mother and child.

The **Boran** are Eastern Cushitic, originally of Ethiopian-Oromo origin, and they presently number some 70,000. They are relatively recent migrants into Kenya having arrived at the turn of the 20th century when the Emperor of Ethiopia, Menelik II, pursued a policy of excessive tribute and, more drastically, extermination, forcing the Boran to migrate south. The Boran raise cattle, sheep and goats as well as the camels that are indispensable for their nomadic life in the arid northeast of the country around Marsabit, Moyale, in Isiolo dis-

A local man finding an alternative use for the ear.

trict, and along the Ewaso Nyiro River.

Those Boran who migrated the furthest south into Kenya, have forsaken their traditional religion for Islam whereas the others believe in a tribal deity called *Wak*.

The Boran have many elaborate rituals and customs, beginning with the *jilla* ceremony when a new born child is named. If the baby is a boy, a tuft of hair known as *gutu* is shaven off and before he is allowed to grow it again as a young man, he has to prove his manhood. To do this, either he must kill a man from another tribe or a lion or an elephant, or he must marry and have a child. The Boran are divided into five "generation sets" each of which is separated by four initiation cycles of eight years each, meaning that 40 years separate the initiation of a father and his son.

There are currently around 22,000 **Rendille** who are Cushitic. They live in the rocky, empty northeast of Kenya in the Korante Plains and in the Kaisut Desert, in Marsabit District. Their neighbors are the Samburu, and despite the differences in language and tradition, the two tribes have centuries-old ties of kinship and economy. The Rendille live in large settlements, which are semi-permanent, as well as in mobile camps, comprising young men and the older boys who move with the herds of camels. Large flocks of sheep and goats are tended by young girls. In common with many desert people, the camel is of vital importance to the Rendille

Myths of the Tribals

Hardly surprisingly for a country with a strong oral tradition, Kenya's tribes have a wealth of legends and myths dealing with everything from God to the rules of their tribe. Early tribal society was family based, most people were illiterate and so story telling became a way of explaining and teaching the younger members of the community. Among the Luo tribe for example, stories were traditionally recited in the evening, after the day's work was completed, in *siwindhe*, the house of a widowed grandmother.

One of the Siwindhe legends is called "Why Man must Dig." The legend tells how, in far off days, *Nyasaye-Nyakalaga* or God used to speak to people and help them, and how food was easily available without any effort needed. One day God spoke to a newly-married woman called Mieha and told her, "Take your hoe to the garden. When you get there, cut the ground once and leave the hoe alone. Your garden will look after itself and harvest itself."

The next day Mieha took her hoe but decided to cut the ground not once, but several times. God was so angry at her disobedience that he said, "Now you must dig for the rest of your life and your food will grow only as a result of your sweat. Woe to your children and your grandchildren who from now on must all labor for their food."

The Gusii tribe recounted its tales in a similar manner to the Luo. In the evening, the homestead owner would gather his sons and grandsons together and teach them about warfare, medicine and land ownership while the young women would learn from their grandmother. Often though, the young Gusii would be encouraged to tell stories and legends among themselves with one of the elders listening in. At the end, the elder would question the young men and women on the significance of the story they had just told.

One such Gusii tale concerns the cock and the ostrich who, long ago, were rivals, each one fearing that his many wives actually loved the other bird. One night, the ostrich decided to pay a visit to the cock and perhaps steal one of his wives. When the ostrich arrived, he found the cock asleep with his head and neck tucked under his wing, and he was so astonished, he cried out, "Cock, where is your head?"

The cock did not move but said from under his wing, "I instructed one of my wives to cut off my head and place it high on a pole in the middle of the homestead. That way, even if I go out or go to sleep, I can still watch all my wives and be sure that they have not run off with someone like you."

The ostrich was very impressed by the logic of this, went home and ordered one of his wives to do exactly the same thing. The poor wife initially refused, but the ostrich insisted, so she duly cut off his head and fastened it to a long pole in the middle of the homestead. When the cock heard of the death of the gullible ostrich, he visited the bereaved wives and offered to take them all to his own homestead. They agreed to go with such a handsome bird and he was delighted to have acquired many more beautiful, long-necked wives.

That night, he advised his son and heir, "Son, never lose your head over a woman. Some are bound to stray but if you are a clever fellow, it is not you who will lose your head, but others, and you will be richer as a result."

lifestyle. Not only is it used as a pack animal capable of carrying up to 80 kg (176 lbs) for 50 km (30 miles) a day, but it also provides milk for the Rendille, even during the dry season when water may only be available for the animals every two weeks. The Rendille mix camel's milk with blood to make a staple of their diet.

Rendille girls are circumcised immediately before marriage whereas the boys, along with their age-set, are circumcised together. There are two major tribal festivals, or *soriu*, one usually in

The children of Mombasa look on with uncertainty as they straddle tradition and modernity.

January or February and the second in June or July, after the rains.

At one time, the numbers of the **el-Molo** tribe had fallen to less than 500, but now intermarriage with the neighboring Samburu and Turkana tribes has helped save them from extinction. The origins of the el-Molo are uncertain, but they are thought to have travelled a relatively short distance south from the Omo delta to Lake Turkana. Their name *molo* means man, and the Maasai-Samburu plural *il* was added to it and subsequently anglicized as "el". The el-Molo call themselves **Ldes**. Most el-Molo today speak Samburu with only a few elders still speaking their indigenous language. They believe in a deity called *Wak*, suggesting an earlier link to the Rendille.

Life for these Cushitic people is changing rapidly. They have already abandoned their former homes on two small islands in Lake Turkana and they are now resettled at Loyangalani, on the south-eastern shore of the lake. They still fish the lake but as this only provides a subsistence level income, they are increasingly turning to cattle herding and to commercial fishing. Fish, either fresh or dried, is a staple part of their diet supplemented by crocodile, turtle and hippopotamus meat, and, when available, wild game and birds. Their principal means of transport and fishing along the lake is a small raft made of doum palm but since the wood absorbs water, these rafts inevitably do

A Maasai family compound with various family members.

not last for long.

The **Bajun**, the **Swahili** and the **Shirazi**, who are all Eastern Bantu, share much in common. They all inhabit the coastal region and they have a common language, Kiswahili. They are Muslims and much of their culture is similar having been open to Arab influence at about the same time. Their language, Kiswahili, is of Bantu origin and has become the national language of Kenya and is also widely spoken throughout east and central Africa.

The Bajun live on the Lamu archipelago and along the coastal strip north towards the Somalian border. Currently they number 37,000. The Bantu-speaking Swahili people have, over generations of trading and immigration, absorbed much of the language and customs of their trading partners who were mainly of Arabic and Persian descent. Increasingly, the word "Swahili" is coming to mean any Muslim from the coast although that is not a totally accurate description. The Swahili and the Shirazi together number only about 5,500.

The Shirazi, as their name would imply, claim to originate from Persia. They used to form the aristocratic dynasties of the Ozi kingdoms of Malindi and Mombasa. Today though, they lead much simpler lives as fishermen and farmers.

Not all tribal names are ancient as the name **Kalenjin** illustrates. The word *Kalenjin* means "I tell you" or "I say to you", and has been used only since the

Heavily out-fitted Pokot women.

late 1950s to describe a group of tribes that were earlier referred to as Nandi-speaking tribes. A Kalenjin is essentially anyone whose mother tongue is one of the many Kalenjin dialects : there are eight major groups of Kalenjin languages, some with further sub-divisions.

The best known of these dialects are Kipsigis, Nandi and Pokot. When the British began their exploration of the African interior, they had many problems with the warlike Nandi tribe which was even beginning to challenge the military supremacy of the Maasai. The

early British administrators, whenever they heard another tribal language that resembled that spoken by the Nandi, described them, unimaginatively, as "Nandi speakers". The missionaries who followed hard on the heels of the early explorers, made it a point to study African languages, later producing written versions, and then, as befitted their calling, African language versions of the scriptures. The first of the Kalenjin dialects to be written down was Nandi and the missionaries continued to use the Nandi language for the rest of the Kalenjin.

The **Pokot** herd their flocks of cattle and goats across the semi-arid lands north of Lake Baringo, from the Taita Hills across to the Karasuk Hills on the Ugandan border. The Pokot can be described either as militant pastoralists from the plains or as the slightly less militant "corn people" from the hills. These militant warriors share several customs with their neighbors, the Turkana to the north and the Karamoja from Uganda, further to the west. Like both of these tribes, the Pokot wear painted clay headdresses even when sleeping, when they are protected by a wooden headrest. Despite these similarities, the Pokot are aggressive in their search for pasture and water which often brings them into conflict with their neighbors. The Pokot eat any kind of meat except that of the hyena and the jackal, as well as honey and milk mixed with blood.

The Nilotic Tugen are a semi-pastoral people who speak Kalenjin and are thought, originally, to have come from around Mount Elgon. Now they are settled mainly in a thin rectangle of land on the floor of the Rift Valley, which is bordered by the Kerio river to the west, and by the Tugen and Kamasia Hills to the west. The President of Kenya, Daniel Toroitich arap Moi, is a Tugen.

Religion

Generalizations are always dangerous, but if one has to generalize about Kenya's religious make-up, then it is true to say that about 70 percent of Kenyans are Christians of one sort or another. Muslims account for the remaining 30 percent of the population living mainly along the coast and in the eastern part of the country.

Islam

Islam is an older religion in Kenya than Christianity, preceding it by several centuries. When the early Arab traders first started coming to the coast on the monsoon winds, they brought with them not only goods to barter but a new religion. Many of the Arabs settled on the coast, intermarrying with the local people and giving rise to a unique **Swahili culture**, which is a distinctive feature both of Mombasa and of the string of ancient

Friday Mosque in Shela village, Lamu. Islam has an essential place along the coast.

All Saints Cathedral, Nairobi. Missionaries poured into Kenya in the 19th century after her doors were opened by European explorers.

city states along the coast.

Most Swahili Muslims are **Sunni** Muslims and just a very small minority of the population is **Shia** – and these are mainly among the Asian community. The Shias have many sects, one of which is the **Ismaili** sect who are followers of the Aga Khan. Look out for a picture of the Aga Khan in a shop, travel agency or office run by Asian Muslims. He is the spiritual head of the Ismaili community and all over Kenya, you will see schools and hospitals set up by Aga Khan foundations. Many Kenyans of Indian origin

are **Hindus** and most large towns will have a Hindu temple or a **Sikh temple.**

Christianity

The 19th-century missionaries who followed hard on the heels of the early European explorers preached **Christianity** all over the country, and today just about every Christian sect is represented in Kenya. European missionary work was very often linked to education and medical aid, which were used to instil confidence and arouse people's interest in their preaching. It is a link that still persists in some of the remoter parts of the country where rural schools

A chapel built by the Italian prisoners-of-war in World War II.

and clinics are often run quite successfully by missionaries.

Many purely African tribal beliefs have mingled with "main stream" Christianity leading to what can only be described as indigenous African Christian sects. These churches believe in the Bible but they may choose to interpret it in a radically different fashion from a more "established" church while incorporating certain traditional practices. At the beginning of this century, there were social and cultural clashes between Africans and the European missionaries, especially over rituals such as female circumcision which the Europeans found repugnant but which featured largely in traditional tribal society.

In the case of the **Kikuyu**, the clash with the missionaries led, ultimately, to the Kikuyu setting up their own schools which in turn led to their own independent church movements such as the **African Orthodox Church** and the **African Pentecostal Church**. Essentially, these churches believe in the Old Testament of the Bible but not the New Testament.

Although so-called urban "modern" society is weakening many of the bonds, **tribal rituals** and customs still hold sway in the villages and in the more remote areas. (See the chapter on People.) Although each tribe naturally has its own individual rituals and customs, some aspects of tribal life can be discussed generally, always bearing in mind that each group may alter certain aspects.

Kikuyu witch doctor explaining his role in 20th-century Kenya.

Traditional Customs

One feature that appears in various tribes such as the Maasai, the Kalenjin and the Samburu, to name just a few, is the concept of **age-groups** and **age-sets**. Authority within a tribe usually derives from these groups. Certain **rites of passage** within a tribe take place communally and as each generation embarks on these rites, they form an age group. This group will stay together, perform certain ceremonies together, pass through various rituals together until the designated time arrives for them to give way to the next generation or age-set.

Within **Kalenjin** society, everyone

Traditional practices like the reading of beads still persist.

An essential feature of the social make-up of many tribes is the age-set where people are divided into groups according to their age.

belongs to an age-set, the basic purpose of which is to divide people into groups according to age, and to which certain responsibilities are then attached. Usually, the first male age-set, after their ritual initiation forms the **warrior group**, since, as the youngest and fittest members of the tribe, they are best able to defend it. Among the Kalenjin, each age-set takes a specific age-set name, which, after the full cycle of age-sets has been completed, will be used again by another age-set.

Among the **Maasai**, the young men are circumcised, marking their entry into warrior-hood. Before the circumcision ceremony which is a group ritual carried out on all the young men of the right age, one natural leader or *olaiguenani* is chosen. This young man will lead his peers – his age-group – through a whole series of rituals until old age when that whole generation will make way for the next age-set.

All members of an age-set live together in a group of anything up to 100 huts called *i-manyat*. The prospective warriors leave their families, and march away together to start building their *i-manyat* where they will live for the next eight to ten years. This will be the time that the young men learn the traditions of the tribe as well as the legends and the songs and dances. They will be taught the art of warfare and if the occasion arises, they will be expected to defend their tribe, their land and their cattle against enemies.

The Prophets of Africa

In 19th-century tribal Africa, long before the first Europeans penetrated the interior of the continent, tribal prophets had foretold the coming of the white man. A Kikuyu prophet called Chege wa Kibiru told his people to expect the arrival of "white strangers who look like butterflies." He told them that although these butterfly people would deprive the Kikuyu of their lands which they later did, especially the fertile lands around Mount Kenya, they were not to fight them. If the Kikuyu did fight, the butterfly people would kill them with their "fire" – presumably he meant their guns.

Luo tribal prophets foretold very much the same thing although the butterfly analogy was dropped. The Luo were warned that the white people had "sticks which vomit fire" – certainly a description of a rifle.

Long before the first white face appeared in Gusii country, on the shores of Lake Victoria, a prophet called Sakawa also told his people about the Europeans. He was much more precise than many prophets for he actually showed his people where the future European buildings would be built, where the electric poles would be and he also advised the Gusii that although the white people would stay and rule the country, they would later leave. Which, of course, they did.

Sakawa is thought to have been born around 1840 and is also thought to have died in November 1902. No one is quite sure because he disappeared and his body was never found. Two years later the British arrived in the land of the Gusii who were quickly defeated by the superior gun power of the British. By 1907, the Gusii were under British control, still harboring the hope that their prophet, Sakawa, would come back to earth – a belief which was to last for many years.

When the ritual leader or priest considers that the young men have completed their training, they will be ready for the circumcision ceremony. At that stage, they pass into the age-set of junior warriors and the existing age-set of junior warriors then becomes senior warriors. And so it continues : the senior warriors will in time become junior elders and then senior elders.

A new age-set is initiated into warrior-hood together at regular intervals, roughly every 12-15 years. The chosen *olaiguenani* shares some of the responsibility with a few other leaders, with ultimate authority being vested in a ritual expert called the *oloiboni*. Once the young Maasai have been circumcised, they are considered to be warriors or *il-murran*, and must follow certain rules. They are forbidden from drinking milk in their parents' home and from eating meat in their *i-manyat*. Instead, the animals are slaughtered away from their huts. The warriors hunt and carry shields whose markings designate their status.

The **Samburu** tribe shares much of the language and cultural heritage of the Maasai and there are similarities in the conduct of their rites of passage and other rituals (see the chapter on People). All ceremonies are conducted at auspicious times which are fixed according to the moon, and these take place in especially constructed settlements known as *lorora*. The circumcision of boys, considered part of the initiation into the warrior group known as *il-murran*, is often carried out by a non-Samburu. After a

The elders have a revered status in the tribes.

month or so, the circumcised young men are considered to be *il-murran* and over the ensuing years, the junior warriors will pass into the age-set of senior warriors at which point they will be allowed to get married. As married men or *lpayan*, they enter into the community of elders who are the real decision makers among the Samburu. Samburu girls are also circumcised but this is done individually, not in a group, as it is for the boys. The girl is circumcised on the morning of her marriage.

Nowadays, among the **Kikuyu**, female circumcision is less frequent than male circumcision which is still considered a necessary rite of passage into adulthood. The young men are divided into age-groups called *riika*, and among themselves they choose their own leader who will henceforth be their delegate at tribal meetings. Each *riika* also chooses a distinguishing characteristic which will be theirs : it could be a special song or a dance or a decoration that they all wear – anything that will mark out that particular age-group.

In common with other Bantu tribes, the Kikuyu have a **council of elders**, called the *kiamia* or court which sits in judgement over the rest of the tribe, judging, solving problems and meting out punishment. A few, select members of the council of elders are chosen to become *njama* or a secret council. Although the Kikuyu have probably adapted more readily than any other tribe to a more westernized way of life, parts of their traditional way of life have still been retained.

The **Kipsigis** attach a great deal of importance to both male and female circumcision to such an extent that the full initiation rituals actually last a number of years although with the advent of a more westernized education, the time spent over such rituals is being reduced. Traditionally, however, the initiation rituals for girls last about 20 months

In some tribes young girls are also subjected to certain rites of passage.

and a little longer for boys.

The beginning of the rituals is accompanied by much drinking of beer, which is stored in a hole in the ground, specially lined with banana leaves to keep the liquid in. Among the Kipsigis, the candidates for circumcision must keep their faces covered. The boys wear a hood with two eye-holes, whereas the girls use the skin of a monkey. After the circumcision ceremony, the girls are segregated from the rest of community for nearly two years during which time the age-group all live together in special huts. Whenever one of the young girls leaves her hut during that time, she covers her face with a hood leaving only her eyes showing. The hut for these girls is unfurnished, and since, in addition, they are not allowed to use chairs, they build themselves little seats of mud. Seven months after the circumcision, female elders of the tribe start to teach the girls the secrets of the tribe and the girls begin to prepare their bridal "trousseau". They choose an animal skin which is then softened with oil and decorated with pearls and shells.

After 18 months of secluded life, a ceremony called *ngetundet*, or coming out, takes place, when the girls can at last put aside the hood that has covered them for the last year and a half and wear instead a *nariet*, which is also a cover, but only for the eyes, made out of shells and little chains. Two months later, the girls are married and have become full members of the tribe.

In a society like Kenya where **tribal bonds** are still very strong, much of the culture is less on a national basis than on a regional one. Different tribes have their own dances, their own stories as well as their own way of dressing and decorating themselves with their own distinctive jewelry and tattooing.

Many of Kenya's tribes were, and still are, **nomadic**. This has naturally meant that such societies have not constructed monuments, or left behind a legacy of permanent buildings, or formal works of art in the conventional sense of the word. Kenya, other than the coast with its separate cultural legacy, has very few ancient structures. Before the arrival of the Europeans in the late 19th century, virtually no towns or villages existed other than the ancient Swahili city states along the coast. The interior of the country was populated by scattered settlements and it was the Europeans who set about founding permanent towns and cities both along the coast and in the rest of

Maasai dancers from the Maasai Mara Reserve.

The National Archives was established to preserve traditions and cultural links.

the country.

The Kenyan government, although keen to see the country "develop", realizes that there is naturally a price to pay for progress, 20th-century style. Many traditions are lost and cultural links are broken as people migrate from their villages to the towns. In an attempt to help preserve the country's traditions, various institutions have been set up. The government has established regional **museums** and **libraries** and the **National Archives** where much restoration work is done. The **Kenya National Theater** in Nairobi, stages not only international plays but also works by Kenyan playwrights. The **National Theater School** was founded in 1968 with the aim of not only teaching students dramatic skills, but also how to write plays. The school also teaches the traditional dances and music of the different regions and tribes.

Rhythm and Dance

Both **music and dance** have long been important in Kenyan social and religious life. The **drum** is

Tribal dances celebrate a variety of events.

Maasai wives singing a welcome song.

widely used and is the basic source of rhythm in much Kenyan music. Instruments are usually very simple and made from locally available sources such as reeds which are used to make simple pipes, or two sticks with which to beat out a rhythm. Most of the instruments may have slight variations but are common to many tribes – such as drums, simple stringed instruments, pipes and horns. They have different names or more or less strings, but the basic principles of these instruments remain the same. The **Kalenjin** use a six-stringed lyre made from a wooden bowl with the skin of a goat or a dikdik stretched over it. The strings are made from cow-fiber. The **Luo** make a simple instrument out of animal horn and also have a single-

Music and dance are intrinsic in the life of the people.

Maasai men applying decorative body paint before dancing.

stringed violin called **orutu**. The **Gusii** have their own version of the lyre which has eight strings and is called **obokhano**. They make drums from a hollowed-out piece of tree trunk, the ends of which are covered with stretched animal hide. The **Pokot** use a six-stringed guitar with a sounding box made from the shell of a tortoise.

Tribal dances celebrated, and still do celebrate, many things: war, although that is less frequent these days, religious events, births, marriages. Usually all the community dances are uniquely masculine and women are prohibited from taking part.

Much of **Swahili literature** belongs to an oral tradition but increasingly young authors are writing down their

Tribal dances tend to be a male domaine.

Swahili Dances

The "stick dance" in the Maulidi festival.

Among the Swahili people living in the Lamu archipelago, song and dance are of great importance during festivities and special occasions. The **Maulidi festival**, which marks the birthday of the prophet Mohammed, is probably the most important event in the island's calendar and is the occasion for much dancing.

A Maulidi is a eulogy on Mohammed's exemplary life. It is celebrated for several days during the six months after Ramadan. The tradition of Habshi Maulidi began about 1900 when it was started by Sheikh Habib Salih, a very religious man who settled in Lamu in the 1880s. He made the little island a respected center of Koranic teaching and it was he who decided that local dances should be performed to entertain the many guests who were in Lamu for Maulidi. Dances seldom include women for local customs prohibit them from participating in public dances.

One of the most famous dances is the **Kirumbizi**. This is a dance where men form a large circle, each person carrying a staff or stick. Two men at a time step into the circle and execute threatening gestures. As the music quickens, the two have a mock combat clashing their staffs.

The Maulidi festivities last about a week and include religious meetings as well as dancing and feasting. Muslim pilgrims flock to the island from all over Kenya as well as from the rest of East Africa.

stories. **Visual arts**, such as the Makonde sculptures and the Kisii soapstone carvings are beautiful pieces of art but very often have their genesis in the tourist trade rather than a purely artistic spirit.

The best known of the country's

The interior of the National Museum, Nairobi.

museums is the **National Museum** in Nairobi which was originally founded in 1910 by the then newly formed East Africa and Uganda Natural History Society, although it did not move to its present site for a number of years. As befits a country primarily known for its superb wildlife, much of this excellent museum is devoted to the flora and fauna of Kenya as well as its topography. There are, however, several important non-wildlife related galleries. The Lamu gallery has a lot of artifacts and information about the islands of the Lamu archipelago. The ethnography gallery has displays of many different examples of jewelry, musical instruments and utensils from the country's many tribes.

Of the country's provincial museums, one of the most attractive is the delightful **Lamu Museum** which is almost an obligatory first stop for all visitors to the island for it has a mass of information about the history of Lamu, its restoration and its present day existence (see chapter on Lamu). **Fort Jesus** in Mombasa is a well-preserved fort in its own right and as such is very interesting to visit. It also has a small, very informative museum inside the walls of the fort. (See chapter on Mombasa.)

Religious and Festive Events

Kisumu Museum, like many of the

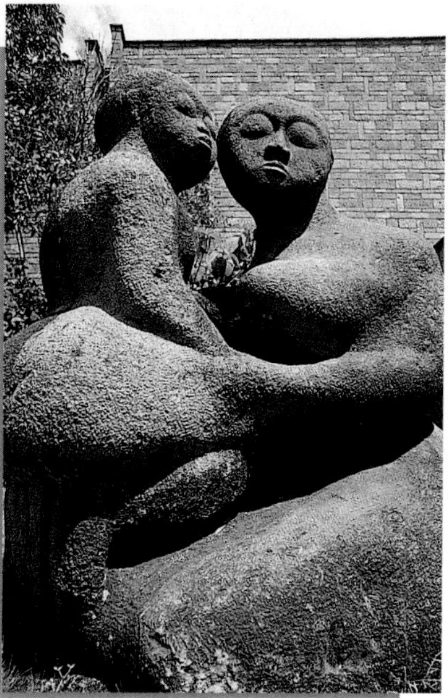

Sculpture in the garden of the National Museum.

Lamu Museum.

country's museums, devotes many of its rooms to wildlife but it also has excellent displays of the implements and objects used by the different tribes who inhabit the region.

There are 11 public holidays a year in Kenya, some of them internationally known holidays and some special to the country. **New Year's Day** is a holiday as are the major **religious festivals**. The Christian festivals of **Good Friday**, **Easter Monday** and **Christmas Day**, as well as the day after Christmas, **Boxing Day** and the Muslim festival of **Id-ul-Fitr**,

marking the end of the holy month of Ramadan, are public holidays.

The **political** holidays are **Labor Day** on 1 May and **Madaraka Day** on 1 June which celebrates self-government. **Nyayo Day** on 10 October is the anniversary of President Moi's inauguration while **Kenyatta Day** on 20 October commemorates the midnight arrest of Jomo Kenyatta by the colonial authorities. The event took place in 1952. **Independence Day** on 12 December actually has two names, **Jamhuri** and **Uhuru Day.** They celebrate both the anniversary of independence in 1963 and also the formation of the Republic of Kenya which took place exactly a year later on 12 December 1964.

Several annual events also mark the calendar in Kenya. In January each year there is an **International Bill Fishing Competition** in Malindi after which anglers can move just a little way south down the coast to Mombasa, where in February there is the **Mombasa Fishing Festival**. In February each year, there is also the **Mtwapa Off-shore Power Boat Race** at the little town of Mtwapa, close to Malindi. March is the time for the prestigious **Kenya Open Golf Championship** which takes place at the Muthaiga Golf Club. The country's biggest sporting event, the **Safari Rally** takes place around Easter each year.

For the next few months, a series of agricultural shows follows. In the middle of June, there is the **Nakuru Agricultural Show**, towards the end of August there is the **Mombasa Agricultural Show**, and a month later, at the end of September, the **Nairobi International Show**. This is the biggest of the agricultural shows lasting six days and regularly attracts about half a million people. The event is often used by politicians as a forum for making major speeches. Then the year ends as it begins, at Malindi for the **Malindi Fishing Festival**.

One of the most dazzling images of Kenya is the sight of a Pokot or a Maasai woman, striding swiftly along a simple country road, wearing a stunning array of **jewelry**. She may well be wearing an elaborate headdress, bracelets, long earrings, and a breathtaking collection of necklaces and beadwork collars, with row upon row of brightly colored beads and buttons, which will sometimes be decorated with incongruous items like a front door key. Kenyan tribeswomen do not wear a single string of beads, as their western sisters would, but dozens of strings, in bright, cheerful colors. Since each Kenyan tribe has its own tradition of beadwork, so the way of wearing them differs. Sometimes the beads are fixed onto a hard collar-like base while others wear the many individual strands of beads loose, worn one on top of the other.

Women from Loita Hills tribe working on elaborately beaded jewelry.

The Language of Beads

Beautiful to look at, formerly a source

Beaded jewelry adapted to contemporary styles.

of wealth and prestige to the wearer, **beads** represent an ancient strand of African culture and history for their origins go back hundreds of years. Beads were used by early explorers and traders as gifts and a means of currency. Often referred to as "trade-wind beads", they were originally made by the Romans and early Egyptians, but the most beautiful examples were Venetian and were brought over by dhow to Africa from the early 15th century onwards. The beads were traded for gold, ivory, palm oil and slaves. Thus, with time and changing fashion, over the generations, necklaces were decorated with a mixture of items. Trade beads from Venice or other European glass-making centers were combined with local handmade elements, as well as with Ethiopian handworked silver beads, or with more ornate silver beads from North India.

Generally speaking, necklaces of a highly structured fixed form are rare in Africa, although two of the most complex occur, in fact, among two neighboring Kenyan tribes, the **Samburu** and **Rendille**. The women wear glass beads, palm fibers (although when elephants were more common, their tail hairs were supposedly used in place of the current plant fibers), and cloth-bound necklaces or neckpieces that form huge ensembles around the shoulders and necks. These ensembles are formed by three to four, or more, wrapped tiers of fibers.

Among the Rendille, these fiber or

In tribal society beads used to be the currency indicative of social status and wealth.

Basketry in the Bombolulu Workshop preserves a traditional handicraft.

cloth neckpieces are called *Mpooro-engorio*. Such necklaces were usually worn on top of wire-strung glass bead necklaces which provided a stiff foundation. The neighboring **Maasai** also use a form of base to support their layers of necklaces, whereas Samburu women tend to wear accumulations of strung glass bead necklaces instead of these wrapped fiber neckpieces.

The women of the Maasai and **Wakamba** tribes are famous for their colorful beadwork whose designs, color combinations and patterns signify the age and status of the wearer. Wakamba weave beads into geometric patterns usually based on the spear or the arrow, a natural enough motif for a tribe so preoccupied with hunting. Maasai women string beads onto wire collars which are worn by married women, although Maasai men also make and wear beaded jewelry.

As well as glass beads, many Kenyan beads are made of **clay**. One method of making clay beads is to arrange the pat-

Maasai wedding necklace made from cowrie shells.

tern of handmade beads, in a log, with layers of special clay building up the design. The clay is then stretched to reduce the size, creating a condensed form of the pattern which is then sliced according to size. Then it is baked, transforming the clay into a hard, durable material. The clay retains its color and the beads are waterproof.

An unusual element in Kenyan jewelry is the frequency with which **wire** is used. In the 19th century, successive European explorers had brought with them large amounts of wire, as well as the highly popular beads, to trade with the local tribes. After the British began constructing the Mombasa to Kampala railway line across the country, and establishing telegraph links, many African tribes found a new source of jewelry – the metal rails and the telegraph wires, which were appropriated to make weapons and jewelry.

The British fumed at what they called stealing whereas tribes such as the Nandi felt they were doing their bit to keep out the unpopular invaders, as well as beautifying themselves at the same time. Since metal became plentiful, thanks to the railway's apparently inexhaustible supply, ever more uses were found for it including specific jewelry to indicate particular ailments and injuries. This in turn meant that a carrier of an infectious disease could be safely identified at a distance, thanks to his jewelry.

Following on from the ancient tribal

A craftsman engrossed in work.

Bombolulu

Bombolulu Workshop trains the physically disabled and blind in handicrafts as part of a rehabilitation program.

As you drive along the busy main road leading north out of Mombasa, heading towards the beaches and the five-star hotels, follow the bright yellow road signs until you turn off down a tree-lined track. This leads to Bombolulu, an interesting, friendly, successful and heart-warming workshop. The Bombolulu Workshop for the Handicapped was founded in 1969 as a pilot project for the physically disabled of Kenya, and in less than 25 years has become one of Kenya's success stories in rehabilitation.

Scattered around the grounds are various workshops making jewelry, clothing and fabrics and turning out woodcarving and leather work. Over 220 physically handicapped and blind people are trained and employed here.

The jewelry workshop department is the oldest in the center, and employs 60-70 disabled workers who are provided with free housing for themselves and their families in addition to earning either a monthly salary or being paid per piece produced. It was started in 1969 with the help of Peace Corps Volunteers who developed a series of jewelry-based ethnic African designs.

The handcrafted jewelry produced in the workshop is made from a variety of materials including copper, brass, local beads, Somali wooden beads, old East African coins as well as a huge array of "natural" materials including banana fiber, beatnik bone, slices of bone, bambakofi seed, ngolokolo seed, krita seed, grass seed, coconut seed, brawn seed, lily seed,

beadwork traditions, modern Kenyan craftsmen now make bead jewelry in more **contemporary** shapes and sizes, and which are much more "wearable" by both urban Africans and non-Africans, than the much more ornate traditional pieces.

One workshop making jewelry based on traditional materials and designs, is **Bombolulu**, an organization which aims to rehabilitate handicapped workers, while the Nairobi-based **Kazuri co-operative** provides much-needed employment, essentially for women. Most of the women working in the Kazuri factory, in the suburb of Karen a few kilometers from central Nairobi, are untrained single mothers from rural areas.

In Kazuri, they have regular employment, on-the-job training and they get health care for themselves and their children. In the workshops, each bead is made of clay and painted entirely by hand before glazing, and so no two are exactly alike. Kazuri, which means machakof and the delightfully named "lucky seed". Each piece of jewelry is based on a traditional African design and is then hand-tooled and finished by the disabled workers. Some of the copper jewelry is then 18-carat gold or silver-plated.

At present there are over 500 different designs of jewelry alone. Every month about 20,000 pieces of jewelry are exported to USA, Canada, Europe, Australia and New Zealand and Japan. Prices are kept very low with only a small profit margin which enables Bombolulu to provide better facilities for the workers. All sales prices are therefore fixed.

In addition to jewelry, Bombolulu also produces both finished cotton clothes and fabrics which are block-printed in the workshops. The tailoring workshop was started in 1987 with German assistance, and in addition to making clothes, each year 12 tailors are trained and are eventually offered either employment in Bombolulu or the necessary capital to help them start up their own business back in their own community.

Recently, a leather workshop and a woodcarving workshop have been founded and as the finances of Bombolulu become increasingly healthy, more development in the future is almost certain. This will certainly open avenues for tradition being kept amidst modernization.

"small and beautiful" in Swahili, was founded by Lady Sue Wood, the widow of Dr Michael Wood, the founder of the "Flying Doctors of East Africa".

Nature is the Source

Far simpler than beadwork jewelry, are items handmade from Kenyan **cow horn**. These items of jewelry come from the horns of steer, mostly owned by the Maasai tribe, and the finished article

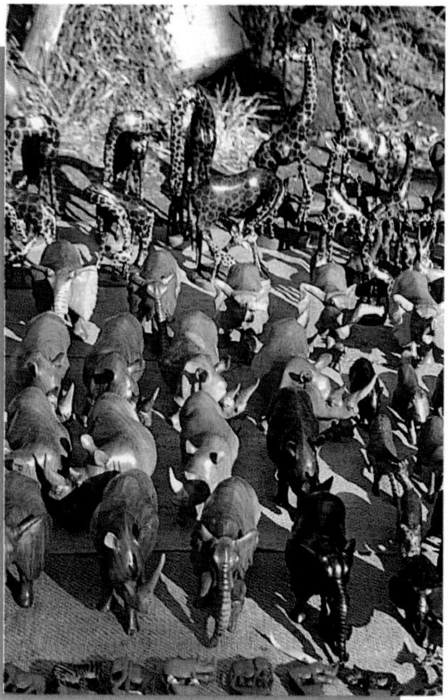

Woodcarving is a favored handicraft.

bears no resemblance to its original state. Processing the gigantic Zebu oxen horns involves using strong chemicals to remove the inner core and outer husk, special tools to cut and smooth out natural imperfections and heat to mold the horn.

Hand carved and hand polished to highlight the natural beauty and grain, typical objects made of this material are bracelets, rings and hair slides. There is no known reason for the variance in color of each horn, but the thickness denotes the amount or lack of nourishment during the animal's life span.

Woodcarving is one of Kenya's most popular handicrafts, and one of the woods most prized for carving is ebony. Ebony, which is one of the hard-

Brightly woven kiondos in a village market in the Kikuyu highlands of Maua.

est of African woods, is easily identified by its burnished beige outer wood, encircling a heart which is dark brown in hue. It is a durable, heavy wood which sinks in water, it is unaffected by termites and other destructive insects and it rarely cracks when seasoned. Being brittle, however, means that this beautiful wood must be carved by very skilled artists. Ebony is used by **Makonde** carvers to produce their unique abstract sculptures as well as household items and combs with a dark sheen.

Wherever you travel in Kenya you will see **baskets** used by the local people for their shopping. These baskets are often made from sisal and are called *kiondos*. Kenyan basketry is always made from natural fibers such as grass, sapling, palm, split reed papyrus and bark. The Nubian women who migrated to East Africa during the last century from southern Sudan, use palm fiber in their trays, baskets or planters that are woven in bold, geometric patterns using bright imported and natural dyes.

In the hills around Kisii, in western Kenya, are soapstone quarries whose soft marble is used in beautiful **Kisii soapstone carvings.** The color of the stone can range from deep rose to ivory white, striated with honey and gold and tinged with deep purple. The stone is turned into gigantic sculptures, tiny safari animals and contemporary household items. Some of the most dramatic pieces are huge, simple, carved hippos and rhinos, whose cool, smooth sur-

The fabric department in the Bombolulu Workshop.

faces invite you to caress the pale pink stone. However, they are quite heavy.

Clothing

Traditional Kenyan **clothing** is simple, designed for the heat and for ease of movement. There is a Kenyan version of a sarong, which is widely worn by both men and women with some stylistic variations.

One version, often worn by women is called a **Kanga** which had its origins along the coast of east Africa, in the mid-19th century. The idea started in Zanzibar when ladies began to sew rectangular cotton handkerchiefs into one big piece to cover their entire bodies, leaving only a slit for their eyes. This style was called "Leso", and it quickly became popular. Soon the handkerchief Leso was being made in one single piece. Originally, the cloth was made in India and China, then later in Kenya and Tanzania. The earliest designs had a border pattern and white spots on a dark background. This resembled the spots on a guinea fowl known as *Kanga* in Swahili – hence the name.

In time, Swahili sayings were added to the design often including a proverb such as *Kanga Naenda Na Urembo* – "The Kanga struts in style". Kangas are printed in bold designs and colors. A kanga is as long as your outstretched arms and wide enough to cover you from neck to knee. Kangas are often sold in pairs and most

Traditional Swahili decoration.

traditional outfits require a pair of at least two different ones. Kangas are worn by both men and women and are reputedly used in over a 100 different ways.

A **kikoi** is a cloth worn as a wrap mainly by Swahili men as well as by other men along the coast of East Africa and Zanzibar. Kikoi cloth was first imported into the East African coast by the dhow trade from the Middle East, the cloth itself coming from China, India, Indonesia and Yemen.

Earlier versions were large, solid blocks of color with brightly striped edges. Kikois were not only limited to the coast for historically they were traded as far inland as Uganda, Zaire and other central African countries. Nowadays, kikoi is woven in Kenya in solid colors with striped borders and a variety of multi-striped patterns.

The Swahili Tradition

Along the coast, where the cultural influence was very different from the interior, the trade and interaction with both Arab and Indian cultures led to the development of a distinct Swahili tradition which is unique being an assimilation of Muslim and African cultures. The external influences on the region's decorative art can be seen in **wood carving, silver work** and other **metal work.** Swahili woodcarving is very different from the abstract Makonde work of the interior, finding its expression in a more formalized, intricate design.

On the island of **Lamu**, still today one of the strongholds of Swahili culture, local craftsmen specialized in carving ornate wooden doors, many of which are still in use and as you wander around the little town, you can see many beautiful examples.

There are four basic types of carved doors in Lamu : the Zanzibar, with deep, carved designs; the Bajun door with a more geometric style; the Indian type, which usually has an arched top, and the Siyu colored doors with small, lacy carved designs. Among the Kikuyu and Maasai tribes, their **shields** were decorated with distinctive polychrome designs which traditionally designated the status of the warriors to whom they belong.

The shield and spear, traditional elements of tribal warfare, are still commonly seen in Kenya.

1914
1918
THIS IS TO THE MEMORY OF
THE NATIVE AFRICAN TROOPS
WHO FOUGHT; TO THE CARRIERS
WHO WERE THE FEET AND HANDS
OF THE ARMY; AND TO ALL OTHER
MEN WHO SERVED AND DIED
FOR THEIR KING AND COUNTRY
IN EASTERN AFRICA
IN THE GREAT WAR, 1914 - 1918
IF YOU FIGHT FOR YOUR COUNTRY
EVEN IF YOU DIE, YOUR SONS
WILL REMEMBER YOUR NAME
HAYA NI MAKUMBUSHO YA ASKARI
WA NTI ZA HUKU AFRICA
WALIOPIGANA KATIKA VITA
PAMOJA NA WATUKUZI
WALIOKUWA NI MAGUU
NA MIKONO YA HAO ASKARI
NA WATU WOTE WENGINE
WALIOTUMIKA WAKAFA
KWA AJILI YA MFALME WAO
NA NTI ZA MASHRIKI YA AFRICA
KATIKA VITA VIKUBWA 1914 - 1918
MUTAKAPO PIGANA KWA NTI ZENU
HATTA MUKIFA VIJANA VYENU
WATAKUMBUKA MAJINA YENU

Nairobi

There can be few capital cities in the world which owe their existence to a railway line. Nairobi certainly does for the capital of Kenya is exactly as old as the halfway point of the "**Lunatic Express**", the improbable railway built by the British to link coastal Mombasa to Kampala.

On 30 May 1899, construction of mile peg 327 of this "impractical, extravagant and uneconomical railway" reached an unhealthy, swampy stretch of land known to the Maasai as "**Nyrobi**" or "place of the cool waters". Despite its poor soil, a swampy black cotton soil which is possibly the worst kind of soil for building, it was the only logical place to construct the upcountry railhead for after Nyrobi came the steep sides of the Great Rift Valley. With the arrival of the train and the construction gangs of indentured Indian laborers, huts and small shops rapidly sprung up and Nairobi began to take shape.

The War Memorial in Nairobi erected to commemorate the struggle for independence.

From a squalid shantytown, Nairobi grew in less than a century

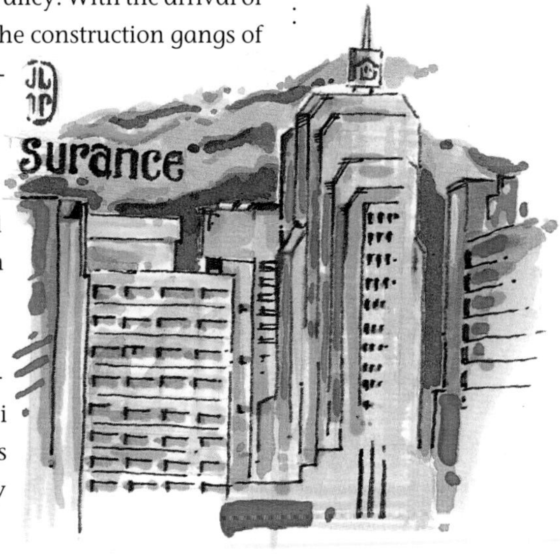

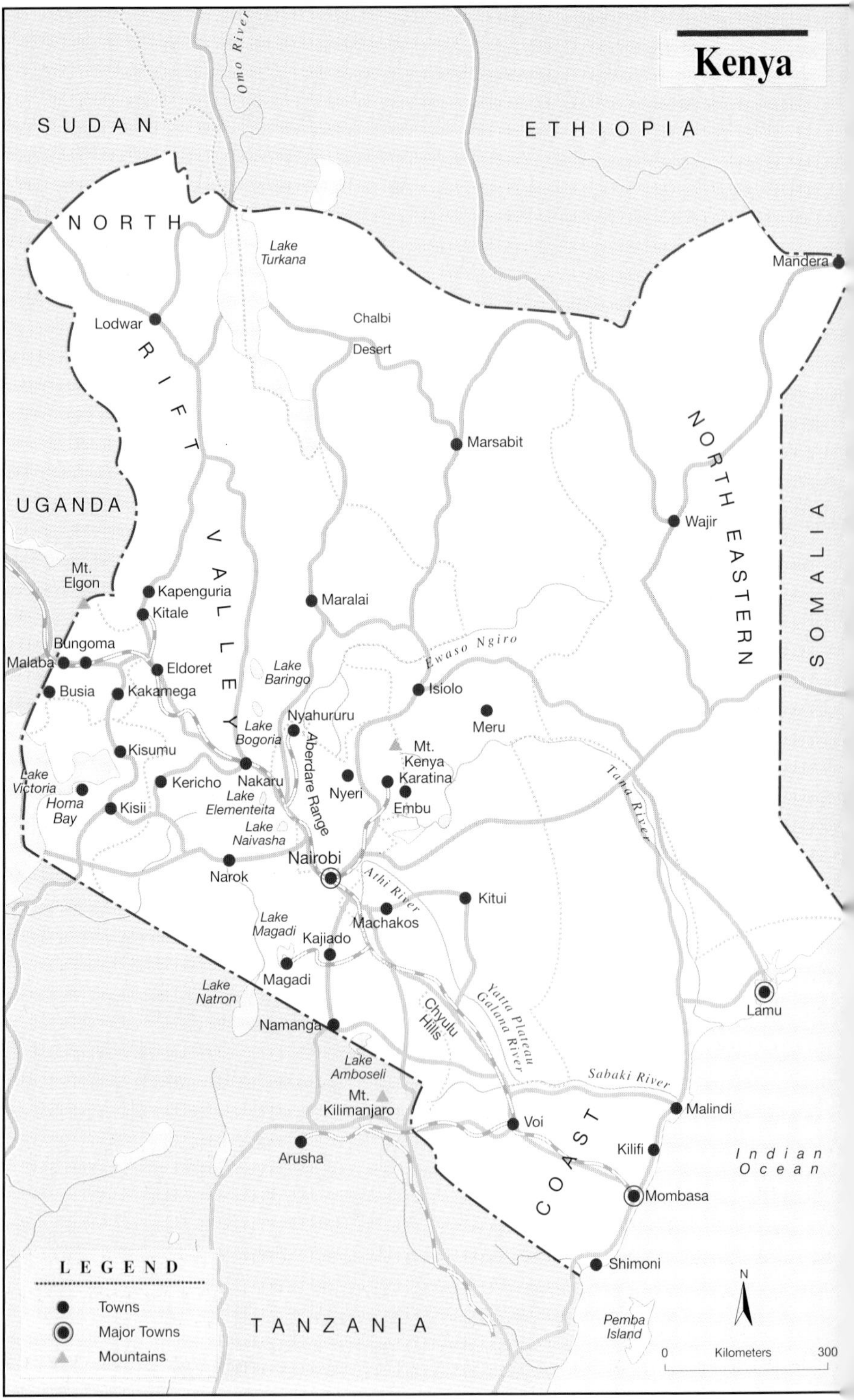
Kenya
SUDAN
ETHIOPIA
UGANDA
SOMALIA
TANZANIA
NORTH
RIFT VALLEY
NORTH EASTERN
COAST
Omo River
Lake Turkana
Chalbi Desert
Lodwar
Marsabit
Mandera
Wajir
Mt. Elgon
Kapenguria
Kitale
Maralai
Ewaso Ngiro
Bungoma
Malaba
Eldoret
Lake Baringo
Busia
Kakamega
Isiolo
Meru
Lake Bogoria
Nyahururu
Aberdare Range
Mt. Kenya
Kisumu
Tana River
Lake Victoria
Kericho
Nakuru
Nyeri
Karatina
Homa Bay
Kisii
Lake Elementeita
Embu
Lake Naivasha
Nairobi
Narok
Athi River
Kitui
Machakos
Lake Magadi
Kajiado
Magadi
Lake Natron
Yatta Plateau
Galana River
Chyulu Hills
Lamu
Namanga
Lake Amboseli
Sabaki River
Mt. Kilimanjaro
Malindi
Voi
Arusha
Kilifi
Indian Ocean
Mombasa
Shimoni
Pemba Island
LEGEND
Towns
Major Towns
Mountains
N
0 Kilometers 300

Nairobi from the Maasai word meaning "place of cool waters" is an international communications and commercial center.

into what is today the largest and most important city between Cairo and Johannesburg. A few years away from its 100th birthday, Nairobi is an efficient, friendly city, bristling with tower blocks and bustling with an ever increasing population. Yet, in the league of world capitals, it remains a small place, a city where you can comfortably walk around most of the city center in a short time, and where else in the world do lion, cheetah and rhino roam around silhouetted against the tower blocks of five-star hotels and office blocks?

Most visitors to Kenya arrive in Nairobi, most safaris leave from there, so it is a place of transit, a place to stock up on supplies, do your paperwork and administration and rest between safaris. After a week or two of bumping along dusty roads and rising at dawn to watch the wildlife, a day in Nairobi comes as a welcome break for it is one of the most traveler-oriented cities in the world. You can get your films processed, buy more maps and films and books for the next safari, catch up on the newspapers, relax, and generally enjoy a day of city life.

Nairobi is 140 km (84 miles) south of the Equator and at an altitude of 1,650 m (5,500 ft) above sea-level, making it pleasantly temperate and invigorating. It is home to Kenyans – African, Asian and white – as well as Somalis, Ugandans and many other African peoples. There are Hindus and Muslims, U.N. officials and tourists, the very rich,

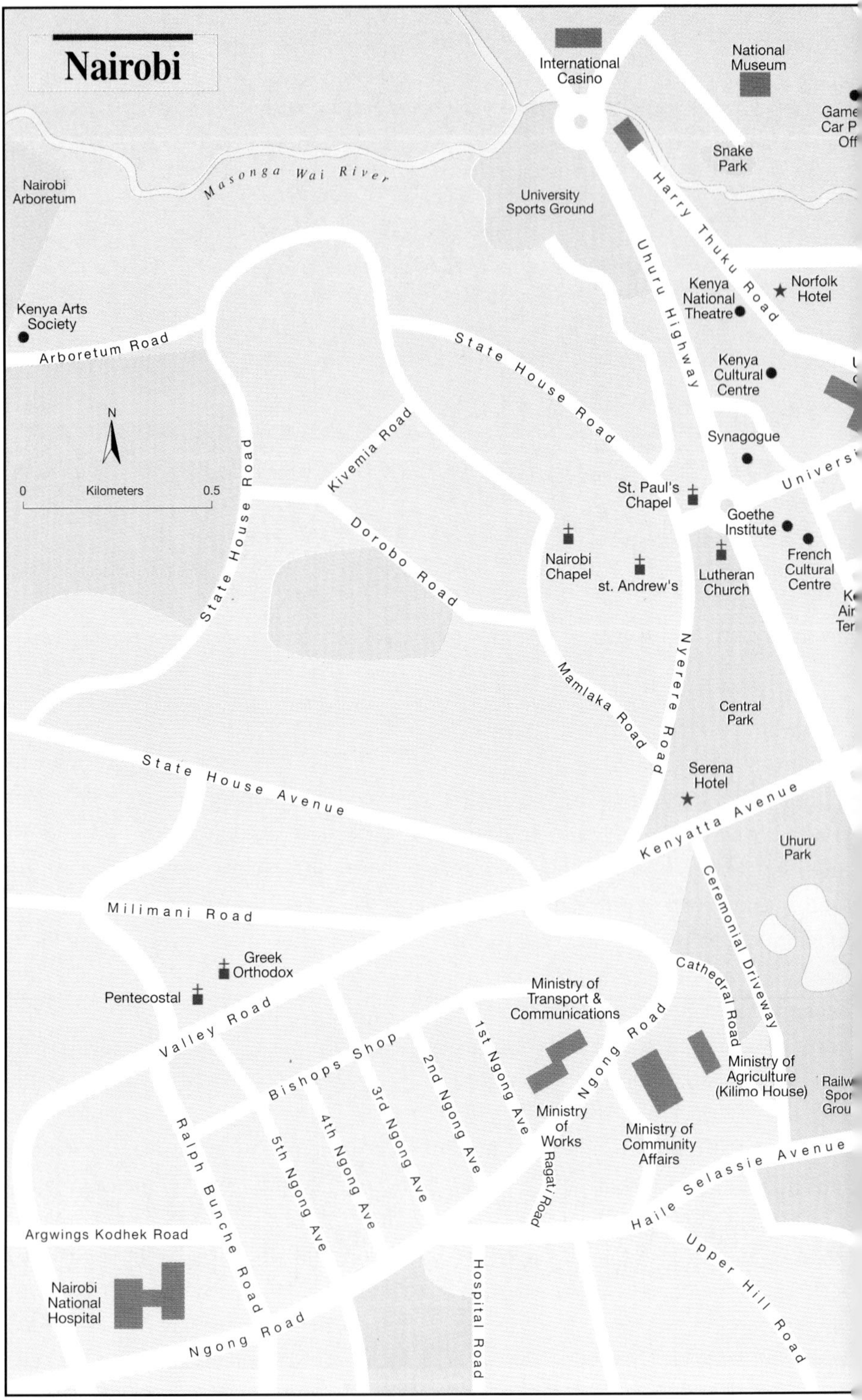
Nairobi
International Casino
National Museum
Snake Park
Masonga Wai River
Nairobi Arboretum
University Sports Ground
Harry Thuku Road
Uhuru Highway
Kenya National Theatre
Norfolk Hotel
Kenya Arts Society
Arboretum Road
State House Road
Kenya Cultural Centre
Synagogue
Kivemia Road
N
0
Kilometers
0.5
State House Road
Dorobo Road
St. Paul's Chapel
Goethe Institute
French Cultural Centre
Nairobi Chapel
st. Andrew's
Lutheran Church
Mamlaka Road
Nyerere Road
Central Park
Serena Hotel
State House Avenue
Kenyatta Avenue
Uhuru Park
Milimani Road
Ceremonial Driveway
Greek Orthodox
Pentecostal
Cathedral Road
Ministry of Transport & Communications
Valley Road
Ngong Road
Bishops Shop
1st Ngong Ave
2nd Ngong Ave
3rd Ngong Ave
4th Ngong Ave
5th Ngong Ave
Ministry of Works
Ministry of Agriculture (Kilimo House)
Ministry of Community Affairs
Ralph Bunche Road
Ragati Road
Haile Selassie Avenue
Argwings Kodhek Road
Upper Hill Road
Nairobi National Hospital
Hospital Road
Ngong Road

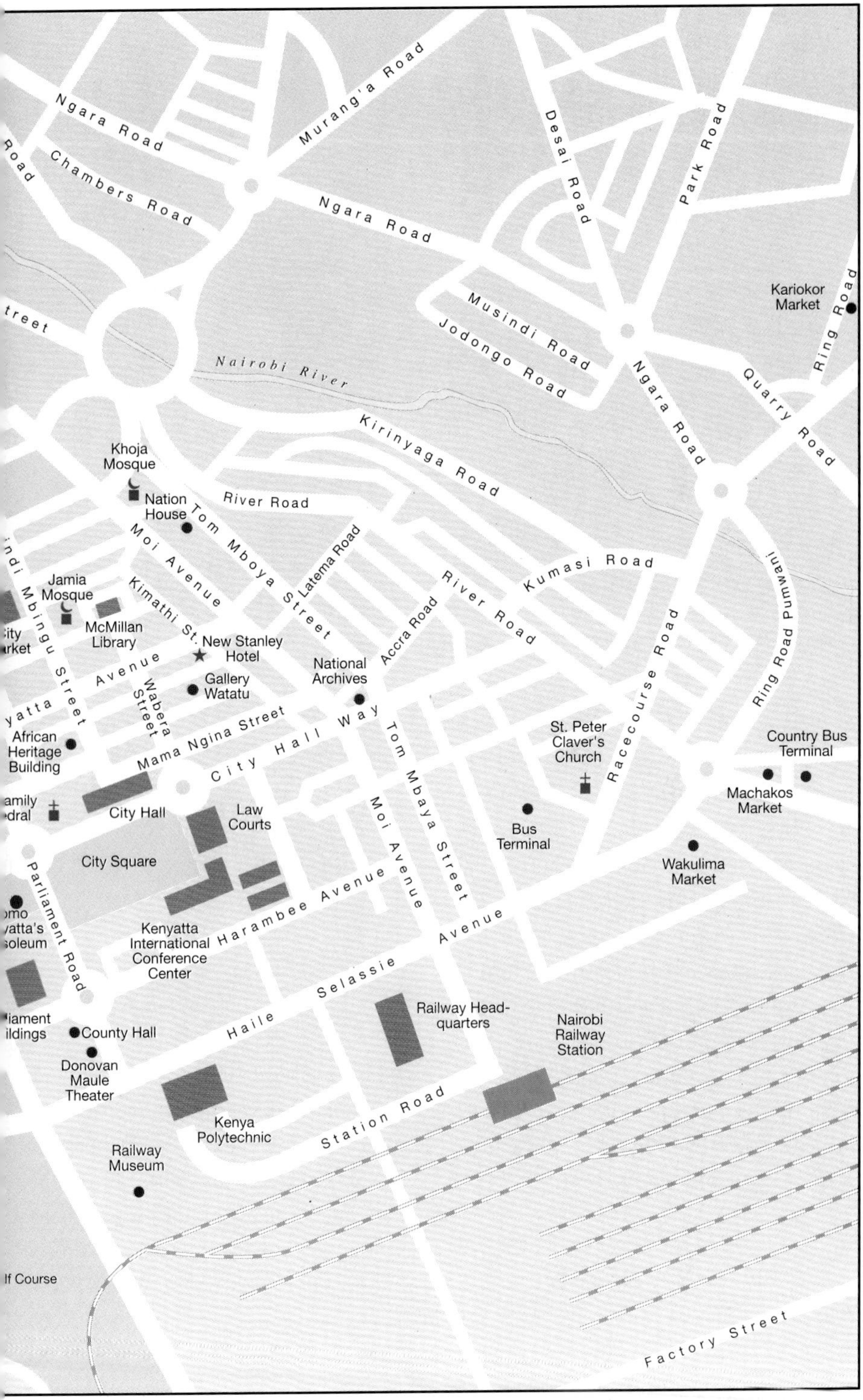
Ngara Road
Murang'a Road
Road
Chambers Road
Ngara Road
Desai Road
Park Road
Kariokor Market
Ring Road
Musindi Road
Jodongo Road
treet
Nairobi River
Ngara Road
Quarry Road
Kirinyaga Road
Khoja Mosque
Nation House
River Road
Tom Mboya Street
Moi Avenue
Latema Road
Kumasi Road
Jamia Mosque
Kimathi St.
River Road
Accra Road
McMillan Library
New Stanley Hotel
National Archives
Racecourse Road
Ring Road Pumwani
Gallery Watatu
Wabera Street
Mbingu Street
Avenue
City Hall Way
Tom Mbaya Street
Mama Ngina Street
St. Peter Claver's Church
Country Bus Terminal
African Heritage Building
City Hall
Law Courts
Moi Avenue
Bus Terminal
Machakos Market
City Square
Wakulima Market
Parliament Road
Harambee Avenue
Kenyatta International Conference Center
Avenue
Haile Selassie
County Hall
Donovan Maule Theater
Railway Headquarters
Nairobi Railway Station
Kenya Polytechnic
Station Road
Railway Museum
Factory Street

Nation Building.

and, sadly, the very poor. The population of Nairobi is growing too rapidly for its own good or for its civic capacities. Nairobi has its share of poverty like any large city, and although the short-term visitor is unlikely to encounter any problems, petty crime does exist such as pickpockets finding the busy **River Road** irresistable. It is not wise either to go to the parks or gardens alone, and certainly never at night. Other than these basic precautions one would take in any larger city, you will find Nairobi's citizens very friendly and helpful.

Exploring Nairobi

The city center is roughly delimited by

the busy Uhuru highway to the west, Haile Selassie Avenue to the south, Tom Mboya Street to the east, and University Way to the north, and within this compact square are the major shops, offices, Parliament and City Hall, the Law Courts and the Kenyatta Conference Center. A good place to begin to explore the city center is the **New Stanley Hotel**, the

Jamia Mosque of the Muslim Sunni sect was built in Arabian style.

oldest hotel in Nairobi and still a favorite meeting place for locals and visitors alike. Many safaris were planned at the **Long Bar** and among a host of famous hunters who stayed there was Ernest Hemingway while the hotel's **Green Bar** claims to have been open 24 hours a day since 1919. Sit in the open-air **Thorn Tree Café** dominated by a huge thorn tree planted in June 1961, whose trunk serves as a message board for travelers, and sip a cold drink and watch Nairobi go by. There are office goers, newly arrived tourists decked out in pristine

MacMillan Library was given to Nairobi in memory of Sir Northrup MacMillan.

safari jackets and un-broken-in walking boots, seasoned safari hands looking sunburned, hustlers selling safaris and "elephant hair" bracelets, shoeshine boys and crazy *matatu* drivers whose overburdened, brightly painted vehicles hurl themselves around corners with careless abandon.

To your right, is the tower of the **Hilton Hotel** in whose shopping center are many of the safari companies and safari outfitters. Opposite the Hilton are the **National Archives** housed in an elegant building which was originally

the Bank of India building. The archives are open to the public and there is a small exhibition of paintings, African artifacts and historical photographs. To your left is the futuristic looking **Nation building**, cheek by jowl with the quiet gardens of the pretty **Jamia Mosque**, and the imposing lion-fronted **MacMillan Library**. Lady MacMillan

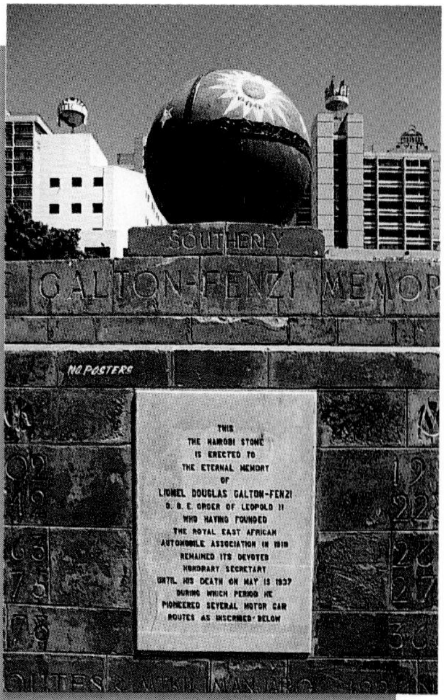

The Galton Fenzi Memorial.

gave the library to Nairobi in 1930 in memory of her husband, Sir Northrup MacMillan, a veteran of World War I. Close to the mosque is one of Nairobi's busiest and most colorful markets, the **City Market**, housed in a huge brick building which was designed in 1930 as an aircraft hangar.

Walk one block to busy, dusty **Kenyatta Avenue**, originally designed so that a cart drawn by a team of 16 oxen could turn in it without difficulty. As you walk along, you will pass the **war memorial** and an intriguing looking memorial, the **Galton Fenzi Memorial**. Galton Fenzi was a passionate motoring enthusiast, the first man to drive from Nairobi to Mombasa, and the founder of the Automobile Associa-

The neo-classical Law Courts.

tion of Kenya. Opposite the General Post Office (G.P.O.) is an attractive building dating from 1913, now home to the Kenya Commercial Bank, but still known as **Kipande House.** Previously, residents had to be fingerprinted and they were issued with their *kipandes* or identification cards in this building. Further along is one of Nairobi's most interesting shops and a "must" for every visitor, **African Heritage**.

From Kenyatta Avenue, walk south to the administrative heart of the city where the elegant pillared **Law Courts** and the soaring modern 28-storeyed **Kenyatta International Conference Center** form an interesting architectural contrast. The Kenyatta Center was built in 1974 and is supposed to resemble a Maasai hut and to symbolize the meeting point of traditional and 20th-century Africa. Whether or not it does, it is still a striking building and if you go up to the roof of the center, there is a panoramic view of the city and the surrounding countryside. Close by is the **Parliament Building** and the **mausoleum of Jomo Kenyatta** which is not open to the public.

A short walk from Haile Selassie Avenue is **Nairobi Railway Station** where Nairobi began its life, and the interesting **Railway Museum**. There is an open-air display of old trains and engines, including relics of the old "Lunatic Express" and Number 301 which was used in the film ***Out of Africa***. The covered section of the mu-

The Kenyatta International Conference Center was built to resemble a Maasai hut to symbolize traditional and 20th-century Africa.

seum has some fascinating exhibits. There are wooden engine seats, which, when time was plentiful and speed was slow, were placed in the front of the engine so that very important people could have an unrestricted view of the country, the wild game, or could, more prosaically, inspect the railway track if necessary.

There are old railway posters and some interesting menus. Passengers traveling on the Kenya and Uganda Railways on 14 May 1931 paid three shillings for a lunch of celery soup, fried

Railway Museum. The railway has a significant place in Kenya's history.

fish and tomato sauce, chicken, mashed potatoes and French beans, lemon jelly and steamed fruit. Four and a half years later, the price and one of the courses was exactly the same for lunch on 19 December 1935 consisting of thick soup, fried fish and tomato sauce, haricot of mutton and rhubarb blancmange.

A short walk back along Haile Selassie Avenue brings you to **Uhuru Park**, a much needed lung in an increasingly crowded city – but do not walk alone across the park at night. The park is bordered by one of Nairobi's most expensive hotels, the **Nairobi Serena**, and the Anglican **All Saints Cathedral** whose foundation stone was laid in 1917 but which was not consecrated until 1952. Haile Selassie Avenue climbs uphill between the **Railway Golf Club** and the **Railway Sports Club**, past government offices, past the **National Library** and where it joins Ngong Road is the elegant, elite and peaceful and very private **Nairobi Club**. The club is almost as old as the city for it was established in 1901 and the low stone buildings date from 1913. The grass on the cricket pitch is still covered to keep it a lush green and upcountry settlers doze in armchairs over the London papers.

On University Way is another exclusive haunt, an expensive hotel called the **Nairobi Safari Club** where you have to be a member in order to stay there. Walk a short distance north past the **University of Nairobi** and you come to one of the city's most prestigious and

The beautifully landscaped Racecourse grounds have been preserved.

atmospheric hotels, the venerable **Norfolk Hotel** which opened on Christmas Day 1904. Its mock-Tudor architecture was rebuilt after a terrorist bomb blast in 1980, and today it is a favorite place for drinks on the terrace. Opposite is Kenya's **National Theater**.

A short taxi ride out of the city center is the **National Museum** which has a good collection of Kenyan fauna, a lot of information about the geography and anthropology of the country, and a superb collection of watercolors painted by the talented and multi-faceted **Joy Adamson**. Although she is best known for her experience with raising wild animals in Kenya, described in her successful books ***Born Free*** and ***Living Free***, Joy Adamson was also an accomplished artist.

When she came to Kenya in 1937, Joy began collecting the indigenous flowers of Kenya and recording them in watercolors. A selection of the five books she illustrated depicting the flowers, trees and shrubs of East Africa is on display. Another of Joy's talents was portrait painting and in 1949 she signed a contract with the Government of Kenya to paint 20 ethnic groups, later extended to cover all of Kenya's peoples many of whose traditions and cultures were rapidly disappearing. The result was an impressive, nearly 600 portraits painted between 1949 and 1955, many of which are in the museum.

In the garden of the museum there is a fiberglass model of an elephant, but

The Norfolk Hotel in mock-Tudor architecture.

not just any elephant, for in 1970 President Jomo Kenyatta decreed that the huge tusker Ahmed be placed under a permanent 24-hour honor guard protecting him from poachers. At his death in 1974, Ahmed stood 9 ft 10 in (2.95 m) high, his right tusk was a massive 9 ft 9 in (2.92 m) long, his left tusk was 9 ft 4 in (2.8 m) long and each tusk weighed 147 lbs (67 kg). Opposite the museum is the **Snake Park** which has examples of most of the species of East African snakes.

Out to the west of the city is **State House**, the residence of the President and in colonial times the residence of the Governor General, and the extensive grounds of the **Nairobi Arboretum**, pleasant for a walk during the day among its 300 labelled species of trees, but it is not advisable to go there alone.

There are several worthwhile things to see and do outside Nairobi. As you drive out past **Wilson Airport** on the Langata Road, you come to one of the country's most famous and popular restaurants, **The Carnivore.** As its name implies, it caters to the committed meat eater (see box story p.354). Just beyond the restaurant are the **Uhuru Gardens** whose striking granite column had to be reduced in size because of the low-flying planes from Wilson Airport.

Nairobi National Park

Some distance further along is one of Nairobi's most impressive sights, the

The Nairobi National Park is unique for the wildlife it supports in their natural surroundings so close to a city.

superb **Nairobi National Park**, 117 sq km (44·5 sq miles) of parkland where lions, rhino, elephants, giraffes and wildebeest roam free within sight of residential blocks and with jumbo jets landing at the nearby Jomo Kenyatta International Airport. Nairobi National Park was the first national park to be gazetted in 1945.

As an introduction to safaris or for the business visitor on a short trip to Nairobi without the time to travel far afield, it cannot be bettered. More than 80 species of mammal and 500 species of bird have been recorded there, all within the city limits, and the rhino has been sighted silhouetted against the Kenyatta Conference Center. The best times to visit the park are either in the early morning or in the evening, avoiding the heat of the day when the animals sleep. Just by the gates of the national park is the **Animal Orphanage**.

Close by is the **Bomas of Kenya** cultural village where you can see traditional dances and visit models of typical Kenyan villages, and the **A.F.E.W. Langata Giraffe Center**, an educational foundation, where you can hand-feed the five Rothschild's giraffes. The Rothschild's giraffe, which comes from the western part of Kenya, is distinguished from the Maasai and Reticulated giraffe by the fact that its markings only go down to its kneecaps, and it is also slightly paler in color. The founders of A.F.E.W. or the African Fund for Endangered Wildlife were Jock and

Karen Blixen's Out of Africa

Home of Karen Blixen, author of "Out of Africa".

One of the most evocative books about Kenya begins in a deceptively simple way : "I had a farm in Africa, at the foot of the Ngong Hills." From this opening line, the Danish author Isak Dinesen goes on to write about her turbulent, passionate years in Kenya in the early years of this century. Karen Christence Dinesen was born in 1885, in 1914 she married her cousin, Baron Bror Blixen, and together they left for Kenya to run a coffee plantation in the author's beloved Ngong Hills, outside Nairobi.

The couple quickly became part of the "Happy Valley" set, the high-living, wildly socializing white settlers and soon Bror left Karen for another woman. By 1921 Karen was divorced but decided to stay on in Kenya and run the farm. However, ten years later, mismanagement, drought and a severe fall in coffee prices forced her to sell up and return to Denmark penniless. It was there that she wrote the best known of her many books, the beautiful, sensitive portrayal of the Kenya she so passionately loved in ***Out of Africa***.

When Karen wrote her autobiographical book, she was nostalgic for the African way of life that she once knew and so liked and admired. She was also celebrating the life and mourning the death of her lover, the Honorable Denys Finch-Hatton, an English hunter who was killed in a plane crash at Voi. Karen built a simple obelisk in his memory which still stands in the midst of maize fields on the eastern slopes of the Ngong Hills. Years after, writing of Denys's death, there is a mystical quality to her words. She describes how, after she had left Africa, a friend wrote to tell her that "at sunrise and sunset, they have seen lions on Finch-Hatton's grave in the Hills. A lion and a lioness have come there, or stood, or lain, on the grave for a long time."

The area where she had her farm, now a wealthy Nairobi suburb, has been named Karen in her honor, and Karen's former house has been restored and is now the Karen Blixen Museum. It was presented by the Danish government to the new Kenyan government at Independence.

The house was built in 1912 and Karen bought it in 1917. As you wander round it, you can feel some of the spirit of her writing. The verandah is there as she described it; the clock whose hands have stopped, the dining room where she used to sit and write "with papers spread all over the dining table", her house boys standing silently in the corner watching the progress of her book, believing it to be their last hope of saving the farm from financial ruin.

Karen died in 1962 long before her book became the inspiration for the highly successful film of the same name – one of the best writers and worst farmers to have lived in Kenya.

The library in Karen Blixen's house.

Giraffe, an icon of African wildlife.

Betty Leslie-Melville, whose beautiful manor house, Giraffe Manor, is opposite the circular feeding platform. One of the very laudable aims of this center is to expose Kenyan schoolchildren to wildlife for many of them do not have the opportunity to go on safari despite living in a country famed for its game.

The **Ngong Hills**, to the west of Nairobi, used to be the haunt of white settlers which accounts for the unlikely sight of half-timbered houses, landscaped gardens and the **Racecourse**. The suburb of **Karen** is named after one of the most famous residents of the Ngong Hills, the Danish writer **Karen Blixen**, whose classic book ***Out of Africa*** inspired the highly successful film of the same name.

Amboseli & Tsavo National Parks

One of the classic images of Kenya, indeed of Africa itself, is that of the African continent's highest mountain, **Mount Kilimanjaro**, with its snowy cap, and walking sedately in the foreground, a herd of African elephants. It is an enduring vision of Kenya that has almost become a cliché but it still remains a magnificent, unforgettable sight.

There is, however, one qualification that needs to be made. Mount Kilimanjaro is actually across the border, in Tanzania, but visitors to Kenya's **Amboseli National Park** have a perfect view of it. The mountain, known as "Kili" to local residents, looks so close that you feel you could walk to it but it is about 40 km (24 miles) away from Amboseli. Legend has it that Queen Victoria gave the mountain to her grand-

A perfect evening at Amboseli.

Classic image of Kenya with Mount Kilimanjaro and
a native of the terrain, the giraffe.

An alternative terrain, the swamp is also a natural home to wildlife.

son, Kaiser Wilhelm of Germany – but that is only a legend after all. What definitely happened is that under the terms of the 1886 Anglo-German Agreement, the mountain was handed over by the British, who were based in what is present day Kenya, to the Germans, who were settled in current Tanzania.

Mount Kilimanjaro is the highest free-standing mountain in the world and it is an extinct volcano. The water that runs down the mountain from its snow-capped Uhuru Peak and through its porous volcanic rock collects in two swamps in Amboseli, **Enkongo Narok swamp** and **Longinye swamp**, which attract abundant wildlife and bird life as well as the nomadic Maasai who bring their herds of cattle to these water sources. *Enkongo Narok* means "black and benevolent", an apt description of the water bubbling out of the fissures on the black volcanic lava.

Visitors with limited time can conceivably visit Amboseli as a day trip from Nairobi, 480 km (288 miles) there and back over fairly good roads, or a short flight away. To "do" Amboseli in a day, though, defeats the real purpose of going there for you will most probably not see Mount Kilimanjaro which is covered by cloud for most of the day.

The perfect time for seeing the **snows of Kilimanjaro** is at dawn and at sunset when there is little cloud cover and the light is perfect. The clouds of Kilimanjaro offer little attraction. Aim, therefore, to spend at least one night at

Whistling Thorn Galls or Ant Galls are not very friendly.

Amboseli to view the mountain and enjoy the wildlife. As many visitors drive on from Amboseli down to **Tsavo National Park**, an overnight stop makes good sense.

The drive from Nairobi takes you south on the Uhuru Highway, in the direction of Mombasa, past the little town of **Kajiado**, the seat of the local government for the southern part of Maasailand. After Kajiado, the land becomes a little hillier and after 58 km (40 miles), you arrive at the small town of **Namanga**, which stands at the foot of a rock, **Oi-Doinyo Orok** or Black Mountain, sacred to the Maasai. The road continues on through Namanga towards the Tanzanian border, past endless stalls selling Maasai handicrafts. The nearby **Namanga Gate** is one of the entry points into the national park.

Amboseli National Park

Amboseli National Park covers 392 sq km (149 sq miles), and is one of Kenya's oldest game sanctuaries. As well as serving as a perfect viewing area for the 5,895-meter (19,336-foot) high mountain, it has a spectacular range of wildlife. The national park adjoins **Lake Amboseli**, situated at 1,200 m (3,936 ft). For most of the year the lake is a dry, flat plain of blindingly white evaporated salts and a land of shimmering mirages, hence it is more of a seasonal lake. The lake tends to flood during the

Ostriches galore.

rainy season, so be careful when driving at that time of the year.

From the Namanga Gate, you drive for about 80 km (48 miles) into the heart of the park called **Ol Tukai**. Mount Kilimanjaro increasingly dominates the landscape and the arid desert turns green and swampy due to the run-off from the snow cap. There are palm trees, acacia and rolling grassland, all of which attract abundant wildlife.

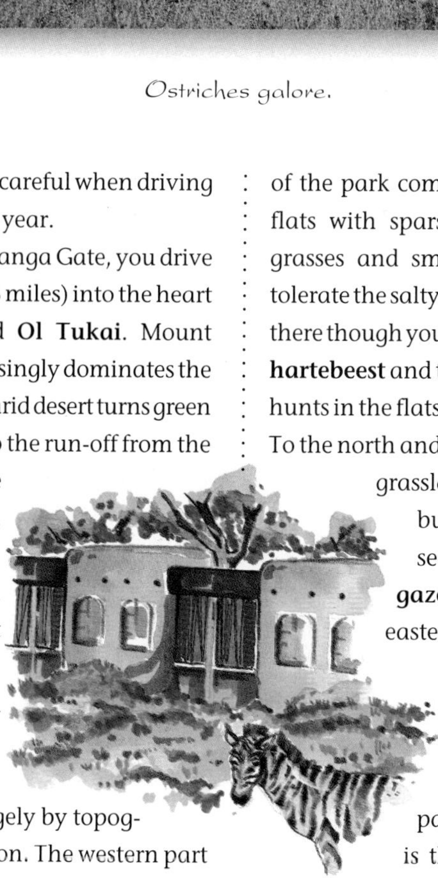

Amboseli can be divided into four areas which are determined largely by topography and vegetation. The western part of the park comprises mainly dry lake flats with sparse vegetation such as grasses and small shrubs which can tolerate the salty soil. There is little game there though you can see **ostrich**, **eland**, **hartebeest** and the **Kori bustard** which hunts in the flats for reptiles and insects. To the north and the east of the park are grasslands with acacia thornbushes, and here you can see many **antelope** and **gazelle** species. The south-eastern part of the park is little more than scrub with hardly any game.

The best area of the park for spotting wildlife is the south-central area,

Oblivious of their size, a herd of moving elephants would leave a trail of broken shrubs and small trees.

The spectacular crowned crane is common in the national park.

for here are the swamps. From **Observation Hill**, you have an excellent panoramic view over the green swamps and the plains beyond. **Elephants**, **buffalo** and **giraffe** are common, **leopards** may be seen further south in the forested area around Kitirua, and, if you are lucky, you will see the rare **black rhino**.

More than 420 species of **birds** have been recorded in Amboseli and the swamps are home to many of them, making them an ornithologist's paradise. You will see buffalo and giraffe with tiny birds seemingly attached to them : these are **red-billed oxpeckers** and **yellow-billed oxpeckers** who pick off parasites from the animals. You can often see **cattle egrets** standing close to a herd of elephants, waiting to find insects that are disturbed by the lumbering passage of the elephants.

Around the various lodges that are in the park, you will see **marabou stork** always on the look-out for garbage. The **crowned crane** is common, large flocks of **sand grouse** may be seen, and between August and April, many species of **migrant waders** live in the swamps. The **Taveta golden weaver** occurs only in the Amboseli region. Ironically for a region which has six species of **vulture** recorded, the film ***Where No Vultures Fly*** was filmed there !

The 1940s classic film, ***The Snows of Kilimanjaro*** was filmed on location, in the park, and Paramount Pictures built *bandas* or simple huts to accommodate the film crew. Today, these have be-

Serena Lodge in Amboseli.

come the inexpensive **Ol Tukai Lodge**, a series of self-catering cottages. Crockery and cooking utensils are provided. You can rent bedding but you must bring your own food – and despite their Hollywood connection, or perhaps because of it, the cottages are beginning to show their age.

Amboseli's Bane

A note of caution with which to leave Amboseli. The richness of its wildlife attracts many visitors but like the Maasai Mara, this very popularity is, sadly, a potential problem. Too many jeeps and mini-buses risk turning Amboseli's fragile grasslands into a **dust bowl**. Even

A chronic problem of the terrain – dust bowl syndrome.

Kilaguni Lodge in Tsavo West, Kenya's first national park lodge.

the name, Amboseli, is somewhat prophetic, for it is the Maasai word for dust devils. Amboseli's future, like most of the national parks, depends on tourism, yet off-road driving by safari companies wanting to give visitors even closer sightings of the wildlife is aggravating the dust problem. To protect the park's fragile **ecosystem** drive only on the designated roads so as not to damage such a precious heritage. This will not inhibit any visitor from seeing the ample game around. Ecologically-minded visitors will help preserve Amboseli for the future.

The pink frangipani is a pretty transgression of flora in a dominantly fauna landscape.

Tsavo National Park

Tsavo is the largest national park in the country and also one of the largest in the world, covering 21,283 sq km (8,088 sq miles). For administrative reasons, it has been split into two national parks, **Tsavo West**, covering 9,536 sq km (3,624 sq miles) and **Tsavo East**, which covers 11,747 sq km (4,464 sq miles). The former **Chyulu Hills National Park** has also been integrated into Tsavo.

Tsavo is nearly mid-way between Nairobi and Mombasa and over the huge area of the park, the altitude ranges from 230 m to 2,000 m (754-6,560 ft). There are many volcanic hills such as the 300-kilometer (180-mile) long **Yatta plateau** in the eastern part of Tsavo. Four rivers drain Tsavo, the **Athi**, the **Tsavo**, the **Voi** and the **Tive**. Over 60 major mammal species have been recorded in Tsavo, the bird life is extensive and there are more than 1,000 kinds of plants.

With such a huge area for one national park, more than four percent of the country's total land area, in fact, **poaching** became a thriving occupation during the 1970s and even into the 1980s. This unpleasant business was a highly profitable one, and elephant, rhino and other species were slaughtered in large staggering numbers. The Kenyan government is getting to grips with the whole deplorable business and Tsavo National Park is now manned by

Along the road in Tsavo.

efficient anti-poaching rangers.

The northern part of Tsavo West, with its convenient access to the main A109 Nairobi-Mombasa highway, is the most developed, and therefore the most visited. Currently, the northern sector of Tsavo East, which means everything north of the Galana River, is closed to the public. It is in this area of **Tsavo East** that the government is still fighting a battle against poachers. The authorities are slowly winning but the statistics are appalling. In 1970, the rhino population of Tsavo was estimated to be around

8,000. Twenty years later, less than 50 animals were alive. The elephant population has also suffered at the hands of poachers, though some legal culling was also done in the 1960s, plummeting from between 50,000-60,000 in the 1960s to 5,000, just 20 years later.

Tsavo West has two major watering holes and as they attract a vast

The leopard caught napping.

amount of wildlife, a lodge has been built by each of the holes, almost guaranteeing that visitors will see a large amount of game during their stay. **Ngulia Lodge** is built on top of cliffs which overlook forests, and this area is one of the rare places in Kenya, other than the Maasai Mara, where you stand a chance of seeing **leopard**. The terrain is ideal for leopards – craggy hills and cliffs, with plenty of tree cover. The water hole attracts large numbers of game including **elephants** and the area is renowned for its **bird life**. During the short rains of October and November, huge flocks of migratory birds become disorientated by the mists and the lights from the lodge and fly down to investigate. Ornithologists have ringed many

The Man-Eaters of Tsavo

In early 1898, Colonel J. H. Patterson, an officer in the Indian Army with a long experience of railway construction, was sent by the British Foreign Office to take charge of a section of the Mombasa to Uganda railway line – the Lunatic Express. One of his tasks was the particularly challenging one of building a bridge over the Tsavo River. The construction of this railway encountered many delays and problems ranging from hostile terrain to hostile tribes. There were also hostile animals, and in one of the most dramatic incidents in the long drawn out, colorful saga, Colonel Patterson waged a one-man crusade against the **Man-Eaters of Tsavo**, two lions who terrorized the railway gangs.

The couple, a male and a female, who stalked the Tsavo construction gangs, had taken to eating Indian coolies who would be carried off during the night to the obvious terror of their fellow workers. Patterson, with all the moral superiority of a colonial, Victorian *pukka sahib* at first put the coolies' deaths down to "scoundrels from the gangs (who) had murdered them for the sake of their money." The Colonel was forced to change his opinion in the third week of March 1898, when one of the workers, a sturdy Sikh, was carried away by a lion and the horrified Patterson was treated to a first hand description of the incident by one of the other workers sleeping in the tent, "the lion suddenly put its head in at the open tent door and seized Ungan Singh...by the throat."

Patterson had very severe time constraints in which to build his bridge but he was well aware that he could expect little in the way of productive labor from the already terrified coolies, so he decided then and there to "rid the neighborhood of the brutes." Brave words, but it was to take the unwitting Colonel 10 months to carry out this pledge. A frustrating game of chase began whereby Patterson would spend all night in a tree only to hear the screams of a victim being dragged away a mile or half a mile away from him.

Thorn barricades were built around the camp, fires were lit and a night watchman would sit up all through the long, night hours, making a loud noise with half a dozen empty oil tins, all in the hope of driving the animals away. All of this was in vain and coolies continued to be dragged away screaming in the middle of the night. Poor Patterson was desperate and wrote, "No matter how likely or tempting a spot we lay in wait for them, they invariably avoided that particular place and seized their victim for the night from some other camp."

The lions even attacked and destroyed the hospital tent despite its extra thick barricade of thorn bushes. The cat-and-mouse game went on. Patterson knew that lions usually revisit newly vacated camp sites, so he changed the site of the hospital tent on several occasions, waiting up all night at the old site only to find that the lions had coolly visited the new site. Attempts at second guessing the man-eaters was proving to be a waste of time and Patterson wrote bitterly of his tormentors, "Except as food, they showed a complete contempt for human beings." As if to add insult to injury, one night the lions brought their prey right up to Patterson's tent where he could hear them crunching the bones and purring contentedly after their gruesome dinner.

As if all this were not enough, Patterson still had his railway bridge to build and he faced the additional challenge of seething unrest among his coolies, who, unimpressed by his game hunting were even planning to murder him at one point. In September, a murder plot was uncovered but Patterson, in true 19th-century

of them as a means of trying to track the distances flown during the migration process.

Close by Ngulia Lodge is a heavily protected **rhino sanctuary**, where a few animals live in peace far from the threat of poachers in a much needed attempt to regenerate the species. The **Tsavo River**, which is seasonal, flows along the base of the Ngulia Hills escarpment.

sahib style, deliberately confronted his would-be attackers, spoke angrily to them in fluent Hindustani and quelled the rebellious workers.

News of Tsavo's unhappy claim to fame had spread and poachers, sportsmen and hopeful heroes descended on the camp, killing lots of innocent lions while the two man-eaters continued to dine in style. Meanwhile the suspicious coolies began to think that the lions were in fact devils while Patterson, hovering on the brink of a breakdown from chronic exhaustion, produced what he hoped would be the answer to his problems — a huge trap, built of two compartments, in one of which human volunteers would sit as bait. This was greeted with universal scepticism much to Patterson's indignation.

By December, he was faced with a general strike and some 500 coolies managed to make the Mombasa train slow down enough for them all to swarm on board and flee. The by-now desperate Patterson was left with less than 50 coolies and all railway construction work came to a halt. For the next three weeks, the remaining coolies spent all their time re-enforcing their camp against the persistently hungry lions.

At long last, one night, one of the lions entered Patterson's trap but the terrified volunteers panicked, fired everywhere except at the lion and by hitting one of the locks, actually made it open and the lion calmly escaped. On 9 December, Patterson finally came face to face with one of the lions, got within less than 15 m (50 ft) of it, shot, but, with the kind of luck that seemed to dog the poor Colonel, his rifle misfired. The shot from the second barrel only wounded the animal who escaped, to Patterson's quite understandable fury.

A wooden scaffold-like perch was built for Patterson who had decided to spend that very night in a place he felt the lions would visit. One of them did appear circling his weak structure for two hours while the poor man could do nothing but sit tight, holding his rifle, hardly able to see in the pitch darkness. Realizing that the animal was too close for comfort, Patterson at last opened fire, "blazing away in the direction in which I heard him plunging about." One lion was at long last, dead. It was huge, requiring eight men to carry it off to camp. A second man-eater remained at large, however.

At the end of December, Patterson once again found himself in the unenviable position of sitting in a tree while a man-eating lion circled around underneath him. Patterson shot the lion twice but it escaped and as day broke, the Colonel and his Swahili gun-bearer, Mahina, stalked the wounded animal following the trail of blood. They found it, wounded, in a thicket but the adventure was far from over.

Patterson fired. The lion charged. Patterson fired again but missed the next shot. He reached for the carbine which should have been in his gun-bearer's hand but both Mahina and the weapon were half way up a tree by now. The desperate Patterson having no choice, quickly climbed up to join them. He shot the animal again from the tree and then in true heroic style, leaped down to the ground to face the lion's dying charge. Two more shots and Tsavo's second man-eater was dead. Patterson, ever the perfect Victorian gentleman, noted that the animal "died gamely."

Both the man-eaters are today in the Field Museum in Chicago. Patterson was presented with a silver bowl by his coolies along with a long poem in Hindustani, extolling his virtues and his bravery which rather glossed over the nine-month long ordeal when it claimed, "Lions do not fear lions, yet one glance from Patterson Sahib cowed the bravest of them."

The other main lodge in Tsavo West is **Kilaguni Lodge**, the first lodge ever opened in a Kenyan national park. Kilaguni Lodge has been built facing two large water holes with the beautiful **Chyulu Hills** in the background and far away in the distance, **Mount Kilimanjaro**. It is an attractive site with superb views and such an abundance of game that the visitor almost feels tempted not

View of Chyulu Hills from Kilaguni Lodge.

to stir from the lodge.

The lodge has been constructed as a narrow central building with a long verandah fronting the dining room and overlooking the two water holes. The verandah is the focal point of the lodge where everybody sets up their tripods, cameras and telescopes, and then just sits and watches the show. **Giraffes**, **zebras**, **elephants**, **oryx**, **eland**, **baboons**, and **marabou storks** are out by the water holes having a quiet drink before dinner, while you do exactly the same thing on the verandah where a

The pensive marabou stork looking for garbage to feed on.

bar has been set up at one end ensuring a constant supply of tea and coffee during the day. Many of the tamer birds fly onto the verandah itself, hopping under the tables in search of crumbs – **hornbills**, **starlings** and even a **hyrax**, scuttling from table to table.

As evening falls over Kilaguni and the Chyulu Hills, the animals begin to emerge from the bush and head for the water holes. All along the verandah are dusty guests, recently returned from their afternoon game drives. Everyone pops along to the verandah "just to see if there are any animals at the water hole" and stays for hours. Day fades into night, the cameras give way to binoculars and the pots of tea to cold beers as the constantly changing scene at the water hole mesmerizes everyone. As in all the lodges, there is no need to dress for dinner at Kilaguni but one "accessory" that is advisable to carry everywhere is a pair of binoculars. In fact, whenever you go for a meal there, take your camera and binoculars along with you (and a tripod if you have one). At meal times the hard-core naturalists and photogra-

Congregating at the water hole in the evening.

Mzima Springs

At the end of the hippo trail.

Located in the vast and semi-dry wilderness of Tsavo, the sight of Mzima Springs is reminiscent of a desert oasis. The clear water bubbles out from a mass of **volcanic boulders** after traveling underground from the Chyulu Hills which lie to the northwest. The Chyulu Hills are composed mainly of porous volcanic ash and lava which make the hills virtually a giant sponge for any rainfall falling onto the hills. Under the volcanic layer are non-porous rocks and the water flows between the two emerging in several springs, Mzima being the biggest. Smaller springs exist along the Loolturesh river, near Kitani Lodge and to the north of the Chyulu Hills. The volcanic rocks through which the Chyulu water passes, act as a filter, hence the water's clarity.

Flora and Fauna

There is lush tropical vegetation along the banks of the springs including wild date palm, raphia palm, doum palm, figs and reeds. Some of the vegetation provides forage for hippos as well as being home to a wide range of migrant and endemic bird species. Fish are found in the springs, notably barbels and "mud-suckers", as well as eels and crocodiles. Vervet and Sykes monkeys also live around the springs. Elephant, rhino, buffalo, zebra, lion and buck all use the spring as their only watering place in the dry season.

The palm which gives Mzima Springs much of its luxuriant tropical appearance is the **wild date palm**. A passable wine is made from this palm, but unfortunately, its dates are unpalatable.

Further downstream, is one of the most beautiful of all palms, the **Raphia Ruffia**, with its huge, red-stemmed fronds about 12 m (40 ft) long. A wax, which is used locally for shoe polish and floor polish, comes from the lower sides of

Mzima Springs.

the leaf.

Next to the river, there is a tree called the "water pear", a member of the myrtle family. When the tree is in bloom, innumerable insects are attracted to its fragrant white flowers. The purple black fruit, the size of a small cherry, is edible when ripe and is eaten by birds and even fish when any fruit falls into the water.

By the side of the pool are some very large **fig trees**, a species of fica. Although the fruit of the tree are not particularly palatable to humans, monkeys love them and when they are ripening, vervet monkeys, and the shyer, darker Sykes' or blue monkeys can be seen in the trees along with baboons.

And Civilization

Mzima Springs plays a vital role as the **source of water** for Mombasa and other towns en route and is connected by a pipeline to Mombasa. There are two pools, the top pool and the long pool, from which the Mzima River flows away to join the Tsavo River, 7 km (4 miles) away.

One section of the path through the springs is marked "hippo trail". The path leading to the pool has been worn by hippos on their way to and from the river. They rarely use these trails in the daytime but at night they may walk for several kilometers in search of food. There is a submerged viewing tank which was constructed in 1969 and you can sit and enjoy the unique experience of watching hippos swim past you.

Lush tropical vegetation around the springs include the doum palm.

The black rhinoceros in a rhino sanctuary.

phers constantly shuttle between the buffet table and their tripod for the activity at the water hole is compelling.

In the morning **guinea fowl** come in one long, single file down to the largest water hole to drink. **Baboons** are everywhere as well as the **saras cranes** and **partridges**. Even in the heat of the day, at lunch time, the water holes are crowded with **elephant**, **giraffe**, **zebra**, **wart hog**, **marabou storks** and **monkeys**. In the evening, a little after sunset, more elephants come, along with buffalo and the ever noisy baboons. During dinner **hyenas**, **civet cats** and **white-tailed mongooses** hang around underneath the restaurant downstairs . The baboons at Kilaguni are as curious as they are the world over but here they have got used to human beings. All it takes is the rustle of a sweet being unwrapped on the first floor balcony outside a bedroom, for a young male to climb quickly up the railing and swing himself cheekily onto the balcony, calmly take the whole packet of sweets, and then swing back over the balcony to climb down.

Just 10 km (6 miles) away from Kilaguni is one of the most important areas in the whole of Tsavo, an oasis called **Mzima Springs**. At the extreme southern edge of Tsavo West and straddling the Tanzanian border is **Lake Jipe** which attracts a lot of bird life, against the backdrop of the **North Pare Mountains** just across the border in Tanzania.

The **Taita Hills**, a series of craggy,

Bird-feeding, a typical scene at Kilaguni Lodge.

volcanic hills, are outside the national park boundaries, situated almost equidistantly from the two sides of Tsavo. The summit of the Taita Hills is at 2,130 m (6,986 ft), and much of the surrounding area has become the **Salt Lick Game Sanctuary** which is privately owned by the Hilton Hotel Group.

The sanctuary covers 11,000 hectares (27,170 acres) and used to be a sisal plantation before it became a successful sanctuary with abundant game and two curious looking, though luxurious, lodges. The **Taita Hills Lodge** resembles an Austrian fortress while the neighboring **Salt Lick Lodge** is a luxury village on stilts. Overhead walkways link the individual buildings while elephants wander at ease underneath.

The oryx is known to impale its victim.

Maasai Mara

Of all Kenya, it is possibly the **Maasai Mara** that seems the most familiar even to first-time visitors who feel that they somehow know this landscape already. For the Maasai Mara is the Kenya of films and books with the wide open spaces of the Serengeti plains, its rolling grasslands dotted with thorny acacia bushes and teeming with wildlife, peopled by proud Maasai warriors who wander for miles following their herds of cattle.

The butterfly chooses a lovely backdrop.

Maasai Mara is in the southwest corner of Kenya bordering on Tanzania, with which it shares the vast Serengeti plain. The 25,000 sq km (9,750 sq miles) expanse of the **Serengeti-Mara Ecosystem** straddles the two countries' national boundaries and the wildlife wander freely between Kenya and Tanzania in search of food.

The game reserve, which was set up in 1961, is divided into two sections. The inner reserve of 518 sq km (202 sq miles) has been developed as a national park where permanent human settlement is not allowed

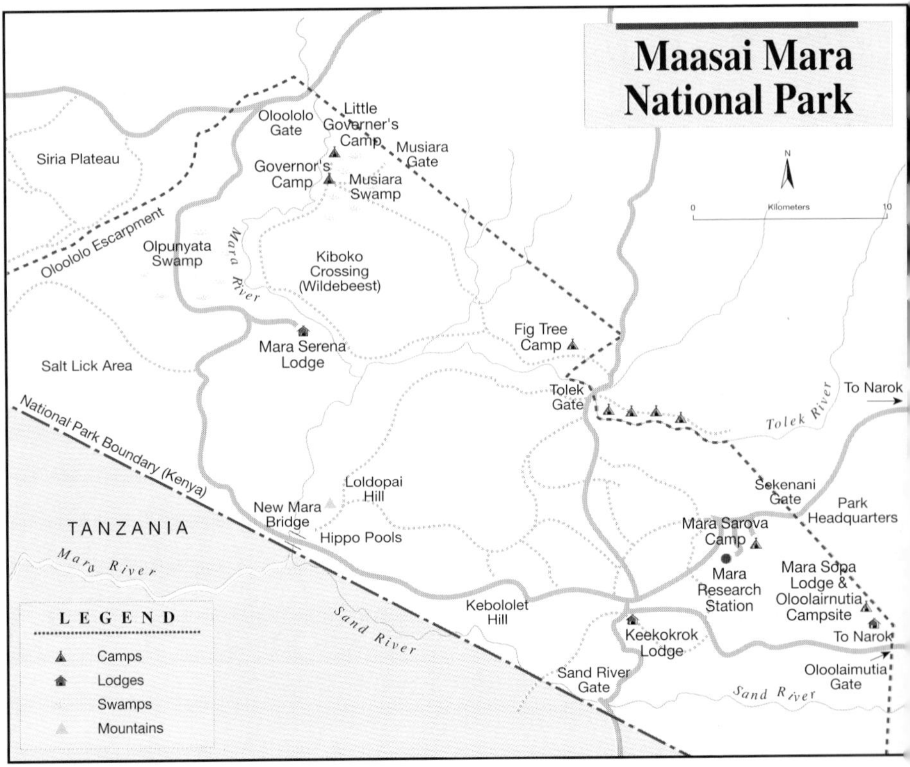

and where roads have been specially laid out for game watching. The outer area is undeveloped and the local Maasai are allowed to graze their cattle here.

The lack of development and the absence of villages have meant that the concentration of **game** in the Mara is impressive and visitors will see wildlife in vast numbers, on a scale that has all but disappeared from the rest of the country. Maasai Mara is justly famous as one of the most spectacular game reserves in Kenya and it is one of the rarer areas of the country where visitors are likely to see the **"Big Five"** all in the same reserve – for elephant, rhino, buffalo, lion and leopard all live in the Maasai Mara.

The Mara landscape is on just as impressive a scale as the wildlife. It is a land of endless vistas of vast plains, of herds of animals wandering against a backdrop of gently rounded hills and of miles of stunted acacia trees. The Mara River runs through the Maasai Mara providing a cool, welcome oasis of water and trees.

The drive from Nairobi to the Maasai Mara takes you through the **Great Rift Valley**. Stop at one of the viewing areas along the road for a sweeping view across the valley, and, in the distance lies M**ount Longonot**, a long

Aerial view of the reserve from a balloon.

extinct volcano, and at 2,776 m (9,105 ft), the highest of Kenya's volcanoes. An hour's drive out of Nairobi, ask your driver to stop at the roadside and show you a tiny chapel built by Italian prisoners of war in 1942.

After you have passed the **Longonot earth satellite station**, you start seeing animals wandering around on the plains that border both sides of the road, herds of giraffe, zebra and gazelles, and you may well see small sandstorms spinning dizzily across the horizon. Most cars stop at **Narok** where you can have a drink, stretch your legs, and haggle for a Maasai shield from one of the many stallholders. Shortly after Narok, the roads branch off for the different parts of the Maasai Mara since there are sev-

A young Maasai on the Maasai Mara Reserve.

A portrait of a Maasai family in their home compound.

eral different entrance gates and a selection of camps and lodges both within and just outside the boundaries of the reserve.

The history of this area can be dated back at least 2,000 years for **Neolithic Man** left behind fragments of his pottery and arrow heads which archeologists uncovered in the **Lemek Valley**, a little to the north. Any written history of this area is non-existent before the arrival of the first Europeans. in the 19th century but it is known that the **Maasai** people lived in this area from the 17th

Bright colors are favored by the Maasai women.

century onwards (see chapter on People). Since the Maasai do not hunt wild animals for food, living instead from their huge cattle herd, for centuries they lived in harmony with the abundant wildlife of the Maasai Mara.

In 1891, a dreadful disease, **rinderpest**, struck East Africa and it spread like wildfire through Maasai Mara. Within a year, the disease had wiped out 90 percent of the cattle and wild animals and famine and smallpox quickly followed in its wake. Once a vaccine against rinderpest was found, the Maasai returned and the herds of cattle and wild animals started to increase. In the years immediately after World War II, hunting was permitted in the area until it was declared a national game reserve in 1948 and hunting was regulated.

Maasai Mara's Community

The Maasai Mara National Reserve can be divided into four geographical zones: the **Ngama Hills** to the east of Keekorok,

The acacia tree's leaves and pods are the staple of many animals.

the **Oloololo Escarpment** to the west, the **Mara Triangle** which runs from Oloololo to the Mara River, and the **Central Plains** which stretch from the river to the Ngama Hills. Since the rainfall and composition of the soil vary between these zones, different ecosystems have evolved, each supporting different plants and animal life.

Grasslands predominate in the Maasai Mara, especially in the Central Plains and the Mara Triangle, kept in balance by a combination of grazing and fire. After the rains, the grassy plains are covered, briefly, with small flowering plants. **Topi** and **kongoni** are closely related antelope, both of which are found in the grasslands. **Eland, elephants** and **Grant's gazelles** all live on the plains as do **buffalo, wildebeest** and **zebra.**

In the course of the last 30 years, much of the **bushland thickets** of the Mara have been reduced by fire and by elephant. There are still scattered pockets of bushland on stony ridge tops and the most extensive are to be found to the east, between Keekorok and Sekenani Gate. The **black rhinoceros** can be found in the bushland as well as a tiny antelope called **Kirk's dikdik. Wart hog** live in the old termite mounds which can be found in the bushland but are also common in the grasslands. Impala are seen around the bushlands where they find both food and protection.

Where the grasslands are dotted with trees, they are called woodlands or **savannah woodlands**. The predomi-

Buffalo at their principal occupation, grazing and lazing.

nant tree in the Maasai Mara-Serengeti plain is the **acacia**, and although the species is abundant, it is nevertheless under threat from the enemies of fire, grazing and the destructive elephant. There are seven species of acacia in the Mara and its leaves and pods are eaten by a wide variety of animals despite the tree's impressive thorns. **Baboon** climb the trees to eat the young pods while **Grant's gazelle** and **impala** pick up those that the baboons drop onto the ground. The animal that is the most dependent on the woodlands is perhaps the **giraffe** which feeds almost entirely on the leaves of the acacia tree and the **desert date**, or, to give it its technical name, the *Balanites aegyptiaca*. Given their advantage over the other animals, giraffes can strip off the tender leaves from branches up to 6 m (20 ft) above the ground. The Mara woodlands are open like the grasslands, and so are home to a similar range of animals including wildebeest, zebra, kongoni, topi and gazelles.

The **Mara River** flows year-round to Lake Victoria and is home to its own community of wildlife – **hippopotamus, crocodile, monitor lizard**, and, frequenting the river banks, the **defassa waterbuck**. Forest borders much of the Mara River and provides food and shelter to a wide range of animals including **bushbuck, red duiker**, the **vervet monkey**, the **olive baboon**, the **blue monkey**, the **copper-tailed monkey**, the **bushbaby** and the **tree hyrax**. Although

Wildlife inevitably seek the Mara River which flows into Lake Victoria.

not all of these species are confined only to the riverine forests, they are most often found there.

The abundance of herbivores in the Maasai Mara attracts, inevitably, predatory carnivores, chief among them being the "big cats", the **lion**, the **leopard** and the **cheetah**. There are also the less majestic scavengers including the **spotted hyena** and the **wild dog**.

Over 450 species of resident and migratory birds have been listed in the Mara, ranging in size from the huge **ostrich** to the tiny **sunbird**. The ostrich can be seen frequently on the plains and grasslands as can other large birds such as the **secretary bird**, the **Kori**, the **black-bellied bustard**, the **white-bellied bustard** and the **ground hornbill**. In the woods, you will find **red-necked spurfowl** and **helmeted guinea-fowl** while near the rivers and streams you will see **Egyptian geese**, the **saddle-bill stork** and the **yellow-necked stork**, the **sacred ibis** and the **blacksmith plover**.

Birds of prey are to be found in all habitats including the **black-shouldered kite**, the **augur buzzard**, and the **Bataleur eagle**. There are six species of **vulture** on the Mara, and they can always be spotted around kills, waiting to pick over whatever the predators may have left for them.

Away from the checklists of animals and birds and the knowledgeable naturalists who can identify all and every species of animal, how does the non-specialist visitor make sense of such

The hyena, a predator which looks like a dog.

an abundance of wildlife ? Quite simply, by relishing the spectacle of huge herds of animals in such close proximity and by enjoying the beauty of the vast, open landscape.

Although animal sightings can never be guaranteed, it is a rare and particularly unlucky visitor to Mara who does not see at least four of the **Big Five**, and very often all five. **Elephants** are common, large herds often wandering calmly across the road in front of your jeep. They amble past, casually ripping up shrubs, pushing over small trees and generally behaving like a group of noisy vandals – except that they are such a magnificent sight and they are, after all, at home.

Sightings of **lions** are also com-

The Kori Bustard in the Maasai Mara.

Cheetah quenching their thirst after a run.

mon, if such a word can be applied to such a majestic animal. You will come across prides of lionesses and boisterous cubs, often with one disdainful male overseeing the whole outing. Huge herds of **zebra** and **wildebeest** roam together, **Grant's gazelles** and **Thomson's gazelles** are abundant, and the poor ugly **wart hog** can frequently be spotted.

Leopards are rarer but they can be seen : if you are lucky, you can spot them in a comfortable branch of a tree, with the half-eaten remains of dinner draped over the branch next to them. Often, that is the best way to spot a leopard for if you see a carcass in a tree, almost certainly the leopard will return at some point in the evening to eat it. **Cheetah** are easier to see, often with their fluffy cubs in tow, and they are reasonably unafraid of jeeps and their human occupants as long as you all remain quiet.

Safari

One of the "big" things to do in the Maasai Mara is to take a balloon safari (see box story p.326). It is a thrilling experience which does not come cheap but floating over herds of animals, seeing the patterns of the Maasai *bomas* from the air, touching down on a flat plain with the back-up cars racing to meet you and sitting down to a champagne breakfast, is a truly unique occasion.

The deserved popularity of the

The Great Wildebeest Migration

The spectacular annual wildebeest migration.

It behaves in a decidedly eccentric way, often running round in circles and rolling in the dust. It is rather strange-looking and clumsy yet the wildebeest or gnu is responsible for one of the world's most spectacular wildlife "events". Twice a year, vast herds of wildebeest, along with zebra and Thomson's gazelles, numbering in total anything up to two million animals, migrate across the vast Serengeti plains in search of pasture. To see hundreds of thousands of these animals marching together across the plains is an unforgettable sight.

The herds start to gather during the rainy season in the plains to the southeast of the Serengeti in Tanzania. It is at this time that a majority of the females give birth and as the rains stop and the dry weather begins, the huge herds start to move northwards, always in search of food. This way, they gradually move north through the Serengeti and, unbeknown to them, across the border into the Kenyan Maasai Mara. The accompanying zebras follow similar routes, although the Thomson's gazelles do not necessarily go as far as the Maasai Mara. There is no one fixed route but every year the overall pattern of the migration stays the same. The herds can travel up to 1,600 km (1,000 miles) during their seasonal migrations.

By June or July, the first of the wildebeest herd arrive in Maasai Mara where they stay eating their fill until they are ready to return "home" to the Serengeti. Slowly, by late October or early November, the wildebeest start retracing their steps.

As with any such mass movement, the annual migration of the wildebeest takes a high toll on the animals. Thousands of wildebeest drown as they cross rivers or are eaten by crocodiles and other predators, or, quite simply, die from exhaustion.

Champagne breakfast at the end of the balloon safari!

Maasai Mara means that the hotel infrastructure is very good indeed and there is a wide range of tented camps and lodges, most of them equally excellent. The obvious drawback to this is that in the Mara you are not alone : it is on virtually every visitor's safari itinerary, but there is space enough and game enough for everyone. At times, you may find several jeeps surrounding the same "kill" or the same cheetah who is waiting to catch her dinner, but most of the time, there will be just you, your driver, and abundant wildlife.

A Day on Safari

A lioness and her kill.

Day begins early on safari, well before sunrise. A cup of tea or coffee is delivered to your tent with a cheery "Good morning", and you sleepily switch on the light and wander outside to drink your tea on your verandah. Slowly the inky black sky with its dazzling canopy of stars begins to turn light, the bird cries get more and more insistent, and another day in the Maasai Mara has begun. Time to pick up your cameras, twice as much film as you think you may need, a warm jacket, and as the sun begins to rise, you head off to your jeep or landcruiser. It is 6.30 a.m. and you are going on the first of the day's game drives.

As the landcruiser bounces its way across the shadow-filled grasslands, keep a look-out for this is one of the best times for animal spotting. Nature is waking up and the animals are ready for breakfast. Herds of zebra and wildebeest, Thomson's gazelle, Grant's gazelle and the occasional jackal wander slowly across the plains.

Suddenly the driver quietly says, "lions" and drives off towards a small clearing, and there, a couple of meters away from you, is the sight that made that 5.30 a.m. wake up call worthwhile. Three lionesses and ten cubs are devouring the carcass of a buffalo. The lionesses look up briefly but knowing that the khaki-colored van and its quietly excited occupants pose no threat, they return to breakfast, and the only sounds are the snuffles and grunts from the animals and the clicking of camera shutters. For 15 or 20 minutes, or even longer, you watch the spectacle in awe. Safari vehicles are open topped, many have raised sunshades as well so you can stand up and watch from the roof in shaded comfort.

The cubs have eaten their fill and start fooling around as any youngster would on such a beautiful morning. They roll over, bite and box each other playfully. One cub tries to sneak away but quick as a flash, a lioness follows him,

....A Day on Safari

cuffs him on the ear and shoos him back towards the carcass. As the van pulls away, the lionesses look up lazily but it is already beginning to get a little too hot even to chase the cubs, and an after-breakfast snooze is clearly on the cards.

The landcruiser bounces off past yet more zebra and wildebeest, more gazelles, a large troop of baboons all arguing about something, their high pitched chattering clearly audible as they run around after each other. From time to time, red-cloaked Maasai shepherds stride past urging on a flock of goats or cattle, waving cheerfully at the heads popping up out of the van. As the last of the early morning chill disappears, the van turns towards the camp and breakfast. It is just nine o'clock.

A huge buffet breakfast is ready and waiting, and scraps of different conversation can be heard. "Three lionesses and ten cubs...wildebeest running past the jeep...four giraffes..." Everyone is there for the animals and so the conversation revolves around them.

As you wander back to your tent after breakfast, one of the camp staff strolls past, smiles and says "*Jambo*". You reply "hello", and then he asks whether you have seen the crocodile and the hippos down by the river. Any thought of sitting down for a short rest is gone as you follow him down to the river bank and there below you is a crocodile sunning himself, and, a few meters away, is a huge mass of black, shiny bodies, all piled against each other, heads resting on backs, snouts resting on stomachs – hippos dozing in the sun. There is just enough time to get more film from your tent, exchange your jacket for a sunhat, and head back to your jeep. It is ten o'clock.

You set off again across the flat plains, not a trace of a shadow now and the chill has long since gone from the breeze. The driver explains that as the predators are usually asleep by now, the other animals emerge without fear. Wildebeest, zebras, baboons, buffaloes, gazelles and topis scarcely bother to look up as you bounce past.

The driver suddenly swerves off the track and heads for a low tree with a small patch of shade. Cheetah. One splendid female, stretched out in the sun. As your vehicle approaches, in true "prima donna" style, the cheetah gets up, stretches and saunters over to the nearest tree where she promptly flops down again in the shade. It is almost as though she knows that it is more difficult to shoot in the shade. Or, possibly, as she realizes that a long photo-session is on the cards, she prefers to be comfortable. Whatever the logic, everyone promptly re-adjusts their cameras for the lower light, the driver switches off the engine and you settle down to watch.

She is least interested in the forest of powerful zoom lenses pointing at her, resolutely refusing to open her eyes. A morning nap is not to be interrupted even for such a perfect "photo opportunity". The minutes tick by until suddenly, the cheetah moves. The cameras start whirring. With an air of disdain that would do a Hollywood film star proud, she strolls slowly past the jeep, its occupants in serious danger of tumbling out as they lean over to record her every step, and disappears rapidly into the bush.

Back to the lodge for lunch, another huge buffet affair and an ice-cold Tusker beer. Coffee on the verandah of your tent and now is the time for a quick snooze, or, for the conscientious, time in which to write up your safari diary or tick off in your reference book the species so far seen, dust your camera equipment, get yet more film ready (what, so much film used up, and only Day One on safari? Thank goodness you brought twice the number of rolls you

Cubs at play.

thought you would need!), and at 4 o'clock, it is time for the evening game drive.

An Evening Drive

Already the landscape is beginning to look a little familiar as you bounce over rough ground and through dried up river beds. The driver stops the jeep by a clump of thorn trees where a lion and lioness are fast asleep. You stare in awe at the lion, such a short distance away. He refuses to wake up and pose for the cameras and videos, but he is almost as magnificent at rest. "Come on, let's go" suggests the driver with a smile, "He's not the only lion in Mara, you know. We'll try and find some more", and you bounce off again.

By now, you are accepting as matter of fact the herds of wildebeest and zebra and the sight of giraffes, their heads at tree level. You pass an unlovely looking wart hog and herds of gazelles dart away as your van mounts a ridge, and, suddenly, there is a collective intake of breath. On a sunny hillock are two lionesses, and five cubs. No, six, there's one asleep over there. Look, there is another one, hidden behind the lioness to the left. Everyone whispers, not wanting to interrupt the animals' siesta in the last of the afternoon sun.

Some of the cubs seem so close you want to reach out and stroke them for they look for all the world like overgrown kittens. One rolls onto his back just begging to be tickled and another keeps nudging his mother wanting her to play but she ignores him and keeps on snoozing. Two cubs roll around in a mock fight while another watches the cameras in wide-eyed fascination, unaware of the yards of film being used up on him. Twenty minutes, then half an hour pass and the sun starts to set. Reluctantly, the driver switches on the engine and you head back to the lodge. "I told you we'd find more lions, didn't I ?" he smiles.

After a much needed hot shower, you wander over to the main room of the lodge where a slide show is taking place. A cold Tusker and the by now familiar swapping of the day's sighting. Another huge meal – well, all that driving around in the fresh air certainly works up an appetite. By ten, back in your tent, you are aware of a satisfied sense of exhaustion, and, unable to write up your diary or read another chapter of *Out of Africa*, you turn off the light and fall asleep to the sound of the wind making the tent cords flap, and the din from the hippos who seem set to grunt all night long. It is 10 o'clock.

Rift Valley & the Northern Game Country

The **Rift Valley** is one of Kenya's decisive geological features separating west from east as it heads south from Lake Turkana, down through the country and on into Tanzania. It is almost as though a knife has sliced neatly down the length of the country. The Kenyan part of the Rift Valley is, of course, only one part of its 6,000-kilometer (3,600-mile) stretch from the Dead Sea, then the Red Sea, and on through Ethiopia, Kenya, and on south into Tanzania, Malawi and Mozambique.

Laikipia region in the Rift Valley.

The floor of the Rift Valley is not uniform. In the north of Kenya, at Lake Turkana, it stands just some 200 m (656 ft) above sea-level, and virtually merges into the surrounding desert. As it heads south though, it rises to 1,900 m (6,232 ft) at Lake Naivasha, and the sides of the valley are clearly delimited by steep

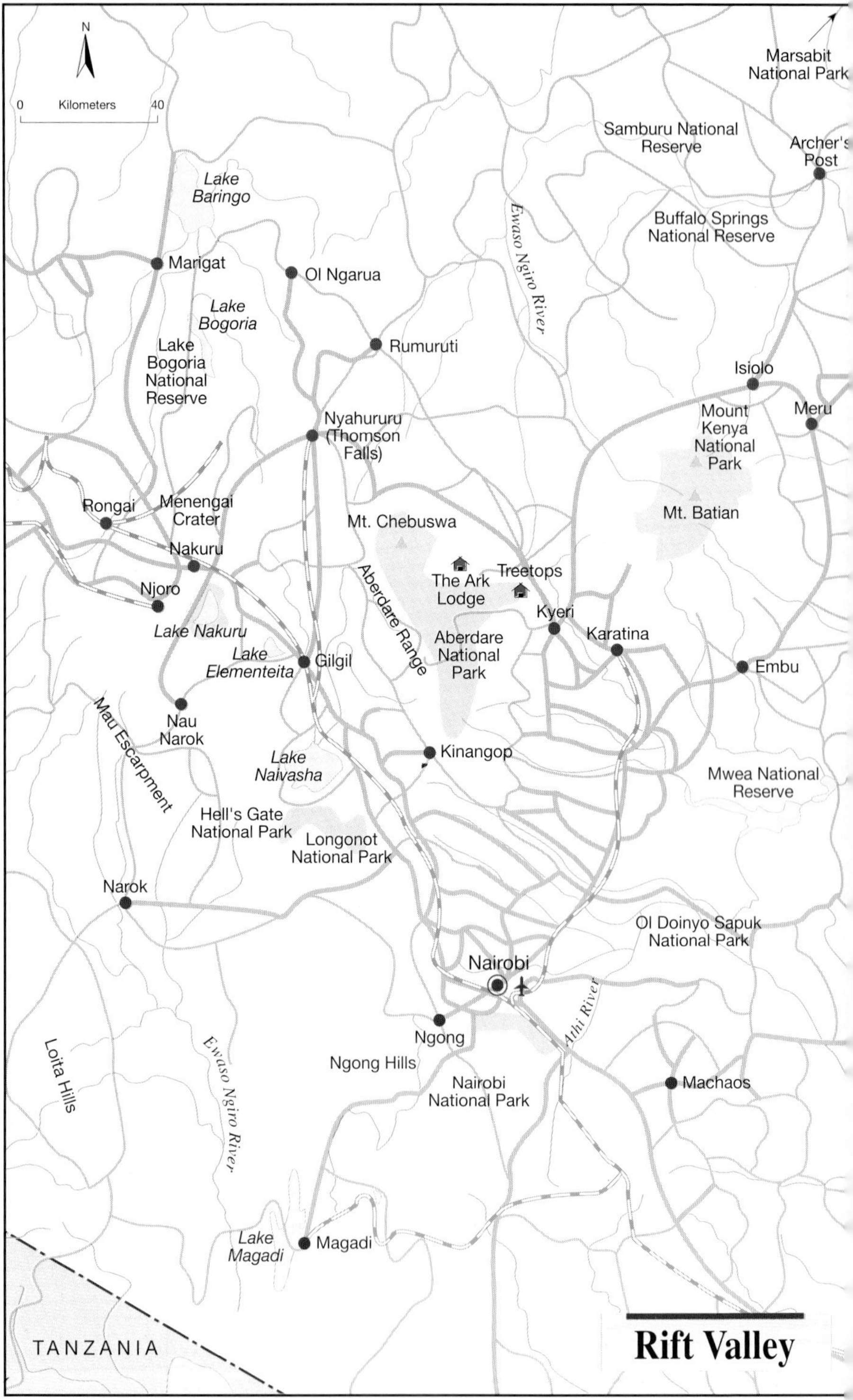
N
0 Kilometers 40
Marsabit National Park
Samburu National Reserve
Archer's Post
Lake Baringo
Ewaso Ngiro River
Buffalo Springs National Reserve
Marigat
Ol Ngarua
Lake Bogoria
Lake Bogoria National Reserve
Rumuruti
Isiolo
Meru
Nyahururu (Thomson Falls)
Mount Kenya National Park
Mt. Batian
Rongai
Menengai Crater
Mt. Chebuswa
Nakuru
The Ark Lodge
Treetops
Njoro
Aberdare Range
Kyeri
Lake Nakuru
Karatina
Aberdare National Park
Lake Elementeita
Gilgil
Embu
Mau Escarpment
Nau Narok
Kinangop
Lake Naivasha
Mwea National Reserve
Hell's Gate National Park
Longonot National Park
Narok
Ol Doinyo Sapuk National Park
Nairobi
Athi River
Ngong
Ngong Hills
Nairobi National Park
Machaos
Loita Hills
Ewaso Ngiro River
Lake Magadi
Magadi
TANZANIA

Rift Valley

The Rift Valley is one of Kenya's major geographical features.

walls. After Naivasha, it descends again to 580 m (1,902 ft) at the Tanzanian border.

Soda Lakes

In Kenya, the Rift Valley has formed one of the country's major geographical features, the string of lakes, some of which are **alkaline lakes**, and **hot springs** that lie like an elongated ribbon to the northwest of Nairobi. **Lake Baringo**, **Lake Bogoria**, **Lake Nakuru**, **Lake Elementaita**, **Lake Naivasha** and **Lake Magadi** in the south have become very important focal points for wildlife especially bird life.

Due to the steep sides of the valley, the drainage out of the Rift Valley is poor in some parts and several of the lakes along its floor have no drainage outlet. The combination of high alkalinity from the surrounding volcanic rocks and the high evaporation of the surface lake water means that the water remaining in the lakes is very often highly concentrated sodium carbonate. This makes an ideal breeding ground for algae, which become the food for certain species of fish resistant to such high amounts of soda, tilapia in particular, which is alkaline-tolerant. The fish and the algae naturally attract birds.

This may all seem very straightforward and nothing more than a simple example of a conventional biological chain, except that in the case of these

Crater Lake, one of the many volcanic lakes in the Rift Valley.

Rift Valley lakes, the last link in the food chain, the birds, exist on a scale that is simply staggering. Birds flock to these lakes, not in hundreds, not in thousands, but in **millions**. The bird life of the soda lakes is one of the marvels of the ornithological world, and lakes such as Nakuru and Bogoria are probably fairly close to paradise for a keen lover of birds (see box story on p.226).

The composition of the lake water is not uniform. Baringo and Naivasha are freshwater lakes which are thought to have subterranean outlets while Magadi

is the opposite, extremely alkaline. The others have varying degrees of salinity and brackishness.

Lake Naivasha was "discovered" by a German naturalist called Gustav Fischer in 1883, and its name is thought to derive from a classic case of European mispronunciation. The early visitors asked their Swahili porters what the

Lake Naivasha, a freshwater lake in a predominantly alkaline lake area.

lake was called and were told *"en-aiposha"*, which means quite simply, "the lake". And so, the pronunciation slightly mangled, Naivasha it became.

The beautiful lake covers 110 sq km (43 sq miles), and with its cool climate and its fertile soil, has become a favorite weekend retreat for city-weary Nairobi residents. Lake Naivasha has farms, vegetable gardens, and, a more recent addition to the agricultural landscape, **vineyards**, where the excellent local Lake Naivasha wine grows unexpectedly well.

Over 400 species of birds have been recorded on the lake which used to be the country's international airport, in the days when the **flying boats** still operated. Between 1937 and 1950, the

Joy Adamson's home, Elsamere, on the shores of Lake Naivasha.

The papyrus is found around Lake Bogoria.

flying boat from London would land at Lake Naivasha where the attractive and popular **Lake Naivasha Hotel** now stands, and the passengers would then get on a bus for the last stage of the journey to Nairobi.

A little distance off-shore, immediately opposite the Lake Naivasha Hotel is **Crescent Island**, a private game sanctuary, which you can visit and where you can walk around and see zebra, dikdik, camel, bushbuck, vervet monkey, spring hares, wildebeest, and Thomson's gazelle, all at close quarters. If you are fortunate, you may also see the elusive bat-eared fox and genet cat.

One of Kenya's more famous resident, **Joy Adamson**, whose best known book ***Born Free*** became a highly successful film, lived on the shores of Lake Naivasha. Her pretty home, **Elsamere**, is today a wildlife education center with an interesting little museum devoted to Joy and her husband George. If you arrive in good time in the afternoon, there is a wonderful tea laid on in the gardens down by the lake. The staff are friendly, helpful, and as there is some accommodation, it is a wonderful place to spend a few days. Priority is given to academics and researchers, so it makes sense to check on room availability before arriving.

Lake Naivasha is a freshwater lake which is used to irrigate the surrounding countryside and it naturally has a different ecology from the soda lakes. To the west of the lake there is a small

Pelicans flying over Lake Nakuru, known for its splendid sighting of flamingoes.

crater lake at the bottom of a very small volcano which makes an interesting side trip from Lake Naivasha. To the south is **Hell's Gate National Park**, one of only two in the country where you are allowed to explore on foot (the other is Saiwa Swamp – see the chapter on Western Kenya). It is thrilling to be able to walk past zebra, antelope, Thomson's gazelles and baboon rather than drive past them.

North of Lake Naivasha is Kenya's fourth largest town, **Nakuru**, a pleasant town whose life centers around agriculture. It is only a short drive from town to **Lake Nakuru**, one of the Rift Valley soda lakes, where **millions of flamingoes** live, making the lake one of the world's most dramatic wildlife sights. Even the casual observer is stunned by the sight of the lake entirely covered with dazzling pink flamingoes: for the keen ornithologist, this must be close to heaven.

To the north of the lake is **Menengai Crater**, an extinct volcano, 2,490 m (8,167 ft) high. The views of the crater itself and over the surrounding countryside are beautiful. Just outside the town of Nakuru is the badly posted sign **Hyrax Hill Prehistoric Site** where excavations carried out in the 1930s indicate that a settlement existed there 3,000 years ago. There is a little museum attached where many of the finds from the archeological digs are displayed.

Lake Bogoria is north of Nakuru, a soda lake with a series of geysers and hot

Excavations have been carried out uncovering prehistoric sites in the Rift Valley dating as far back as 400,000 years.

Samburu

Elephant hunting was one of the principal activities in Samburu in the 19th century.

The 19th-century author of ***Elephant Hunting in Equatorial East Africa,*** Arthur Neumann, would have a shock if he were able to see his former camp on the banks of the Ewaso Nyiro River in Samburu. Gone are the grass and mud huts, the rickety table and his bed, "an exact copy of the native bed, made of sticks tied lengthways, and others tied crossways, most hard and uncomfortable." Now, there is a lounge-cum-bar that has been built out over the river, so that while sipping a sundowner, you can watch the marabou storks and look for crocodiles and hippos. Where Neumann's servant was carried off by a crocodile, there is now an empty, walled-off area where meat is hung out each night as a bait for crocodiles.

Arthur Neumann was a shy man who came to Africa in 1880 to join his brother, and after extensive travels throughout the continent and a variety of jobs including a stint on the proposed Mombasa-Lake Victoria train, the Lunatic Express, he decided that he wanted to devote himself to elephant hunting. And Samburu became his favorite part of the country.

Now, there are cultural shows given by the local Samburu tribes people and there is a swimming pool, a far cry from the rough camp which was always known as *Nyama yangu*, the Kiswahili for "my meat", the nickname given to Neumann. He killed so many elephants and

springs. They are not called "hot" without reason – scalding water shoots out from the ground, so be careful not to get too close to them and do not touch the water. **Lake Baringo** is further north again, a freshwater lake, which is yet another terrestrial paradise for bird watchers.

East of Lake Baringo and to the north of the Aberdares and Mount Kenya, the nature of the countryside changes. The main roads seem to peter out. There are no towns and very few villages for this part of the country is sparsely populated. Turkana lies to the west with one main road connecting it to the populated south of the country. East of Turkana the land is just as empty. One look at the map will show that the main road north from Naivasha stops at Lake Baringo. The main road that circles Mount Kenya has a turn off for thus provided much elephant meat.

Neumann wrote of himself, "Nothing else thrills me, but the spell of the elephant is as potent as ever." Today, the thrill is just as potent in Samburu. Gone are the guns, to be replaced by zoom lenses. As you drive through the reserve surrounded by herds of reticulated giraffe, Grevy's zebra, and elephants, with noisy families of baboons everywhere and a family of cheetah out looking for dinner, it is easy to imagine the quiet Neumann enjoying the same panoramas.

You stop the jeep for a few minutes, by a clump of acacia bushes and suddenly, in one thrilling moment, you come face to face with a leopard. He sits in a low tree branch, the remnants of his dinner next to him, and watches with sleepy interest as you reach for your binoculars, and not a gun, as *Nyama yangu* would have done.

Take heed of the scalding water in the hot springs.

Local Samburu tribes people put on cultural shows for visitors nowadays.

Isiolo and then it stops. The same ring-road branches off to **Meru** where it promptly stops. The **north and north-east** of Kenya is an empty land, a huge expanse of deserts, with only secondary, rough, unsurfaced roads, a handful of villages, and no major towns.

National Reserves

Fifty-three kilometers (32 miles) to the north of Isiolo there are three national reserves which are often considered together, **Samburu, Buffalo Springs and Shaba**. These three reserves cover between them some 300 sq km (117 sq miles), and are spread out along the banks of the **Ewaso Nyiro River**.

On the shore of Lake Baringo, another freshwater volcanic lake.

Samburu is situated on the northern bank of the river and covers 104 sq km (41 sq miles). A bridge over the river, a few kilometers upstream from the Samburu Lodge, connects it with the neighboring Buffalo Springs Reserve. The newer **Shaba Reserve**, covering 338 sq km (130 sq miles), is to the east of **Buffalo Springs** and also on the southern bank of the river. It is less visited than the other two reserves, which are, themselves, considered a little "off the beaten track" by many safari companies. Joy Adamson spent much time in

the Shaba area, rehabilitating leopards.

The countryside is a combination of desert scrub and open savannah plains, with the tree-fringed river running through it. The existence of the river, lined as it is with large acacia trees and doum palms, attracts much game and bird life. Since the river is permanent, unlike many of Kenya's rivers that dry up during the dry season, its 32 km (19 miles) sustain a considerable wildlife population including elephant, cheetah, leopard, buffalo, Grevy's zebra, reticulated giraffe, wart hog and dikdik, as well as crocodiles in the river itself. Visitors who have been to the southern game parks before heading north, will see two species in Samburu for the first time : **Grevy's zebra** is only found in the north of the country and the **reticulated giraffe** is only found in the Samburu-Isiolo region, also in Meru Game Reserve, and in Marsabit, much further north.

Samburu is 64 km (38 miles) north of the Equator and the temperatures are hot with low humidity. The main accommodation is the attractive **Samburu Game Lodge** built along the banks of the river. The lodge has been constructed on the former camp site of a famous Victorian elephant hunter, Arthur Neumann, but he would probably not recognize the place today.

One of Kenya's most remote and least visited national parks is the **Marsabit National Park and Reserve**, a thickly forested oasis in the middle of the surrounding desert. Access to the park is difficult for the road from Isiolo is a long, rough, dangerous one – this is bandit country – so flying to Marsabit makes sense. If you do decide, however, to drive to Marsabit, a 4WD vehicle is a must. You will also need a special permit from the Provincial Headquarters in Isiolo, and you must be a party of at least two vehicles, and be totally self-

Hot springs in Lake Bogoria.

Samburu Reserve.

Samburu Lodge.

Birds of the Rift Valley Lakes

Flamingoes inundate some of the alkaline lakes.

As you approach **Lake Nakuru,** there is a strong, unpleasant smell. The horizon is pink, hardly the expected color for a lake. You park your car on the edge of the lake, and since the water level is low and has receded from the shore, you set off to walk across part of the bed of the lake towards the pink-colored, shimmering water. As you approach, you realize that the pink horizon is not water at all but a huge, moving mass of flamingoes. Thousands and thousands of flamingoes, their colors ranging from the palest of delicate pinks to a deep salmon-red color, cover the surface of the lake which is barely discernible below the constantly shifting crowd covering it.

There are flamingoes as far as the eye can see. Flamingoes are feeding, cleaning themselves, sleeping on one leg, walking around, making a cacophony of noise – and suddenly, there is a whirring sound, and a cloud of pink sweeps by, as several dozen or several hundred birds take off en masse and fly off to another part of the lake.

The bed of the lake is cracked with deep fissures and as you walk, you realize what the smell is. It is a combination of the saline water and the droppings of the thousands of birds. Yet the spectacle is so beautiful that you find that you forget the odors.

The lake is part of the **Lake Nakuru National Park** which was founded in 1960 and which has gradually increased in size over the ensuing 30 years to reach its present size of 200 sq km (76 sq miles). The lake, which measures 62 sq km (24 sq miles), is very shallow and its water level can fluctuate quite considerably, anything up to 4 m (13 ft) in a year. You can tell how low the water level is by the deposits of crystallized soda along its shores.

Lake Nakuru is not only home to flamingoes. Defassa waterbuck and buffalo come down to the shores of the lake, hippos live in the north-

The superb starling.

eastern corner of the lake, among the reeds and in the surrounding bush, you can see Bohor reedbuck and Thomson's gazelle – but the overall memory you will take away with you is of the pink flamingoes.

The number of flamingoes on the lake is not constant, and as water and food conditions vary, so does the bird population. At times, more than a million flamingoes may be on Lake Nakuru, at times the numbers will be less for large numbers of them may temporarily desert Nakuru for Lake Bogoria to the north or Lake Magadi to the south.

Lake Magadi is a shallow alkaline lake, very close to the Tanzanian border, and has a large and varied water bird population, including, of course, large numbers of flamingoes. It is the only place in Kenya where you can see the Chestnut-banded Sand Plover. You will need to get permission from the **Magadi Soda Company** to travel to this little visited, remote lake.

Lake Bogoria, which was formerly called Lake Hannington, is a shallow soda lake and is now the centerpiece of the **Lake Bogoria National Reserve**, set in dramatically beautiful scenery. To the east, a wall of steep hills, the northern edge of the Aberdares, descends almost to the very edge of the lake, while along the flatter, western shores there is a series of hot springs and geysers. If you can tear your attention away from the huge populations of greater and lesser flamingoes covering the lake's surface, you should be able to spot the greater kudu, which live mainly along the eastern shores of the lake. Impala are common and you may also see the klipspringer.

Nearby **Lake Baringo** is quite different from Lake Bogoria, since it is a deep, freshwater lake, and thus sustains a slightly different wildlife population. There are crocodiles, hippos – and birds galore. Of Kenya's 1,200 species of birds, over a third of them of over 450 different

The Goliath Heron.

...Birds of the Rift Valley Lakes

species have been recorded at Lake Baringo. Many of the birds live in the acacia woodlands that border the lake but Baringo has two major ornithological attractions. There is a large nesting colony of Goliath Herons and the escarpment to the west of the lake is home to Verreaux's Eagle, Hemprich's Hornbill and the rare Bristle-crowned Starling.

The fragility of the ecological chain was amply, and very sadly, demonstrated in September 1993 when more than 5,000 flamingoes died in just two weeks on Lake Nakuru and Lake Bogoria. The Kenyan Wildlife Service immediately swung into action, flying veterinary doctors to the two lakes. These experts examined the dead birds and initially decided that they had died from a bacterial infection, *Pseudamonas aeruinosus*, which is usually a harmless bacteria. What particularly alarmed the Kenyan Wildlife Service was the statistical implications, for with a combined population of between two and three million birds on the two lakes, an infection could soon become a horrific epidemic.

To control the infection, the corpses were burned and a plea was made for a concerted effort by the local community to arrest the problem. Afforestation was necessary particularly in water catchment areas and industrial effluent had to be treated. The drought which persisted in Kenya in 1993 could also be responsible for the deaths of the birds for the water in the lakes had become putrid, encouraging bacterial growth.

sufficient in petrol, food and water. This is deserted, difficult terrain, and any trip there needs to be well planned.

Once there, Marsabit is an amazing place for within its huge 2,070 sq km (787 sq miles), it contains a forested mountain which literally surges out of the surrounding parched desert, a group of volcanic craters, and a wealth of rare and little known birds. One of the volcanic craters fills with water during the rainy season and is known as **Lake Paradise**. This is the place to head for if you are camping, for not only is it a pleasant oasis in a harsh climate, but it is where most of the reserve's water birds have been recorded.

To the north lies the inhospitable **Dida Galgalla desert**, an expanse of black lava. Many rare species of birds inhabit this exotic area – 52 birds of prey alone have been recorded around the Marsabit area – and some of the more unusual species to be seen include the **Heuglin's Bustard**, the **Somali Ostrich**, **Swallow-tailed kites**, **Lammergeyer** and **Somali Bee-eaters**. Wild-

Samburu landscape.

life is also abundant and visitors may well see some of the most impressive **tuskers** to be seen in the country as well as the **greater kudu**, **aardwolf**, the **striped hyena**, and the rarely seen **caracal**. Unusually, **reticulated giraffes** spend much time in the forest, not their usual habitat.

The northeast of the country, beyond Marsabit, is a vast, sparsely populated area of desert and semi-desert. The land is flat, with little to break the shimmering monotony of the landscape except the rare village, the even rarer small town, and the occasional group of nomads herding their flocks. Poaching is a sad fact of life here and bandits, known as *shiftas*, discourage all but the truly tenacious traveler.

An abandoned termite mound, sometimes used as a nest by the wart hog.

The Mountain National Parks

The **Central Highlands** of Kenya consist of the **Aberdares** and of **Mount Kenya** itself. Together, they form the eastern wall of the Rift Valley which is a fertile, well-irrigated, forested area. Within these Central Highlands are two of Kenya's most beautiful national parks, the **Mount Kenya National Park**, and, only 80 km (48 miles) away, the **Aberdares National Park.** Together, they consist of some of the country's highest parkland, and with their forests and abundant water, are home to a wide variety of wildlife.

The Central Highlands region is the home of the Kikuyu tribe.

This area is the heartland of the **Kikuyu** tribe for whom Mount Kenya is sacred but with its good climate and its highly fertile soil, the European "white settlers" who arrived in large numbers in Kenya in the early years of this century, coveted the land. The growing resentment of the Kikuyu, who saw their best territory being taken away by the Europeans, turning them, effectively, into

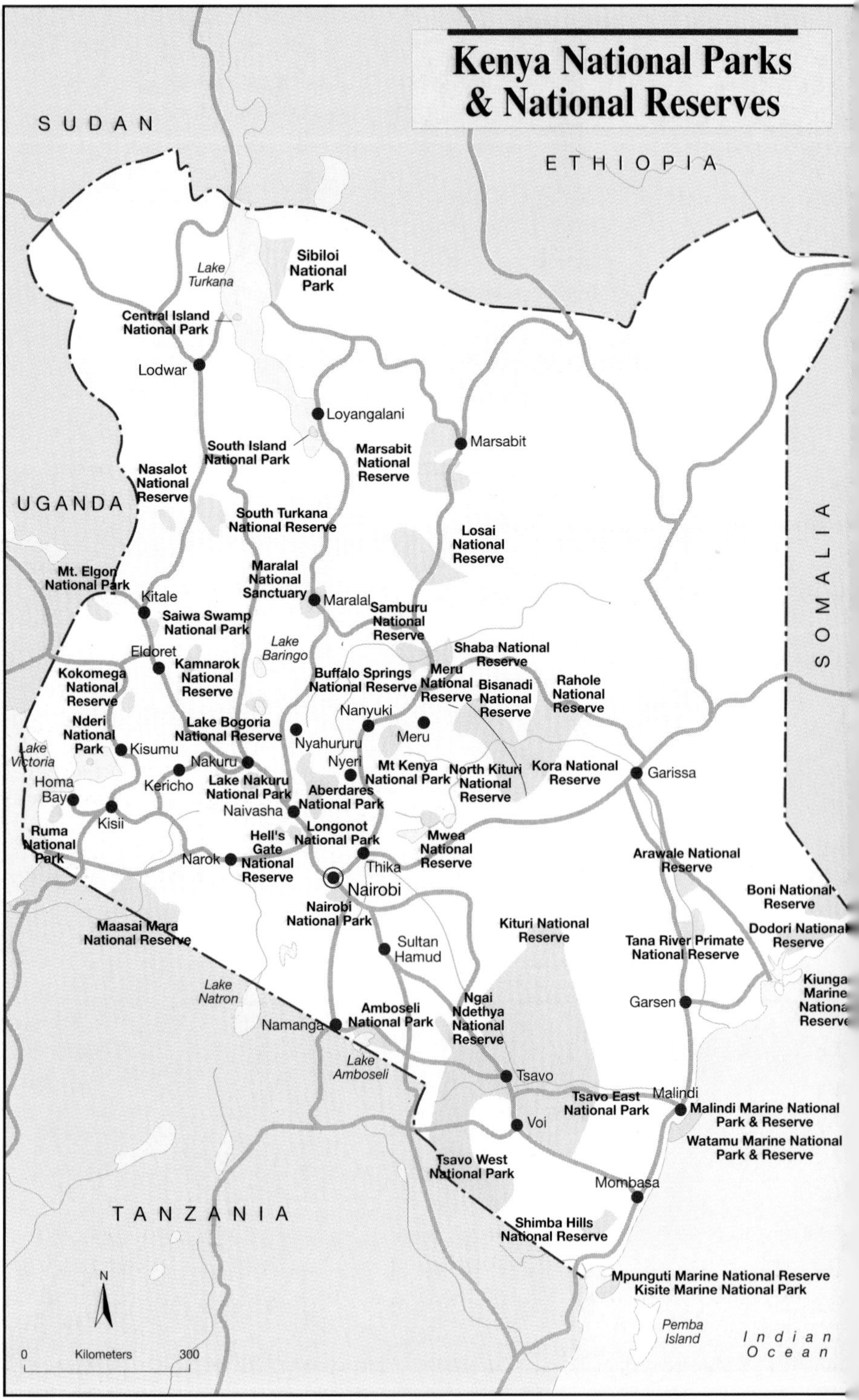
Kenya National Parks & National Reserves
SUDAN
ETHIOPIA
UGANDA
SOMALIA
TANZANIA
Lake Turkana
Sibiloi National Park
Central Island National Park
Lodwar
Loyangalani
Marsabit
South Island National Park
Marsabit National Reserve
Nasalot National Reserve
South Turkana National Reserve
Losai National Reserve
Mt. Elgon National Park
Maralal National Sanctuary
Maralal
Kitale
Samburu National Reserve
Saiwa Swamp National Park
Lake Baringo
Eldoret
Kamnarok National Reserve
Shaba National Reserve
Kokomega National Reserve
Buffalo Springs National Reserve
Meru National Reserve
Bisanadi National Reserve
Rahole National Reserve
Nanyuki
Nderi National Park
Lake Bogoria National Reserve
Nyahururu
Meru
Lake Victoria
Kisumu
Nakuru
Nyeri
Mt Kenya National Park
North Kituri National Reserve
Kora National Reserve
Garissa
Homa Bay
Kericho
Lake Nakuru National Park
Aberdares National Park
Kisii
Naivasha
Ruma National Park
Hell's Gate National Reserve
Longonot National Park
Mwea National Reserve
Arawale National Reserve
Narok
Thika
Nairobi
Boni National Reserve
Nairobi National Park
Kituri National Reserve
Maasai Mara National Reserve
Sultan Hamud
Dodori National Reserve
Tana River Primate National Reserve
Lake Natron
Ngai Ndethya National Reserve
Kiunga Marine National Reserve
Garsen
Amboseli National Park
Namanga
Lake Amboseli
Tsavo
Tsavo East National Park
Malindi
Malindi Marine National Park & Reserve
Voi
Watamu Marine National Park & Reserve
Tsavo West National Park
Mombasa
Shimba Hills National Reserve
Mpunguti Marine National Reserve
Kisite Marine National Park
N
Pemba Island
Indian Ocean
0 Kilometers 300

Vultures of the Central Highlands.

squatters on their own land, was to lead to the **Mau Mau Rebellion**, and eventually, to **independence**.

Some of the white settlers who stayed in Kenya after independence still live in the Central Highlands, but with much reduced land holdings. Land has been distributed to the Kikuyu but the subdivision of the land into small parcels has brought its own problems. Some of the plots are too small to support entire families and there is a consequent encroachment of the forests. Loss of tree cover leads to soil erosion and the ever increasing population naturally puts pressure on the region, and particularly on the forests since trees are cut for firewood and to build houses.

When the first 19th-century European missionaries reported back on seeing the snowy peak of **Mount Kenya**, no one really believed in the possibility of snow on the Equator. Even the first ascent of the 5,199-meter (17,058-foot) mountain, by Sir Halford Mackinder in 1899, aroused little interest. **Kirinyaga** or Mount Kenya, the sacred mountain of the Kikuyus, was only to become truly popular with climbers by the middle of the 20th century.

Today Africa's second highest mountain offers very challenging climbing to the experienced mountaineer, and also several well-established trails. (See Sports chapter.) Since the mountain has been designated as a national park, you will have to pay the park's fees before setting off on any treks.

A Kikuyu village.

Mount Kenya National Park

Mount Kenya was formed between two and a half and three million years ago as a result of **volcanic eruptions**. Its base diameter is 120 km (72 miles). Geologists believe that initially the mountain may have been higher, up to 6,000 m (19,680 ft), but that centuries of erosion has worn away the cone, leaving today's jagged peaks and valleys containing glacial lakes. It is also estimated that there used to be many more

glaciers on the mountain, and even in the 100 years since records of the mountain have been maintained, starting in 1893, seven recorded glaciers have disappeared. The remaining glaciers are steadily getting thinner and if this process continues, along with global warming, the permanent ice cap may soon be a thing of the past.

The combination of volcanic soil and abundant water has made the slopes of the mountain very fertile and agriculture is practised up to about 1,900 m (6,232 ft). The lower slopes are intensively cultivated, with wheat in particular being grown to the north. Above the cultivation level are large swathes of untouched rainforest which harbor a wide variety of trees and plants including **giant camphor**, **vines** and **orchids**. The forest cover is not quite so thick on the northern and eastern slopes of the mountain where the rainfall is less. These slopes are characterized by **conifers**.

The forests are home to a wide variety of wildlife including **elephant**, **buffalo** and many species of **monkeys**, all of which climbers may encounter on the tracks through the forest. In the clearings, you may also see **many species of antelope**, the **giant forest hog**, as well as **lion** and **rhino** which is naturally much more rare in view of its dangerously reduced numbers.

The forests on the western and southern sides of the mountain gradually change to a stretch of tall, dense **bamboo** which in turn gives way to open woodland. As you climb higher, this woodland is followed by a stretch of **giant heather**, and then you pass into a zone of **open moorland**. Here, in an area which stretches right up to the snow line, there are many small flowering plants but as you draw closer to the snow, between 4,500 and 4,700 m (14,760 and 15,416 ft), the vegetation becomes increasingly sparse. Beyond

Mount Kenya, the sacred mountain of the Kikuyu and the second highest peak in Africa.

The Ark

The Ark in the Aberdares.

The one thing you will never get at The Ark is a good night's sleep. If you do, that means you were unlucky and did not see any of the spectacular wildlife on offer. For at his amazing-looking hotel, for all the world a wooden Noah's Ark, right in the middle of the Aberdares National Park, all guests are woken up during the night whenever any animal come to the salt lick. The more interrupted your night's sleep, the more successful your stay.

Your trip to the Ark begins when all the guests for the night meet for lunch at the nearby elegant Aberdares Country Club, just a few kilometers away, where most of your luggage is stored. You should only take a small overnight bag with you to the Ark, for the rooms are very small, with, quite frankly, no space for luggage, and in any case, once at The Ark, you will have no time for anything but animal watching. On arrival, you are briefed on the buzzer system which is in operation during the night : there is a buzzer in every bedroom, and two buzzes mean either rhino or elephant, three mean lion or leopard. Sartorial elegance is not a consideration either, for, you are told, the blanket folded at the end of your bed is to be used in the middle of the night when the buzzer goes. Instead of wasting precious time getting dressed, just wrap yourself up in the blanket and hurry along to the viewing gallery.

Long before night falls, many animals come to the salt lick and during the day, you may also use the various outdoor viewing terraces : at night, you only use the covered gallery. There is also a photographic hide though visibility from the terraces is actually good enough. People sit out on the terraces or in the viewing gallery,

the snow line, only **lichens** and **mosses** can survive.

The woodland and moorland on the upper reaches of the mountain are home to **eland**, **duiker**, the **rock hyrax** and even **zebra**. Much more difficult to spot, though they live in this terrain, are **leopards**. **Bird life** is also rich as you climb the mountain and you will see the **cliff chat** and the **scarlet-tufted malachite sunbird** while larger birds of prey hover overhead, including **eagles**, **auger buzzards** and the **bearded vulture**.

Back down at ground level, the A2 road circles the base of the mountain, and the region's main towns and villages are strung along it, any of which can serve as a convenient starting point for treks up the mountain. **Naro Moru** lies to the west of Mount Kenya and is actually little more than a village but it is one of the most popular starting points

Bird table at The Ark.

reading, scanning the trees for animals or helping themselves to the copious tea that is laid on. In the early evening, there is a trip along the walkway to watch the birds being fed. Then as darkness falls, back at The Ark, people gather round the fire, swapping safari stories, chatting to the wardens who wander around, ready to offer advice and information on everything from shutter speeds to bird species.

The Buzzer Goes Wild

Dinner, and then everyone heads off for bed with a final reminder not to bother getting dressed, but to use the blanket. And that is exactly what happens when the buzzer sounds twice at 3.15 a.m. You wrap the blanket round yourself, trot bleary-eyed along to the glass-walled viewing area, and there, in the moonlight, is a mother rhino, feeding her baby. The darkened gallery is full of other blanket cocooned people, all marveling at the enchanting tranquil scene outside. Since camera flashes are absolutely forbidden at night, there is very little photography and everyone sits quietly for five or ten or twenty minutes, watching in companionable, sleepy silence, while the baby rhino feeds.

Some nights, there may be only one "wake-up call", other nights, you get hardly any sleep at all. A detailed log is kept of all animal sightings, nocturnal or otherwise, and when you wake up for breakfast, you can check to see how good, or bad, a night's sleep yours was. And, with hindsight, who cares about a night's sleep when there are rhinos to be seen ?

for climbers who use the **Naro Moru trail**. All bookings for this trail have to be made through the **Naro Moru River Lodge**, an excellent hotel which owns the franchise on the huts along the trail, so for any information and bookings you must contact the hotel.

Continuing north on the circular road around Mount Kenya, you arrive at the busy little country town of **Nanyuki**, which still has a faint whiff of a frontier town about it. Perhaps it is the sign telling you that you have just crossed the **Equator** (see box story p.56) or perhaps it is the picturesquely named **Settlers' Stores**, a Nanyuki institution since the 1930s, but Nanyuki gives you the feeling of embarking on an adventure. A short drive outside town is the **Commonwealth War Cemetery** with its well-tended, neat little memorial garden. Nanyuki is the departure point for the

The poinsetta grows in the agreeable climate and favorable soil conditions.

Burguret trail or the **Sirimon trail** up the mountain, and is a good place to shop for supplies. It is also en route to one of Kenya's most luxurious, and most famous hotels, the **Mount Kenya Safari Club**.

Back on the circular road around the base of the mountain, the next town is **Isiolo**, another frontier town, this time for the vast empty north-eastern area of the country. As the road begins to head south again, on the western side of Mount Kenya, there is the little town of **Meru**, a busy administrative town which services this area of the central province. If it is rainy, Meru will be blanketed in mist but otherwise there are lovely views from the town over the surrounding plains.

To the east of Meru, is the **Meru National Park**, one of the lesser known and less frequented of Kenya's national parks. Benefiting from the abundant rainfall over neighboring Mount Kenya, Meru is lush and luxuriant. It was here that **George and Joy Adamson** rehabilitated the son of their famous lioness, Elsa, as well as their cheetah, Pippah, whose grave is in the park. Sadly, the story does not have a very happy ending, for the poachers who decimated the imported white rhino population murdered Joy in Meru. Although security has been improved, you should always ask about the prevailing conditions in Meru before arranging a trip there. Part of the park is in any case totally off-limits to visitors since it has been desig-

The eland is the largest antelope in Kenya and one of the nimblest.

nated as a "wilderness area."

Meru is not very practical as an overnight stop for the next trail up Mount Kenya, the **Chogoria trail**, the only eastern one up the mountain since it is still quite a long drive south. Anyone wanting to ascend Mount Kenya from the Chogoria trail will probably have to camp at the base or overnight at Meru and set off very early to start climbing. Further south is another small, administrative town, **Embu**, which has a cool, pleasant climate and is surrounded by hills and farms.

Aberdares National Park

The second of the two principal national parks in this area is the **Aberdares National Park** which was formed in 1950 from a large section of the forest which covers the **Aberdares**. This range of mountains was named after the then president of the Royal Geographical Society, by the intrepid explorer Thomson, in 1848. The national park encompasses moorland and forest on the Kinangop plateau: walking is not permitted in the park without special permission, and since there is no public transport at all, the best way of seeing the wildlife is to base yourself at either of the two lodges, both of which have panoramic viewing platforms over the forest. These two lodges, **Treetops** and **The Ark** are every bit as impressive as their reputation, and they are both very spe-

The terrain is also ideal for the leopard.

Mount Kenya Safari Club

The alternative scene at the Mount Kenya Safari Club.

It is early evening, when there is a discreet knock on your door. Your room attendant has come to light the fire in your bedroom and while he does so, you sit and look out at the view from your room and watch the last of the day's light over Mount Kenya.

Welcome to one of Kenya's most famous, luxurious and beautiful (not surprisingly equally expensive) hotels, the Mount Kenya Safari Club. Sitting exactly on the Equator, which runs exactly through the manicured lawns and well-tended gardens, facing the dramatic profile of Mount Kenya, this is a place for a little well-earned pampering, after the bouncy roads of dusty safaris. This oasis of cool greenery offers everything – swimming in a heated pool, tennis, riding, walking and even its own game ranch, right on the Equator.

The **Mount Kenya Safari Club** was the brainchild of three friends : the late actor and film star, William Holden, Ray Ryan, a Texas oil millionaire, and Carl Hirschmann, a Swiss financier. Since its opening in 1959, it has been a magnet for Kenyans as well as for travelers from all over the world who all enjoy its unashamed luxury and the excellent food – jacket and tie are obligatory for dinner, gentlemen.

In the extensive grounds of the safari club, is the **Mount Kenya Game Ranch**, founded by William Holden and his friends, Julian McKeand, Deane Johnson, President of Warner Communications, and the Hunts, who still run it. The ranch covers 499 hectares (1,216 acres) and has about 2,000 animals from 26 different species. A mixed farm was purchased in 1967 and turned into a game ranch, and as a symbol of the ranch, the founders chose Africa's rarest, most beautiful and elusive animal, the **bongo**, hardly ever seen in the wild and seldom photographed. Today, the ranch is one of the few places in the world where you can see two rare species of game, the bongo and the **white zebra**.

The friends later founded the **Mount Kenya**

The rare and elusive bongo is the symbol of the Mount Kenya Game Ranch.

Animal Orphanage which is open to visitors. As well as providing a natural environment for various game, the orphanage operates as a study-center for Kenya's school children, enabling them in particular to see the bongo. It also serves as a refuge for sick wild animals until they are well enough to be released and returned to the national parks.

William Holden first came to Kenya in 1956 and started a program for Kenyan children, exposing them to animals they had never seen. He died in November 1981, and in his memory, the **William Holden Wildlife Foundation** was formed to carry on his work and meet the ever-increasing demand for conserving endangered animal species. The foundation is located at the William Holden Education Center, on 6 hectares (15 acres) of the ranch. One interesting "import" is a flock of high-altitude llamas from South America which are used by students for their expeditions up the mountain.

The orphanage is a fun place to visit – well, that is, if you actually enjoy being mobbed by hungry zebra and llamas who refuse to believe that visitors could be thoughtless enough to come empty-handed. Luckily, the wardens have pocketfuls of snacks for the animals which are hurriedly handed over to the mobbed visitors.

Among the animals in the orphanage, you can see Speedy, a 135-kilogram (300-pound), century-old giant tortoise, and two rare white rhinos, "Zulu" and "Big Mama". There is also a bush pig called Tessie who simply refuses to let herself be rehabilitated. Each time she is released into the wild, she makes her way back, breaks down the fences and returns "home." As the panel next to her area laconically states, "This animal is not a success story in wildlife rehabilitation. It now thinks it is a person."

Long term residents of the Animal Orphanage, for the purpose of conservation.

An endangered species, the square-lipped or white rhino can still be found here.

cial, unusual lodges. Both are built close to water holes and both have **salt licks** whereby salt is spread out on the soil, attracting animals to it.

Treetops is one of Kenya's most famous hotels and is where, in 1952, the young British Princess Elizabeth was informed that she had become Queen Elizabeth II. Treetops has played host to a long list of European royalty, presidents and celebrities, as the faded photographs on the walls testify, all of which gives the lodge an extra charm.

The original lodge had only two rooms which in time expanded to four, but it was burned down during the Mau Mau Rebellion. The lodge was rebuilt in 1957 and has grown considerably ever since. It is extremely popular despite its undeniably tiny rooms and the shared bathroom facilities.

If you are staying at Treetops, you will be told to rendezvous at the **Outspan Hotel** in the little town of **Nyeri**, a bustling little administrative center, where you will have lunch, leave the bulk of your luggage, and then transfer to Treetops with only an overnight bag. There is no obligation to spend a night at the Outspan which is the headquarters for Treetops, but since it is a lovely, old-style hotel, an extra day or so amidst the beautiful, cool gardens is a real pleasure. **Lord and Lady Baden Powell**, the founders of the boy scout and the girl guide movements, retired to a cottage in the grounds of the hotel which you can visit, and the couple are both buried in

A typical setting of the Aberdare Country Club.

St. Peter's Church in Nyeri. The other luxury hotel in Nyeri is **The White Rhino.**

A similar procedure takes place when you visit The Ark (see box story p.238). All visitors meet for lunch at the elegant, baronial-style **Aberdares Country Club** where the food is excellent and **ostriches** run around on the manicured lawns. You leave all your luggage in storage there, take only an overnight bag and are driven through the forest to The Ark, a short 18-kilometer (11-mile) drive away, although regular sightings of **black and white colobus monkeys** tend to slow down the journey.

From Nyeri, if you follow the B5 road north, you pass through the little town of **Ngobit** and on to **Nyahururu**, a little town sitting at 2,360 m (7,741 ft). Its name, in the Maa language, means "where waters run deep", an appropriate name for the site of **Thomson's Falls.** The explorer, Joseph Thomson named them after his father in 1883.

North to Lake Turkana

Kenya's northern frontiers with Ethiopia and Sudan lie across some of the country's most arid, empty and dramatic country. Few people live in the vast northern desert, even fewer visit, but those who do are rewarded with a glimpse of Kenya's wilder, untouched nature.

Lake Turkana is situated in the Rift Valley, a massive fault-line in the earth's crust which runs down much of the African continent south from the Red Sea. The Turkana area is climatically hostile although its harsh conditions are offset by the friendly welcome from the local people who see few outsiders and are always happy to meet visitors.

Woman and child of the Samburu tribe.

A Historical Document

In late March 1888, an expedition led

Bird life in the more arid terrain include the marabou storks and the vultures.

by the Austrian explorer, **Count Teleki**, and his geographer and friend, Lieutenant Ludwig von Hohnel, arrived at Lake Turkana. Von Hohnel noted in his diary that the explorers came across a stretch of ground "strewn with human skulls and bones."

It was only 80 years later that the significance of this comment would be realized, when another explorer, Richard Leakey, the son of the pioneer archeologists Mary and Louis Leakey, started work in the area around **Koobi Fora** where he unearthed a rich trove of fossil remains (see box story p.256). Over the next few years, Richard Leakey and his team were to find fossil fragments dating back almost three million years. The Lake Turkana area may well be one of the places where **early man** first walked upright, and sat down under the burning sun to make his first crude tools.

When the Austrian expedition saw Lake Turkana, they named it **Lake Rudolf** in honor of their Crown Prince, but by the late 1970s the name had been changed to Turkana. An even more poetic and descriptive name is the **Jade Sea**, an accurate description of this literal and metaphorical oasis amid the surrounding monochromatic, desolate landscape of extinct volcanoes and arid lava beds.

The spectacular color of the lake always stuns visitors, however much they may have heard about it, for it appears to change color constantly. The water varies in tone from gray to blue to

The ibis is found around Lake Turkana.

the wonderful jade of its name. The color derives from the algae in the lake which change as the wind disturbs the particles and as the passing clouds alter the light overhead.

Unfriendly but Pro-wildlife

Lake Turkana, which stretches south from the Ethiopian border, is shaped rather like a dog's leg, for it is long and thin – a little over 257 km (154 miles) long, with an average width of 31 km (19 miles). The lake's surface area is about 7,500 sq km (2,925 sq miles). It is fed by the Omo River to the north which drains from Mount Amara in Ethiopia's western highlands. As the lake has no

Kingfisher in the ubiquitous thorn tree.

The Grevy's zebra has a thick mane and no stripes on its belly.

outlet, its water level rises and falls in rhythm with the Omo River as it floods and abates, producing a difference in level of about 95 cm (37 in).

The lake water is alkaline, making it unpleasant to drink for humans, but it does provide an invaluable reservoir for wildlife. At some point, probably around 10,000 years ago, the lake is thought to have been a source for the River Nile, a theory which is borne out by the fact that today Nile perch can be fished in the lake.

The surrounding dusty plains are broken up by dry river beds known as *luggas* which can, however, become dangerous when there is a flash flood. This region of Kenya has an extreme climate with daytime temperatures sometimes reaching a breathless, stifling 63° C, and with sudden storms ripping through the heat. Despite its shimmering beauty, Lake Turkana is just as quixotic, with sudden squalls breaking out almost without warning, when strong winds can transform the calm surface of the lake into three-meter (10-ft) high waves. The high temperature of this area and the absence of rainfall are causing Lake Turkana to evaporate at a quantifiable rate: the shoreline is receding at a rate of 3 m (10 ft) a year.

The phenomenal water source at Turkana attracts a wide range of **bird life**, more than 350 species, some resident and some migratory, including the tawny eagle, the sacred ibis, the white

A nomadic Turkana woman milking a camel.

The giraffe is within the limited range of wildlife found in the region.

stork, the malachite kingfisher and the Egyptian goose. From March to early May, the lake is visited by vast flocks of European migratory birds, especially marsh sand-pipers and wagtails.

There are also several dangerous **reptiles**, including cobras, puff-adders, night adders and saw-scaled vipers. As far as **mammals** are concerned, you will see Grevy's zebra, the reticulated giraffe, and, naturally in a desert region, camels galore. When Count Teleki and Lieutenant von Hohnel first saw Lake Turkana, they reported that there

were large herds of rhino, buffalo, water buck and elephant there, but, sadly, in a century, they have been wiped out of this area, mainly by poaching.

In such a remote area as this, the road infrastructure is minimal, there is almost no public transport, and petrol is, obviously, a rare and expensive commodity. Some of the existing roads are real bone-shakers and driving becomes an endurance test. Trips to this area are not to be undertaken lightly and travelers will need a sturdy four-wheel drive vehicle, and comprehensive equipment such as ropes and chains to get the jeep out of the inevitable breakdowns in the middle of a sand dune, as well as ample supplies of food and water and suitable clothing for both the high day temperatures and the chilly desert nights. Other items to be packed include an extensive tool kit, a shovel to dig the jeep free, an extra-strong jack and two planks of wood to help get out of dunes, or, if you encounter a flash flood, out of mud. If possible, aim to travel in convoys and always follow the on-the-spot advice of the local people before setting off on any trip.

The only town of sorts in the northwest of Kenya is **Lodwar**, a small, hot and dusty local administrative center, with an airstrip and limited accommodation possibilities. Lodwar, which is 64 km (38 miles) from the shores of the lake, may be small but it administers the Turkana District, all 200,000 sq km (78,000 sq miles) of it. The A1 road forks at Lodwar, one track leading to the village of Kalokol near the shore of the lake, while the other heads off on a lonely route to **Lokichogio** and the Sudanese border. West out of the town is a road that goes through the village of **Lorukumu** and onto the Ugandan border.

Since the water level of the lake has receded considerably in recent years, largely because of the drought in Ethio-

Koobi Fora

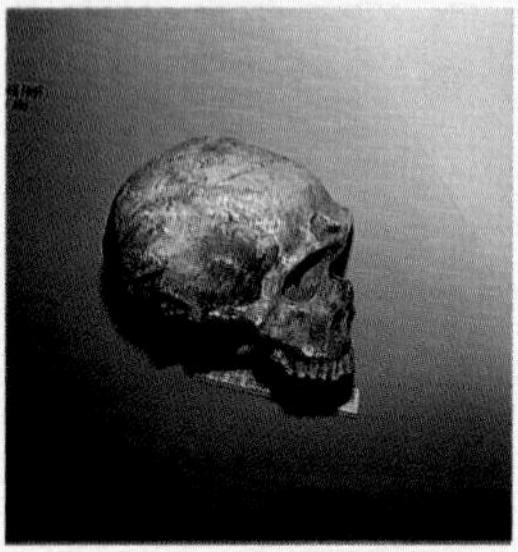

Skull of a prehistoric man.

Koobi Fora Research Project, on the northeastern shore of Lake Turkana, is a vast paleontological site covering some 2,500 sq km (975 sq miles). In 1972, a small fragment of skull was found in the sand, and over the ensuing months another 300 fragments were unearthed. Reconstructed, they helped form a hominid's skull which is known simply as "1470", after its index number. Despite its prosaic name, "1470" is the earliest evidence yet found of man's evolution from the apes. Its high forehead and large cranial capacity place it in the "Homo" category, although its jaw is still primitive.

Lake Turkana is situated in the Rift Valley which has helped immeasurably in the search for fossils for it allows what can only be called a favorable erosion pattern. Rather than staying buried beneath layers of sediment, the fossils are exposed due to the movement of the earth's crust.

During the 1970s the Koobi Fora Research Project grew from a small expedition to become a large, multi-disciplinary research venture of the national museums led by Richard Leakey and involved numerous scientists from many countries.

Koobi Fora is part of the **Sibiloi National Park**, which was established in 1972 by the Kenyan Government on the advice of Richard Leakey as a means of protecting the fossil-bearing shores of the lake. At present, relatively little fossil collection is in progress since much of the actual research work has moved to the western side of Lake Turkana.

The camp, however, is used as a base for training students. Each year two field camps are held when students from Kenya and all over the world are trained in the study of fossils. The **Koobi Fora International School of Paleontology** offers these students a unique opportunity for "hands on" training allowing them to handle fossils and help in their location and identification. The camp is on a sand spit which juts out into the lake and visitors can stay there and visit the nearby museum which has many of the fossil finds on display, including a one and a half million-year-old elephant.

It goes without saying but should you find any fossil fragments in this area, it is absolutely forbidden to pick them up and take them. Not only are you destroying a piece of history, you are also risking a jail sentence. Leave any fossils exactly where you find them for the precise location of a fossil is of vital importance. Valuable geological information can be gleaned from the surrounding soils, which may help significantly with dating a given specimen. The experts are trying to piece together an extremely old jigsaw puzzle. Many of the pieces of this puzzle are missing while others are exposed each year by wind, and rain, and the natural process of erosion, and for that reason, any fragment, however tiny, must be left in place.

pia, you can now walk across part of the bed of the lake, through flocks of flamingoes, although you should always ask advice before doing so – just remember that there are hippos and crocodiles in the lake. In the dry season, you can even drive out across the lake bed towards the little island where the Lake Turkana Lodge is built. The lodge used to be surrounded by the waters of **Ferguson's Gulf**, but they have dried up, effectively leaving the lodge on land, and the shore-based fish freezing factories with reduced catches.

Snakes inhabit the terrain.

Yet the lake still offers good **fishing**, with more than 40 different species recorded, chief among them the Nile perch, which can reach a massive size. Catches of over 100 lbs (45 kg) are not infrequent, and the record currently stands at 238 lbs (107 kg), but other than their sheer size, these fish do not provide much of a challenge for the keen angler.

The tiger fish may not be as huge as the Nile perch, but they put up more of a fight. Nile tilapia are abundant and are fished commercially. One interesting fish in the lake is the small puffer fish, which is usually found near coral reefs, and whose presence gives rise to theories that Lake Turkana may once have been connected to the Mediterranean sea, via the Nile.

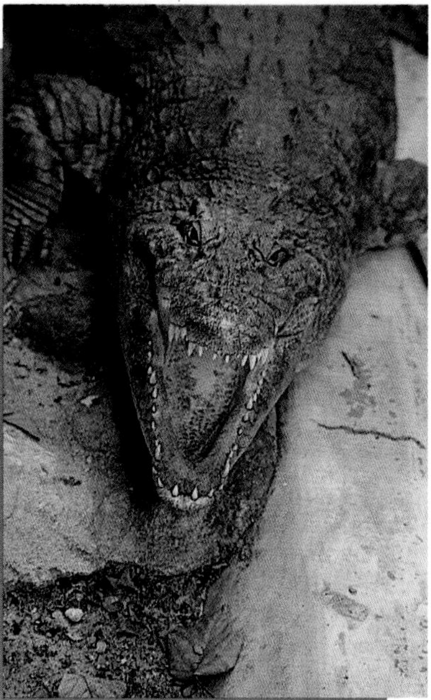

Lake Turkana has the world's largest colony of crocodiles.

When two male topi fight, they drop to their knees and clash horns.

Islands on Lake Turkana

Fifteen kilometers offshore is a small island, **Central Island**, whose 5 sq km (2 sq miles) have been turned into a national park. Sixty-five kilometers (39 miles) further north, close to the delta of the Omo River is another tiny island, **North Island**, home only to snakes.

The three little islands in the lake are the breeding grounds for the **Nile crocodile**, some of which can reach an impressive 5 m (16 ft) in length. Turkana has the world's largest remaining colony of this species – something to bear in mind if ever you feel tempted to go for a swim in the lake. The crocodiles are not reputed to attack humans, but it is not a good idea to put this theory to the test.

A few miles south of Kalokol are **Eliye Springs**, but since there is no road, and the track often goes through 12-meter (40-foot) high sand dunes, you will definitely need a 4WD to reach this tiny oasis. Once there, you will find a handful of huts and a tropical micro-climate with palm trees growing around the springs.

There is no road which circumnavigates the lake, most of which is accessible only via very rough tracks. At the southern end of the lake, the black lava of the volcanic barrier of the **Suguta Valley** separates the eastern and western shores. From Kalokol, a road heads north along the shore to the village and airstrip at **Lokitaung**, and then there is nothing more until the Ethiopian border. There is no road south of Kalokol, and on the eastern shores of the lake, there is just one short distance that is covered by road, the C77, which skirts the lake shore for a few miles near the village of **Loyangalani**.

Samburu dancers.

As it has been for centuries, the Turkana area is home to nomadic pastoralists, tribes people from the **Samburu, Turkana, Rendille, Merille, Gabbra** and **Boran** tribes. Around the village of Loyangalani are two villages hat are home to the entire community of the el-Molo tribe. They now number ess than 500 and live from fishing the ake, although, inevitably, with the introduction of new fishing techniques and the slow intrusions of the 20th century in their environment, their centuries-old lifestyle is changing. As with all ribal peoples, do exercise discretion and a certain amount of caution when trying to photograph the local Turkana people. Many dislike having their picture taken, so always ask first.

A brightly-clad Samburu child.

Western Kenya

The western part of Kenya is the most densely populated in the country and the most productive region, yet it is not on most safari itineraries. Visitors are thin on the ground which means that when you travel around the area, you will be able to experience Kenya in a more leisurely fashion. The countryside is pretty, with gently rolling hills often covered by **tea plantations**. This part of the country is densely populated and so roads are good and getting around is therefore easy.

Thunderstorm in the distance while birds gather at the waterhole.

The drive from Nairobi westwards is an interesting one, on a good road, the A104, taking you on a steep climb up to the town of **Nakuru** which is at 1,830 m (6,002 ft). Here, the landscape of intensively farmed hills seems more like misty Scotland than Africa. After the small town of **Molo**, at the picturesque **Mau summit**, the road divides. One road, the C53, heads off northwest towards, eventually, the Ugandan border, while the other road, the C23, turns to the southwest, heading towards

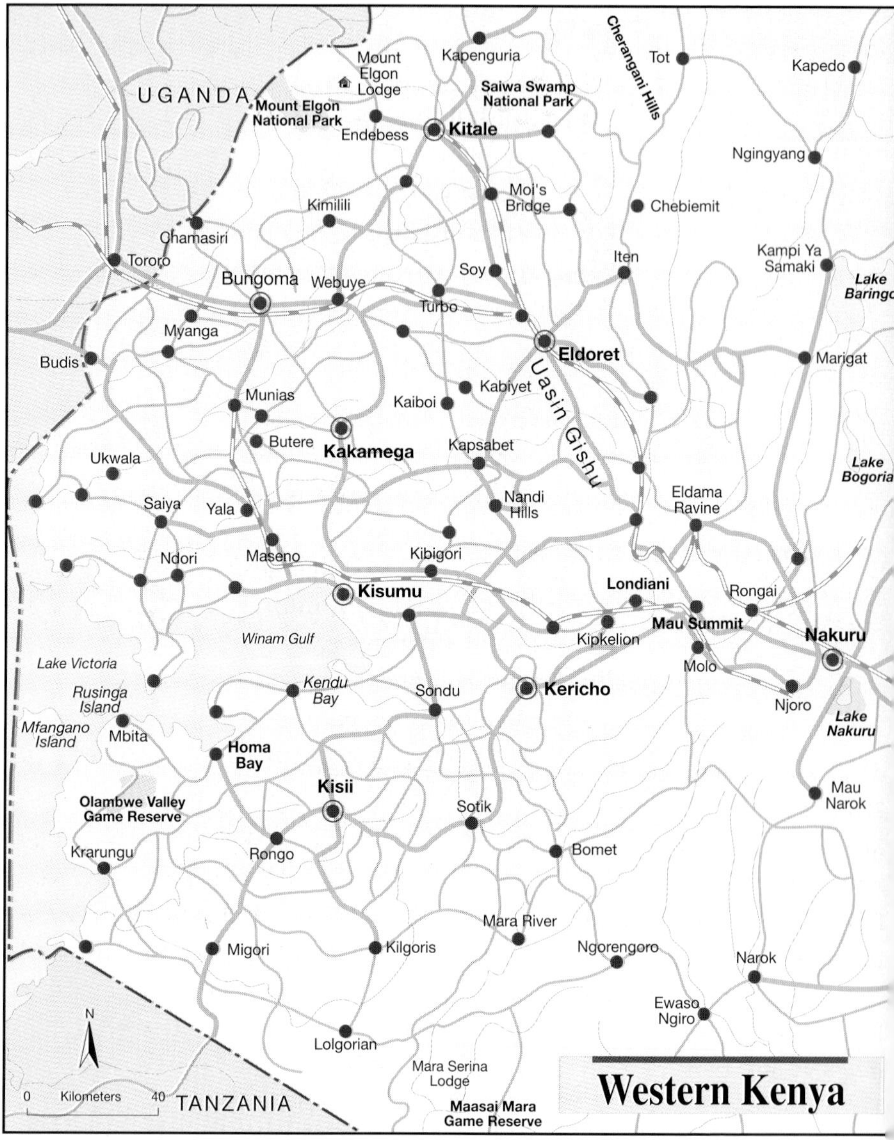

Kericho and onto Lake Victoria.

Lake Victoria

The dominating feature of the region is, of course, **Lake Victoria**, which forms the western boundary of the country Kenya's borders with **Uganda** and **Tan**-**zania** pass through the lake but trave between the three countries via the lak is no longer possible. Lake Victoria is no part of the Rift Valley lakes. It is wid and shallow being only 100 m (328 ft

Farms in Kenya's green country.

deep, with a total area covering some 70,000 sq km (27,300 sq miles) of which Kenya's share is 3,785 sq km (1,476 sq miles). It is the world's second largest freshwater lake and the third largest in the world. One rather depressing word of warning, however: **bilharzia** is prevalent in the lake, so however much you may feel like going for a swim – don't. The lake dominates the region not only geographically, but also climatically, for the moisture that is drawn out of the lake by the sun, falls as heavy, consistent rainfall on the surrounding hills, and this has led to ideal conditions for tea cultivation.

The main ethnic groups of the area are the dominant **Luo** around Lake Victoria, **Luyia** in the sugar-growing areas to the north of Kisumu and to the south-east in the Kisii hills, the **Gusii**.

The main town in the region, and in fact the third largest town in Kenya after Nairobi and Mombasa, is **Kisumu**, situated on the sloping shore of the lake. Having said that, the town has a rather sleepy air about it, partly due to the heat and humidity but also due to the fact that ever since the international ferry services on Lake Victoria stopped operating in 1977, the town lost much of its business. It is a pleasant place, nonetheless, where not too much goes on but it does boast one of the country's best museums, the **Kisumu Museum**.

Kisumu was earlier called **Port Florence**, in memory of the wife of the engineer who completed the last section

Well-developed roads are a feature of the western landscape.

Saiwa Swamp National Park

The pied kingfisher.

The hornbill.

One of Kenya's unknown treasures is the tiny, little visited Saiwa Swamp National Park which was created especially to protect one animal, the semi-aquatic **sitatunga antelope**. It is located in the Cherangani Hills, 22 km (13 miles) east of the town of Kitale at an altitude of 1,870 m (6,134 ft), close to the Koitobos River.

What is unique about this national park is that you can only visit it on foot. After being confined to jeeps and vans in all the other national parks, it is a real joy to be able to walk around Saiwa Swamp. There are well-indicated walking trails which go around the swamps and walkways right across them in some places. Even in its own protected environment, the sitatunga is elusive and the best way of seeing it is to get up early in the morning, climb into one of the observation towers and rake the swamps with your binoculars. The late afternoon is also a good time to see it. There are about 40 sitatunga living in the park. They are unusual in being able to walk about on the surface of the boggy swamps, thanks to their elongated hoofs. For a detailed description of the sitatunga, see the chapter on Wildlife.

Several other animals that are not widely seen in the rest of the country can be found here, including the Brazza monkey, with its white beard, and the nocturnal Potto. You will also be able to see the beautiful black and white colobus monkeys who live in the trees. Watch out for their flowing "cape" of white hair when they move. Leopards have been seen in the park but they are not permanent residents. Birds such as hornbills, kingfishers and turacos may be seen.

of the Lunatic Express, the Victorian feat of engineering which linked Mombasa to Lake Victoria. At four o'clock in the afternoon, on 21 December 1901, Florence Preston rather ineptly hammered home the last nail of the last rail of this momentous, epic railway.

Islands on Lake Victoria

Off shore and still within Kenya's territorial limits are two small islands, Mfangano Island and Rusinga Island. The Kenyan political hero, **Tom Mboya** was born on **Rusinga Island** in 1930, and after he was shot by police in 1969, his mausoleum was built there. Mboya was a leading politician who could well have been destined for a highly successful career. There is a display of memorabilia about him on the island. The anthropologist **Mary Leakey** discovered the skull of "Proconsul Africanus" on the island – an anthropoid ape who lived on the island three million years

The profusion of flowers is not unusual in this more cultivated part of the country.

ago. Even older fossil remains have been found on the little island, which is connected to the mainland by a causeway.

Do not be surprised to meet visitors on the island who have flown in from the Maasai Mara for the day, for the promise of a day's big game fishing lures many anglers away from the lions and the giraffes. Since most of the lodges in the Mara have their own airstrips, it is easy to arrange for the short flight to Rusinga Island. You leave Mara at dawn and have breakfast on the island.

There is excellent fishing around the island especially for **Nile perch**. Records abound for this fish, but catches of 100 lbs (45 kg) are a regular feature. Over 100 species of bird have been recorded on or around the island and you can see **fish eagles** perched on the trees, waiting for their prey. Other residents include **hippos**, **giant monitor lizards**, and the **spotted-neck otter** which is unique to Lake Victoria. Lonrho hotels have built cottages on the island for those who wish to stay over night.

Mfangano Island is far more primitive. There are some interesting prehistoric cave paintings and you can see the local fishermen bringing in shoals of "dagga", a freshwater shrimp and using a lamp to attract the fish.

South of Kisumu and west of Kisii on the lake shore is a fairly nondescript little town called **Homa Bay**. Close by is a little-known national park, the **Lambwe Valley Game Reserve**. This reserve, which receives hardly any visi-

The hippo community at their enviable pastime: bathing and sunbathing.

tors, covers 194 sq km (76 sq miles), and was created to help preserve the small herd of **Roan antelope** that lives in the region. The reserve contains rolling savannah land with some open woodlands and you will almost certainly spot the Roan antelope, **Jackson's hartebeest** and **oribi** as well as seeing extensive bird life. Beware of the **tsetse fly** which thrives there. It actually carries little risk for short stay visitors but it does mean that there are virtually no permanent inhabitants in the area.

Some 30 km (18 miles) north of Kisumu, east of the AI road heading north to Kitale, is the **Kakamega Forest Reserve**, another of western Kenya's little known gems. It is virgin tropical rainforest, almost certainly a small remnant from the West African rainforest that once spread across the width of the continent from the Congo Basin. Today, this surviving stretch of forest is home to a very large number of animals and birds – especially the latter. Many birds in Kakamega are not found anywhere else in the country. Take waterproof clothing since it rains every day there and a good pair of binoculars. Book a room in the clean and comfortable **Forest Rest House** and enjoy a day or so of absolute peace and quiet – just you and the rainforest.

Green Country

The **Western Highlands** separate

A market in rural Kenya.

Kisumu and the lake from the rest of the country and they are the agricultural heartland of Kenya. To the north, around Kitale and Eldoret lies fertile farmland, and to the south, around Kericho and Kisii are tea and coffee plantations.

The most famous product of **Kisii**, the stunningly beautiful soapstone that bears its name, is best purchased outside the area. Since there are very few visitors to this part of Kenya, the best pieces of sculpture naturally enough leave the town for the more expensive shops and galleries of Nairobi. The soapstone is actually quarried in the village of **Tabaka**, a few kilometers to the south. Kisii is the center of the **Gusii** tribe, a community with an unenviable claim to fame – that of the highest population density in the country and the highest birthrate in the world.

Tea Town

A 98-kilometer

Mount Elgon and the National Park

Sykes' monkeys.

Mount Elgon, an extinct volcano and the fourth highest mountain in Africa, straddles the international border between Kenya and Uganda, and the border runs right through the center of the crater. On the Kenyan side, is the **Mount Elgon National Park** covering an area of 108 sq km (42 sq miles). The highest peak of the mountain, the 4,321-meter (14,173-foot) high Wagagai peak is in Uganda while the highest peak in Kenya is only 11 m (36 ft) lower, the Sudek Peak at 4,310 m (14,137 ft). A favorite peak for climbers on the Kenyan side is Koitoboss at 4,231 m (13,878 ft), which offers wonderful views over the crater, **Suam Gorge**, as well as into Uganda beyond. Suam Gorge is a deep rift in the crater.

The floor of the volcanic crater is 3,500 m (11,480 ft) above sea-level where there are hot springs. Other than the beauty of the mountain and the possibilities it offers for climbing, the main attraction of this national park is the herds of elephants. Elephants are especially fond of salt which is found in abundance in the caves on the mountain side, and so they are drawn to this area. The elephants gouge the salt out of the walls of the cave, although, in a classic "chicken-and-egg" piece of logic, some people claim that its was actually the elephants that excavated the caves in the first place. Poaching, especially from the Ugandan side, has reduced the number of elephants over recent years.

Three caves are open : Kitum, where you are most likely to see the elephants eating salt, Chepnyali, and the most impressive cave of the three, Mackingeny. Kitum Cave was the inspiration for Rider Haggard's story "She."

Within the park, there is a variety of natural habitats from savannah woodland through mountain forest to alpine moorlands. The forests here are some of the most impressive in the country. As you climb up the mountain, the forest gives way to bamboo jungle and then

(59-mile) drive north along the C23 brings you to the "tea" town of **Kericho**, situated at the heart of Kenya's **tea plantations**. Kenya is the world's third largest tea producer, after India and Sri Lanka. Tea is one of Kenya's major and vital exports, and all around Kericho are hills covered with hectares of tea bushes as far as the eye can see.

Kericho is a nice little town, with a perfect climate – for tea, that is – since there is a short rain shower virtually every day. Be sure to visit the aptly named **Tea Hotel**, originally built by the Brooke Bond tea company in the early 1950s, which has an olde-worlde charm about it.

While enjoying a cup of tea on the

moorland, dotted with giant alpine flowers such as the giant lobelia and the giant groundsel. Orchids are common and although there will always be some flowers in bloom, the peak flowering season is during the months of June and July.

The lower forests on the mountainside are home to a wide range of animal and bird life including the attractive black and white colobus monkey. You may also see bushbuck, buffalo, leopard, the giant forest hog and Sykes' monkey. Black rhino have been recorded but they are rare. Other rare animals that may be seen in the higher altitude forest or on the moorland are the Golden Cat and the Black-fronted duiker.

Bird life is also rich and inside some of the caves, you will see nesting colonies of the Scarce Swift. When the alpine flowers are in bloom, sunbirds can be seen feeding from them. There are many birds of prey, the most common being the Lanner Falcon.

Mount Elgon is wet for much of the year, so you will almost certainly need a 4WD vehicle – no public transport goes into the park. Make sure you pack waterproof clothing as well as warm clothing, especially for the cold nights, and do not forget a torch for the caves. There is a lodge called the Mount Elgon Lodge but it is a little erratic, so be prepared to camp – but you will need the permission of the national park rangers to do so. It makes sense to avoid climbing during the rainy seasons which are generally the months of April and May, and August and September, and the best months to explore the mountain are from December to March.

terrace, you can ask about arranging a tour of a plantation. Kericho has a village green, a war memorial, and the ivy-clad Holy Trinity Church – all very reminiscent of a far-away English village, complete with the afternoon rain showers, and a cup of tea!

The **Cherangani Hills** are part of the Rift Valley and they head northeast from the town of **Eldoret** for some 60 km (36 miles). The hills are beautiful and are ideal for camping and hiking. Eldoret used to be called quite simply "64" since it was set up at mile post number 64 on the wagon route from **Londiani**. This area used to teem with wildlife but the white settlers soon developed the area agriculturally and wheat and maize are now grown intensively here, changing the landscape somewhat.

Further north is the small agricultural town of **Kitale** which has an interesting enough little museum, and is a transit point for people heading either for **Mount Elgon** or **Saiwa Swamp.** Beyond Kitale, the B4 road heads north and on into the dry vast deserts of Turkana.

The Defassa waterbuck.

NDIA KUU
A.W.S!!!
WEIGHT LOSS PROGRAMME
NOW IN MOMBASA!
AFRICA ACUPUNCTURE
CENTRE
BIMA TOWER 2ND FLOOR
DIGO ROAD (Near G.P.O)
TEL. 223010/316399
P. O. BOX 90582
MOMBASA

Mombasa

Hot, steamy Mombasa, with its ancient culture and its unique way of life, moves at a different rhythm to the Kenyan interior. Blessed with one of the best natural harbors along the coast of East Africa, Mombasa has been a **major port** for centuries, and today is Kenya's second largest city and the country's most important trading city.

Unlike Nairobi, which is, relatively speaking, a historical youngster, Mombasa has had a long and eventful history. Coastal trading towns were mentioned back in the 2nd century AD, and Diogenes, a Greek explorer, visited the coast around AD 111, noting the various types of merchandise at the Mombasa docks. In 1154, Mombasa is again mentioned, this time in the accounts of an Arab geographer called Al Idrisi who was at the court of Roger II of Sicily.

A typical door in the Old Town, Mombasa.

Over the centuries, Arabs came to trade along the coast and many

Fort Jesus on the waterfront.

settled down here, attracted by the wealth of the region. Increasing numbers of Africans were converted to Islam and a unique Afro-Arab culture gradually evolved along the coast known as **Swahili**.

Mombasa flourished and grew steadily wealthier through the export c slaves and ivory as did many of th other coastal city states of Zanzibar an Pemba (now both part of Tanzania) Malindi and Paté (see chapters on Th Coast and on Lamu). Mombasa was c its apogee in the 15th century when th

ast African coastal trade was flourish-
ng and dhows from Arabia, India and
ersia visited the string of ports and
oastal city states regularly.

Mombasa's destiny was to take a
ifferent direction in 1498 when the
ortuguese sailed into the harbor. They
ere highly unpopular visitors whose
esire to convert the local Muslims to

The unique Swahili culture evolved over a number of centuries.

Christianity was not appreciated and who were perceived to be trade rivals. As the richest town on the coast, Mombasa naturally interested the Portuguese but her citizens resisted leading to years of attack before finally succumbing in 1589, under the double onslaught of the Portuguese and the ravages of a tribe of cannibals called the **Zimba**.

With Portuguese cannon battering the city, this Bantu tribe arrived at Mombasa and proposed themselves as anti-Portuguese mercenaries. The pressurized people of Mombasa were left with little choice but to open the city gates to the Zimba who then set about eating as much of the available population who had not already thrown themselves into

Fort Jesus – An Eventful History

Remnants of Portuguese presence in Fort Jesus.

As you enter Fort Jesus, above the outer keep, there is an inscription in Portuguese. Its translation sets the tone for the Fort's aggressive history : "In 1635, Francisco de Seixas de Cabriera, aged 27 years, was made for four years Captain of this Fort which he had reconstructed, and to which he added this guard room. He subjected to His Majesty, the people of the coast, who under their tyrant King, had been in a state of rebellion. He made the kings of Otondo, Manda, Luziwa and Jaca tributary to His Majesty. He inflicted in person punishment on Paté and Siyu which was unexpected in India, extending to the destruction of their town walls. He punished the Musungulos and chastised Pemba, where on his own responsibility, he had the rebel governors and all leading citizens executed. He made all pay tribute to His Majesty..."

Rebellion, punishment, destruction, execution, tribute, chastisement – young Francisco was just one in a line of patriotic Portuguese bent on subjecting the local people to Lisbon's rule, extracting as much tribute as they could manage, and, of course, laying the groundwork for their hoped-for retirement full of glory and titles, which, in Francisco's case, was apparently successful. In 1593, the Portuguese built Fort Jesus as their military base in Mombasa which took them only five years to complete. It was to be the symbol both of their authority over the uncooperative coast for one hundred years as well as of their demise, for, after the long and brutal siege of the Fort, Portuguese power was effectively over.

Fort Jesus was designed by an Italian architect and engineer, Joao Batista Cairato, who was the leading architect of the Portuguese in India. Cairato designed his fort well, an impressive military stronghold with walls built of block of coral to a height of 13 m (43 ft). This height was later increased by another 3 m (10 ft), and you can see the addition as you wander around Fort Jesus today. There was a large moat on the landward side, the sea was to the other side and, with four towers from which most of the city could be covered, the fort was felt to be secure. An additional feature of the fort was the sharp angles of the walls, which meant that anyone trying to attack one wall was in direct firing range from one of the other walls.

Portuguese Tenacity

The defences of Fort Jesus were soon put to the test. In August 1631, the Arab Sultan of Mombasa, whom the Portuguese called Don Jeronimo, entered the Fort, killed the captain and gave the signal to his followers outside who proceeded to kill every single Portuguese in town. However, within six months Don Jeronimo had tired of life in Mombasa, so he captured a passing ship and sailed out of the pages of history as a pirate.

A replacement Portuguese captain promptly arrived from Zanzibar. On 13 March 1696, the Omani naval and land forces, led by the Omani Imam Seif Bin Sultan Al-Yaarubi, laid siege to the Portuguese in Fort Jesus. The original garrison

Inside Fort Jesus.

onsisted of the Portuguese captain, his soldiers nd their families and about 1,500 loyal Swahili oops. When troop reinforcements arrived from oa on Christmas Day, they unfortunately rought with them the plague which quickly ecimated the troops. By July 1697, only four ortuguese had survived along with 22 African ıen and 50 African women, but this patheti-ılly small group still managed to defeat an rab attack.

In September, the ship that had brought the einforcements from India called at Mombasa n their return trip to Goa and was wrecked pposite the Fort. The crew took over the arrison, held off an Arab attack and, luckier ıan most of their compatriots, were soon eplaced by a fresh garrison and continued their terrupted journey to Goa.

During the next year the siege continued hile plague continued to decimate the de-nders. When the final assault came on the Fort in the early hours of the morning of 13 December 1698, there were only 13 people left alive, all of whom the Arab attackers promptly killed. With a marked sense of poor timing, the relief ship from Goa arrived a few days later but seeing the Omani flag flying over the Fort, sailed on to Mozambique.

The Portuguese, however, did not give up the Fort that easily and 30 years later, on 16 March 1728, they re-took it and set about repairing it. But a year later, in April 1729, the town rose up against the Portuguese who fled to the Fort. By late November, when supplies were running low the soldiers capitulated. In a strange footnote to history, some of the Portuguese were converted to Islam and chose to stay on in Mombasa, while the rest were given two ships to take them to Mozambique.

From 1741-1837, the Mazruis, a local family, ruled over Mombasa fairly undisturbed by their Omani overlords until the early 19th century when the Sultan of Oman, Seyyid Said, began to take a keen interest in his African possessions. In 1824, the Mazrui, not relishing the thought of losing their virtual independence appealed to the captain of a passing British ship for his country's help against Muscat even though there was a political alliance between Britain and Oman at the time. Nevertheless, Captain Owen decided to make Mombasa a British Protectorate. When London heard the news, they repudiated his treaty and on 25 July 1826, the British representative was withdrawn from Fort Jesus (see History chapter). On 7 January 1828 Seyyid Said consolidated his powers at Mombasa when he regained full control of Fort Jesus.

Thereafter, the history of the Fort quietened down somewhat. True, there were skirmishes in January 1875, when the Sultan's troops briefly revolted and two British war ships bombarded the Fort. Over the years, however, there was no new construction and few repairs were undertaken. When Mombasa was declared a British Protectorate, once again, on 1 July 1895, Fort Jesus became a government prison which was to remain until 1958. In 1960, the museum was built and the Fort opened to the public as a historical monument.

The Old Town in Mombasa.

the sea or been shot at by the Portuguese. Not surprisingly, little of pre-Portuguese Mombasa architecture survives today.

The most visible sign of the Portuguese domination, the imposing **Fort Jesus**, was built between 1593 and 1596 and it was to be the stronghold of the Europeans for a century. In 1696, the Sultan of Oman laid siege to the Fort starving the inhabitants into submission some 33 months later and the Omanis replaced the hated Portuguese as rulers of the coast.

20th-century Mombasa

Today, the island of Mombasa is small and crowded and its narrow streets, line with coral-rock houses, are always bus and noisy. The city has long since ou grown the 14 sq km (5 sq miles) of th island and is now linked to the mair land by **Makupa causeway** to the wes which follows the earlier railway lin and by **New Nyali Bridge** to the nort There is still only a **ferry** to the south.

The Old Town is still dominated b the imposing 16th-century Fort Jesu but today the crowds of Europeans to b seen are welcomed with open arm holiday-makers from the north an south beaches taking a day off fro sunbathing. Mombasa has found i niche in current Kenyan tourism: th island may not have wild animals an tented camps but it is surrounded b

Serene Beach Hotel.

excellent beaches and good coral reefs. Now many safaris end with a couple of relaxing days in Mombasa in one of the many luxury hotels which have sprung up along the beaches north and south of the city.

Mombasa island has shops and banks and travel agencies and all the paraphernalia of a busy town, and it is an efficient place where you can transact all necessary business effectively. One of the island's main thoroughfares, **Moi Avenue**, is dominated by two huge pairs of elephant "tusks", actually made of aluminium, which were erected in honor of the coronation of Queen Elizabeth II and which have remained for the last 40 years becoming the unofficial symbol of Mombasa.

The **Old Town** is the most interesting part of Mombasa to visit, and the natural place to begin exploration is **Fort Jesus** which has had an action packed history. (See box story p.276.) Nowadays, it is a pleasant place to wander around with pretty views particularly on the seaward side.

The Fort also has an excellent little **museum**, a delightful juice counter tucked away on the ramparts and a good book shop with many local history books on sale that you will probably not come across again during your travels. The museum has a good ceramics collection and an especially interesting set of exhibits raised from the wreck of a 17th-century Portuguese frigate, the "San Antonio de Tanna", which sank in

The luxurious Castle Hotel in Mombasa.

front of the fort in 1697.

Among the exhibits is a model of a Mtepe, a handsewn craft built mainly at Lamu; the accompanying information panel tells a delightful tale. No nails were used in the construction of these ships, the timbers being pegged and sewn together with a kind of coir rope. It was believed that there was a "magnetic mountain" at the floor of the Indian Ocean, so any ships which relied on nails for their construction would founder as they passed over this mountain because their nails would be drawn out like teeth and the timbers would fall apart.

As you explore the fort, look out for the cannons around the ramparts called "carronads" after the Carron works in Scotland where they were cast. In one corner of the fort there is a green goods trolley. These were used in Mombasa at the turn of the century as the local means of transport. **Government House**, which was built in 1898, was also connected to the local transport system for the trolley line swept around the front of the building rather like a carriage drive. There are some nice old photographs on display showing liveried trolley men posing by the Governor's private trolleys.

Near the **Omani House**, there is a skeleton which was found in January 1990. The skeleton was buried in a grave in what would appear to be a formal Christian burial, the body facing west, the hands folded together over the stom-

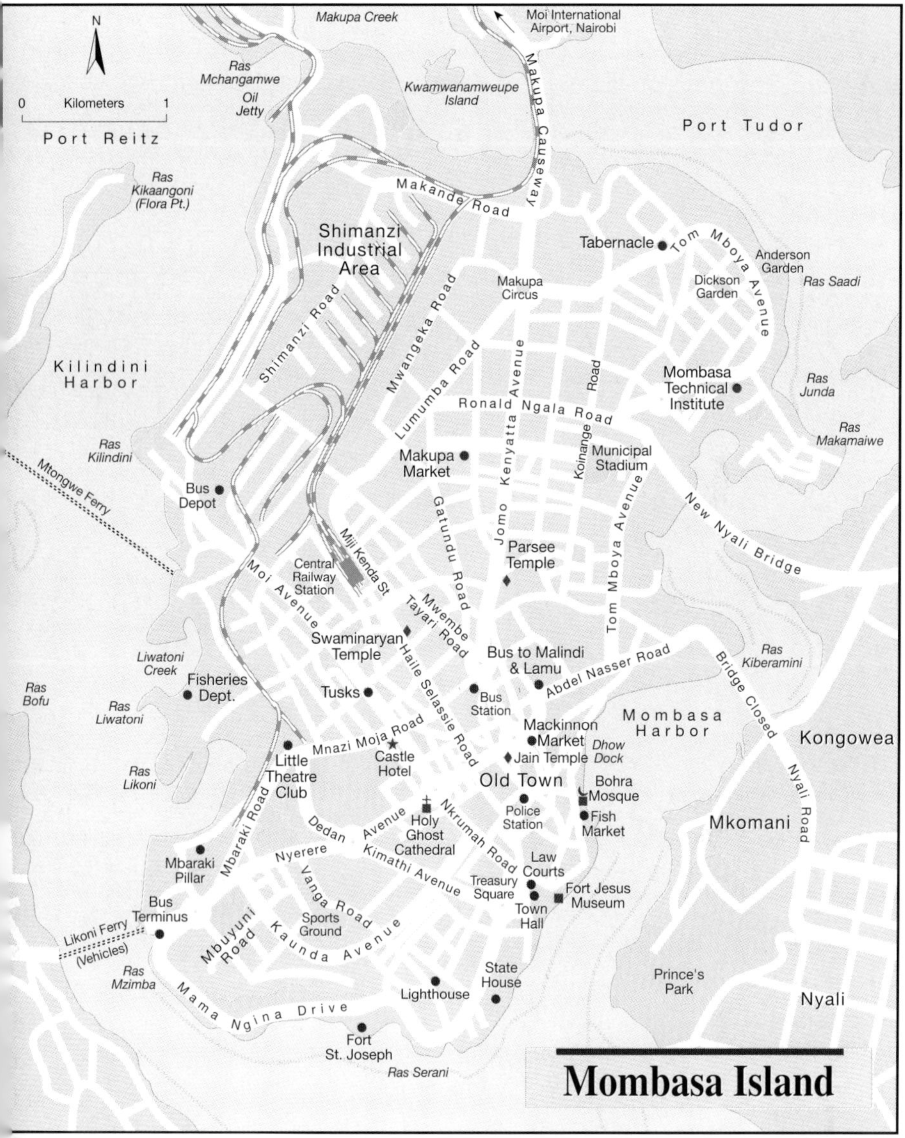

Mombasa Island

ch area and the feet joined together. lthough it is still not possible to give an xact date for the burial, it has been entatively dated as between the late 6th to early 17th century. Outside the **rab House**, which was built in 1800, here is a solid raised gun platform dated 648. It was on this platform that the Portuguese made their last stand against the Arab attackers in the early morning of 13 December 1698.

As you leave the Fort to visit the surrounding maze of old streets, do remember that this is still a conservative Muslim neighborhood. No one objects to your taking pictures of streets and

The aluminium elephant tusks on Moi Avenue.

To Nairobi by Train

You have finished sunning yourself on the beach and are ready to head back to Nairobi, so you go to the airport to take a flight. Well, that is one way of doing the trip but a much more interesting way is to take the overnight train. It takes longer but is much more fun and allows you to see something of the land across which the early 20th-century British built their "Lunatic Express" that has almost become a legend.

There is one train a day for Nairobi which leaves Mombasa Station at five o'clock and you arrive in Nairobi at 8.30 the next morning. When you arrive at Mombasa station, first of all you check your compartment and carriage number on the lists that are pinned up, and then the steward will ask whether you want the first sitting or second sitting for dinner and he gives you a coupon accordingly.

The train is very comfortable with well-equipped sleeping compartments, and as the train pulls slowly out of Mombasa station, the railway staff will begin to make up your bed for you. Night falls quickly but until it is dark, the view is fascinating, and from first light the next morning, you can enjoy the African panorama from your compartment. You pass through many villages where children pour out of their homes to wave enthusiastically at the train, despite the fact that they must see it every morning. You can spot game as well in its natural setting and appreciate the vast emptiness of the Kenyan landscape.

The food on the train is, well, hearty. Hearty, and verging on the British, but all that seems right, somehow, as you thunder through the African evening, your dinner coupon calmly informing you that this is the Mombasa-Kampala train, which, sadly, it is not. For all too soon, after an equally hearty English breakfast, you are steaming into Nairobi station. Perhaps building a railway across the country was not such a lunatic idea after all.

buildings but if you wish to photograph people, especially women, always ask first. Do not walk around in beach attire and if you enter a mosque, remember to remove your shoes.

As you continue to explore the little white-washed streets of the Old Town, look out for **carved wooden doors**, many of them festooned with enormous locks, and keep looking upwards for little balconies often with **carved brackets**.

Beaches

To the north and the south of Mombasa are miles of **beaches**, fringed with palm trees on one side and coral reefs out to sea. The beaches stretch south half way to the Tanzanian border and north almost three-quarters of the way to Kilfi. These are the beaches sun-starved northern Europeans dream of, with endless white sand and nothing more tiring to do than decide whether to swim, to snorkel or to keep dozing in the sun.

The ancient baobab tree has been protected by decree.

Many of the beaches are attached to the big hotels which are usually of a high standard and effortlessly geared to the tourist industry. One of the most prestigious of the southern beaches is **Diani** which has an off-shore coral reef which is excellent for diving and snorkeling. As you drive down the road to the southern beaches close to the Trade Winds Hotel, a road turns off away from the beach. Follow the road, keep asking directions and after a few minutes you will drive into a tiny village which has an enormous **baobab tree**, 22 m (72 ft) wide, and so old that it is protected by decree. You will have to keep asking for the "big" baobab tree otherwise you will be directed to others, not so large nor so famous.

The Portuguese built Fort Jesus as their military base.

The Coast

The 480-kilometer (288-mile) strip of coastline that runs from Somalia in the north down to Tanzania is one of Kenya's most popular areas, and many safaris end with a few welcome and relaxing days on the beach where you can forget about dawn game drives and dusty tracks and do nothing more stressful than go for a swim in the Indian Ocean. The coastal climate is hot and sultry, the vegetation is lush and tropical, and everything is a far cry from the vast, rolling plains of the Kenyan interior. There are extensive plantations of cash crops, the architecture is Islamic and the people are ethnically different, all of which adds up to an interesting contrast with the Kenya of the safari.

The ruins at Jumba La Mtwana were a complex comprising mosques and several houses.

Although **Mombasa** dominates the coast, economically and socially, there is much to see beyond the beach and the luxurious hotels, especially for the history buff for this coastal region has a

Malindi Airport. Travel is greatly facilitated by domestic flights.

long and fascinating history and a culture that is markedly different from the rest of the country. The East African coast has been in direct contact with other continents from at least the beginning of the 1st century AD, welcoming Greeks, Romans, Arabs, Persians, Indians, Malays and Chinese. Arab and Persian merchants began to settle permanently on the African coast from the 9th century onwards bringing with them a new religion, Islam. The Arabs, Persians, and Indians all influenced the coastal culture and the language which came to be known as **Swahili**, after the Arab word *sahil* for coast.

A general definition of the Swahili people is that they are Muslim Africans who are basically, but not always, town dwellers. They speak Swahili as their first language and inhabit the east coast of Africa, from the Somali border to northern Mozambique as well as the islands in the Lamu archipelago, Pemba, Zanzibar, Comores and Madagascar.

Trade was voluminous and often sophisticated, with a marked preference for luxury goods. Imported trade items to the coast included ceramics, jewelry, glass and beads from the Far East, India and the Arabian peninsula. In return, the Swahili settlements offered such items as beads, cowrie and other shells, rhinoceros horn, tortoiseshell, skins, ambergris and ivory among others.

The history of the coast is dominated by trade and it was successive generations of traders who shaped the

Islamic architecture marks the coastal culture.

destiny of the coast. The early Arab traders began to put down some roots along the coast, marrying local women, and by the 12th century a string of settlements had grown up. The first settlements were on islands which were easier to defend such as Lamu, Pemba and Zanzibar, and these were followed over the following centuries by a string of settlements on the mainland. Kilwa to the south and now in Tanzania, Mombasa and Malindi grew up as did the settlement on Paté Island.

City States

The settlement pattern of these city states was relatively uniform. There was a

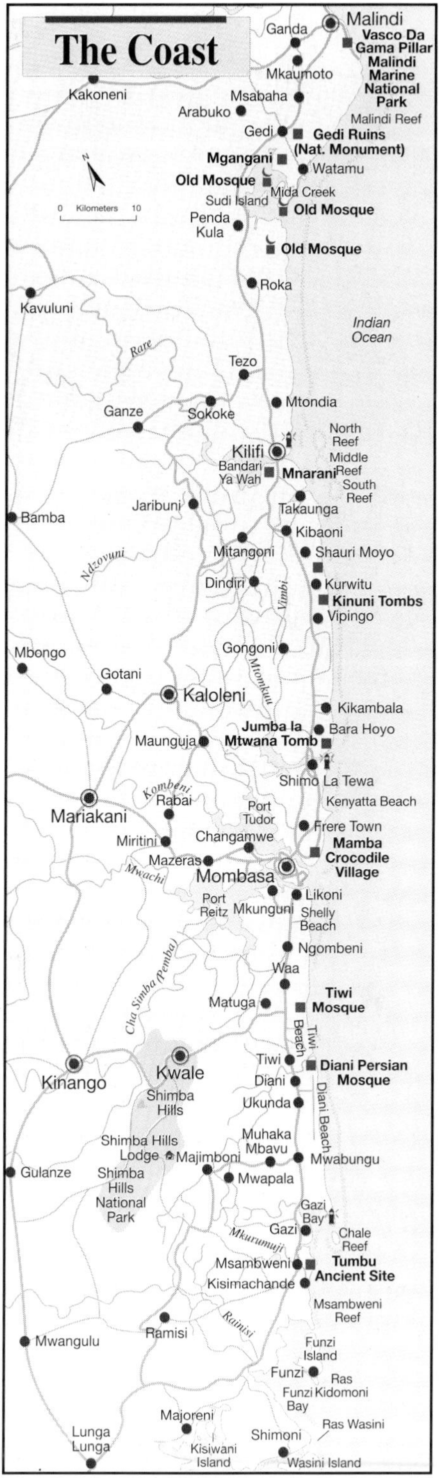

In the Old Town, from colonial days gone by.

cluster of single-storey houses, usually made out of coral, surrounding a mosque. Socially, the hierarchy consisted of the ruling classes, who were Muslims of mixed Arab and African descent, and who were generally traders. The laborers were usually Africans, often slaves. The driving force of the communities was Islam and there w virtually no African impetus as suc These coastal settlements looked res lutely outwards and overseas and th had no influence whatsoever on t East African interior. It was as thou

ıe two worlds were unrelated.

These small, independent city states, .espite their wealth and learning, had ·ne inherent weakness: they were al-ʼays waging war on each other, in enerations long power struggle. Thus, ʼhen the Portuguese arrived in 1498, ıe Swahili city states found themselves ɔtally unprepared, and within just a few years, the Europeans had gained control over the coast. Portuguese rule was always tenuous and extremely unpopular for they sacked the coast and forced people to convert to Christianity, but otherwise showed little interest in their local subjects, who, not surprisingly, began to rebel. With help from the Omanis, the Portuguese were finally driven from the coast in 1898, and their place was speedily taken by the Omanis, whose headquarters was the island of Zanzibar.

The Omanis had their own internal squabbles, into which the British tried to resist being drawn, but since the entire economy of Zanzibar was underpinned by the slave trade abhorred by 19th-century Britain, the British found themselves drawn gradually but relentlessly into the affairs of the Swahili coast. In 1888 the British East Africa company took over the administration of the interior of East Africa but a 16-kilometer (10-mile) wide strip along the coast was recognized as belonging to the Sultan of Zanzibar, in whose possession it remained until independence.

The Beaches and Water Sports

South of Mombasa and stretching to the Tanzanian border are kilometers, of wide, sandy beaches, protected from dangerous currents and sharks by a coral reef. Most of the **southern stretch of coast** is lined with top-class hotels

The Chronicles of the City States

Early records refer to the East African coast as *Zinj*, a Persian word meaning land of the black people, and for centuries this fertile, prosperous area was visited by Arab traders some of whom sailed away on the monsoon winds and some of whom decided to stay on. A dozen or so tiny city states grew up along this coast, owing allegiance to no single ruler and frequently at loggerheads with each other. Much of our knowledge of this area derives from the records kept by these city states, called Chronicles. These are a curious mixture of long catalogues of battles, births and deaths and pure fabrication. Flights of total and utter fancy have to be carefully sifted from the real events.

One of the most detailed of these chronicle is the Paté Chronicle, which records the histor of Paté and the neighboring islands from 120 to the late 19th century. Internecine quarrel were rife and Lamu, Shela, Paté, Manda an Faza appear to have spent most of their tim quarreling and fighting with each other, ofte for the flimsiest of reasons. When a Manda ma was not invited to a council meeting, he wen and betrayed his island to Paté. When the nois from Paté shipwrights disturbed a Manda prince fighting again broke out. Attacks were rarely surprise and long-winded declarations of wa were commonplace, allowing both sides th time to prepare for battle.

and it is a place dedicated to relaxation and unwinding. The best of the southern beaches are found along the 21-kilometer (13-mile) stretch between **Tiwi** and **Diani** and if any one beach had to be singled out as Kenya's "best", it would almost certainly be Diani. The sand here is white and fine, the beaches are shaded by palm trees, and the coral reef a kilometer offshore ensures calm, clear waters, free from major irritants like sharks and minor irritants like seaweed.

There are vestiges of the region's past, hidden among the palm trees and the luxury hotels. At **Kongo** there is a well-preserved 15th-century **Mwana Mosque** while further south at **Msambweni** is a 17th-century slave pen, a sad reminder of one of the area's former sources of wealth.

The tiny **Funzi Island** is only separated from the coast by a narrow channel which you can walk across at low tide. You can dive off the coral reef around the island.

Close to the border is a little villag called **Shimoni**, formerly the headqua ters of the Imperial British East Afric Company and now the jumping off poin for a trip to the interesting little island o **Wasini**. The lack of cars guarante peace and quiet and it is an ideal plac to do some diving and snorkeling fo there are coral reefs and the nearb **Kisiti/Mpungutu Marine Nationa Park**. Day trips to Wasini can easily b arranged in a dhow from Shimoni. In land from Mombasa is the **Shimba Hil National Reserve** (see box story p.296

North of Mombasa are yet mor excellent beaches and the coast ha been developed almost three-quarte of the way to Kilfi. As you drive nort much of the road is bordered with sis plantations. Sixteen kilometers (1 miles) north of Mombasa are the rui

Hotels pepper the beaches along Kenya's coast.

f **Jumba La Mtwana**, one of a string of mall Swahili city states along the coast, hat dates from the mid-14th century. he name means "the large house of the ave" but in the absence of historical ecords, there is no way of knowing hether or not that was the settlement's riginal name. The ruins at Jumba in- ude three mosques, a tomb with an rabic inscription and at least eight ouses, and they are on the seashore. In ommon with some of the other earlier ettlements along the coast, the site had o harbor, so small boats would have een beached while larger vessels would ther have anchored offshore or in twapa Creek. Archeologists estimate at Jumba was abandoned about the iddle of the 15th century.

Kilfi is a pretty little town, built on both banks of the Kilfi Creek. For years, the only means of crossing the creek was by ferry, but a bridge has recently been built which is far less aesthetic but more practical. Kilfi proper is on the northern bank while the small village of **Mnarani** is on the southern bank, with its ruins of the former 14th-century city state. Mnarani was occupied from the late 14th century to the early 17th century when the Galla tribespeople destroyed it. It is a fairly steep climb up to the ruins, but the effort is worthwhile for there are some interesting vestiges including the ruined Great Mosque and a pillar tomb.

After Kilfi, the coast continues in a long straight line until the **Watamu**

Gedi was a larger, more affluent city state.

Marine National Reserve which comprises the inshore lake formed by the Mida Creek and the adjoining coastline, where the coral reefs are spectacular. There are caves at the entrance to the creek where you can dive down and see giant rock cod.

The ruins of **Gedi**, just north of Watamu, are one of the more extensive of the Swahili city states. Gedi, founded in the late 13th or early 14th century, was at the height of its prestige in the middle of the 15th century and was abandoned in the early 17th century. As with many other city states, written historical records are scarce, but historians think that Gedi must have been a large and affluent place whose desertion was probably due to the arrival of the nomadic Galla tribe from Somalia. What remains a mystery is the precise role of Gedi for none of the Portuguese, Arab or Swahili records that exist mention the place, yet it was a large city with a double outer wall, a palace and private houses of some luxury.

Amongst the most impressive ruins are the Great Mosque, the palace, a tomb with the date AD 1399 and a Fluted Pillar Tomb. During excavations, early 16th-century Ming porcelain was found in one of the houses which the archeologists named the House of the Porcelain Bowl. In some of the houses you can see evidence of quite sophisticated bathroom facilities including double "sinks" and a bidet.

In the 14th century, **Malindi** was a major Swahili settlement but its recorded history goes back at least two centuries earlier. The fleet of Chinese junks commanded by Cheng Ho visited Malindi between 1417 and 1419, and it was one of the rare places along the East African coast to offer a welcome to the Portuguese. Out on a small rocky promontory jutting out into the sea, there is a small stone cross bearing the arms of Portugal which was erected by Vasco da Gama in January 1499. Another Portuguese vestige is a little church, which incorporates a 16th-century chapel which was visited by St. Francis Xavier in 154[illegible] when he buried two of his soldiers during his trip to Goa in India.

Today Malindi is home to holidaymakers and sports enthusiasts from all over the world, who come for the good

Vasco Da Gama's cross marks the explorer's visit to the region in the 15th century.

eaweed-free beaches and the surfing. Although surfing is possible all year ound, the best months are between late une and early September. Ernest Hemingway came to Malindi to fish in he 1930s, setting a trend in big game ishing. The coral reefs offshore have been named the **Malindi Marine National Park**, and you can see the reefs from a glass-bottomed boat or go snorkeling or diving. Malindi is well served with hotels, restaurants and cafés and local flights to Mombasa and Lamu.

North of Malindi, the coastline con-

Shimba Hills National Reserve

A pride of lions.

The Shimba Hills Reserve is a few kilometers inland from the coast, its hills running almost parallel with the Tiwi-Diani beaches, and as it is only 56 km (37 miles) south of Mombasa, it is therefore ideal for holiday makers who want to visit a reserve as an alternative to another day on the beach. It covers about 310 sq km (121 sq miles), and is the only reserve in the country where the rare **Sable Antelope** may be seen. They have become relatively tame, making them a joy for photographers.

The reserve has a combination of rolling, park-like country and coastal rainforest, with a pleasanter, cooler climate than the coast. The reserve is very rich botanically, with some beautiful species of orchids flowering in April, July and August.

At the Shimba Hills Lodge, there is a baited water hole, so sightings of animals is more or less assured. As well as elephant, leopard and lion, you may also see Roan Antelope which have been re-introduced though the experiment has not been as successful as was hoped. Duiker, bush buck, Colobus monkeys and Sykes' monkey are also to be seen, as well as a wide range of birds.

tinues for 222 km (133 miles) to the Somalian border, but nowadays, very few travelers visit this part of Kenya. Traveling in this part of the country has always been unpredictable for two main reasons, the state of the roads and whether or not the Tana River is flooded. But now there is a much more disturbing element than floods delaying your ferry crossing, there has been an in

The baobab tree in Gedi, in this history-saturated coast.

crease in banditry on these roads. Nevertheless, for the truly intrepid visitor, this stretch of little visited coastline has its own charms.

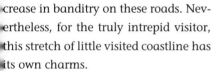

Two kilometers west of the village of **Mambrui** is a gorge called **Marafa**, or "**Hell's Kitchen**", with its dramatically eroded rock pinnacles and colored sandstone cliffs, some of them 30 m (98 ft) high. In Mambrui village, you can see an old pillar tomb in the cemetery. Out at sea, off the village of **Ngomeni**, is a **satellite launching pad** built by the Italians in the 1960s.

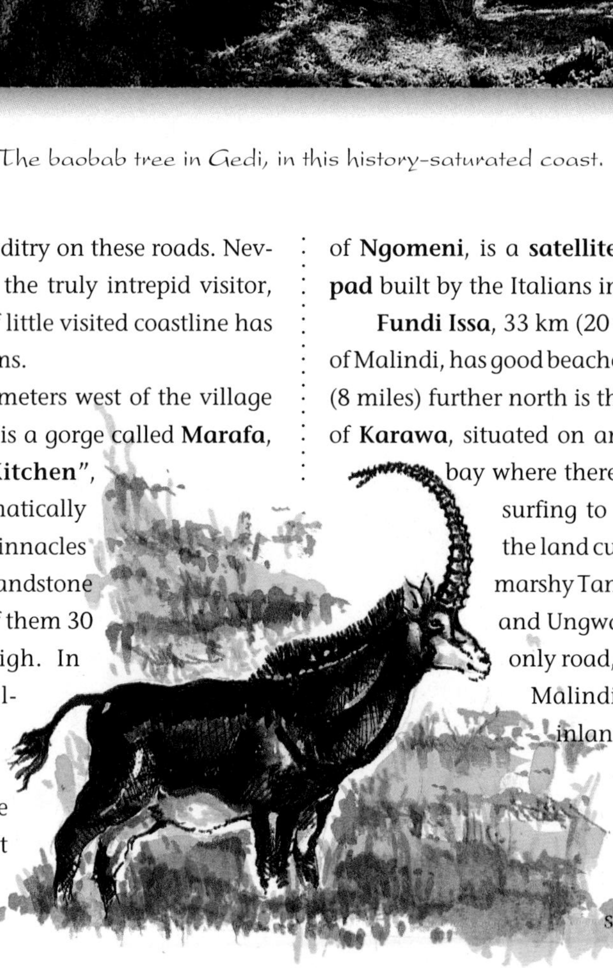

Fundi Issa, 33 km (20 miles) north of Malindi, has good beaches and 13 km (8 miles) further north is the little town of **Karawa**, situated on an impressive bay where there is excellent surfing to be done. As the land curves into the marshy Tana River delta and Ungwana Bay, the only road, the B8 from Malindi, continues inland to the little sleepy town of **Garsen** which has just a few shops and all

A mangrove swamp along the coast.

the time in the world to spare. There is no road across the marshy delta so unless you are continuing inland to the **Tana River Primate Nature Reserve**, at Garsen you head back through the delta towards the coast on the **Witu** road. When the Sultan of Paté quarrelled with the Sultan of Zanzibar in 1862, he fled to Witu, which he grandly designated the State of Swahililand, duly issuing his own currency and his own postage stamps. In 1888, the Sultan signed an alliance with a group of Germans. His son subsequently had a disa

greement with them and it all ended rather messily with a huge British force arriving and all but destroying the town and the surrounding plantations. Today, Witu is a somnolent little place, giving no hint of its former, short-lived statehood.

The road continues for 32 km (19 miles) to **Mkunumbi** and another 25 km (15 miles) to **Hindi**, before apparently running out of steam in the village of **Mokowe**, which is directly opposite **Lamu Island**. Ferries make the short crossing to the island, but today hardly any travelers go to Lamu via Mokowe: everyone flies from Malindi instead.

The bay in which Lamu and the other islands are scattered is deeply indented and poorly served with roads. The only way to cross the creeks is to stay on the road, heading inland to **Bodhei**, and then follow the road back as it skirts the **Dodori National Reserve**. The road rejoins the coast at the tiny village of **Kiunga**, makes one more stop at the border village of **Dar es Salaam** (not to be confused with its more famous namesake in Tanzania) and you have arrived at the **Somalian border**.

Now, the sad fact about all this area north of Malindi, including the various reserves, is that this whole part of the country today is unsafe. Do not travel there unless you absolutely have to, and even so, always take the advice of the local people before trying to travel around the region.

There are bandits and poachers, many of whom have been displaced because of the war in Somalia and who are turning their eyes south to the relative calm and prosperity of Kenya. This is an unfortunate state of affairs, especially for the local inhabitants and also for the visitor who will almost certainly not get to see the various national reserves nor the lush countryside north of Malindi.

Lamu Archipelago

The Kenyan coast is totally different from the interior. It is hot and humid and the people are ethnically different. It is home to sun-worshippers rather than naturalists. There are luxuriant plantations rather than the arid-looking, leafless acacia trees of the inland plains, there are mosques and ruined fortresses rather than tented camps and water holes.

Nowhere is this difference more highlighted than in the remote **Lamu archipelago**, a cluster of islands whose way of life has remained largely unaffected by the mainland and which even today, when travel seems to be getting easier and less mysterious, move at a completely different rhythm from the mainland. On Lamu island, the way to get about is on foot, by dhow along the coastline, or on a donkey – a far cry from the efficient Landrovers of the game parks.

Kijani House Hotel in Shela Village, Lamu.

The archipelago consists of a number of islands and

Lamu waterfront. The sea plays a crucial role in the life of the people.

a host of reefs and rocks. **Lamu** is the largest of the islands, and the center for virtually all of the archipelago's activities. Close by is **Manda**, home only to a small, rotating number of families who look after the impressive ruins of **Takwa.** (See box story p.308.) Off the northern tip of Manda is the even smaller **Mand[a] Toto** island. Further afield are the islands of **Paté**, **Siyu** and **Kiwayu**.

Much of the history of this region has been decided by the sea and the wind, for the early traders arrived with the monsoon winds bringing with them

The port in Lamu has given a distinct color to the coast's history.

exotic goods, news from outside, and, of lasting significance to the region, the Islamic faith. The islands developed at a different rhythm and a different pace from the rest of the country. Each year, the Kaskazi northeast winds, which blow from November to March, would bring to the islands ships from India and Arabia filled with Indian furniture, Chinese porcelain, pottery and cloth, dates, carpets and chests. After stopping at several ports along the way, the voyage would end in Zanzibar. There is a complete reversal of the wind pattern with

Market scene in Lamu.

the Kusi southwest winds which prevail from May to September permitting the ships to East Africa to return home.

Lamu Island

Today, visitors arrive in Lamu rather more prosaically, mainly by air, on one of the little planes that hurtle down towards a grass landing-strip on Manda island. After running the gauntlet of the highly vocal and insistent hotel touts (they cheerfully ignore you if you already have a hotel reservation) you and your luggage are loaded onto a launch and you sail across the channel to Lamu island. This is the beginning of what will be very much a sea-oriented trip. You

will, for example, find yourself hailing a passing dhow when you want to go to the village of Shela. Why walk, when you can sail with a garrulous, friendly and knowledgeable dhow captain?

Lamu is the oldest living town in East Africa and the only Swahili settle-

Lamu Muslims having a tête-à-tête outside the mosque.

nent which retains its original charac-
:er. The town already existed in the 14th
:entury as an independent city state,
:xporting timber, ivory, amber, spices
ind slaves. Manufactured luxury goods
rom across the Indian Ocean, such as
:arpets and porcelain, were imported.

The Portuguese period (1497-1698) had little direct impact on Swahili culture but it did change the pattern of the Indian Ocean trade. The once prosperous Swahili city states lost their middleman positions and gradually declined. In the 18th and 19th centuries, the Sul-

Fishing traps off Lamu.

Manda Island

Takwa was a viable town from the 15th to the 17th century.

Across the channel from Lamu town, and up a narrow mangrove creek on the island of Manda, is the ruined Swahili town of **Takwa** whose ruins are preserved as a national monument. You can hire a dhow to sail across from either Shela or Lamu town, and if the tide is low, as you approach the creek, you have to get out of the boat and walk the last few meters.

Excavations and mapping of the site which flourished between the 15th and 17th century, have revealed 150 buildings including a fine Friday mosque, a pillar tomb with the date 1683, the town walls, the town hall, and numerous limestone and coral houses, all with their doors facing north to Mecca.

Archeologists estimate that approximately 2,500 people lived at Takwa, earning their living from farming, fishing and trading. The crops cultivated included sorghum, cassava, pumpkins, yams and water melons. Takwa was abandoned for two main reasons : the freshwater supply became salt water, and there was endless fighting with the people of Paté. So, in the late 17th century, the townspeople of Takwa relocated to Shela, a village across the creek on Lamu island.

tan of Oman became very powerful, and during this period of commercial revival Lamu's inhabitants built and rebuilt most of the traditional stone houses and mosques.

With the abolition of slavery at the end of the 19th century, Lamu's source of cheap labor disappeared. Trade and

An Afro-European signboard at the hairdresser's.

transport shifted to Mombasa when the railway was built and Lamu fell into oblivion. The small remote island town was sustained only by traditional maritime activities, and, paradoxically, it was this very remoteness that saved Lamu from the process of modernization that has destroyed so many towns around the world.

As the late 20th-century visitor explores the narrow, white-washed streets of Lamu, squeezing himself against the wall to let a line of solidly plodding donkeys pass or suddenly stumbles upon a tiny, brightly painted mosque, he could be forgiven for thinking he was in a time warp. Prayers are called from the many tiny mosques. Women are covered from head to toe in a voluminous black robe called a *bui-bui*.

Elegant dhows line up along the waterfront, many with eyes painted on them as protective charms which help the dhow "see" the dangerous rocks. These dhows are the only means of travel inter-island. There is one token nod to modernity, however, for the island is the proud pos-

Typical architecture in Lamu with a whiff of Arab influence.

sessor of one car which belongs to the District Commissioner, and which can be driven for exactly 2 km ($1^1/_2$ miles) before the track peters out into sand dunes.

Lamu is a strictly **Islamic town**, and as such, it expects certain behavior from its visitors. Foreign women shoul dress modestly which means not wear ing skimpy beach clothes in town, alco hol should not be consumed in publi (though it is available in the hotels and taking pictures of Lamu women i not allowed.

A traditionally carved door in Lamu.

Lamu Architecture

Architecturally, the **old stone town** is almost unchanged since the 18th century and it has a unique and unequalled combination of intimacy and privacy, so much a feature of Islamic culture. The town plan is very well adapted to the tropical climate for the narrow streets offer shade and also produce a slight wind-tunnel effect. The thick walls of the houses give extra coolness and neutralize the disadvantage of narrow streets by acting as sound insulators. The exterior of the traditional stone house is massive and bleak with the thick coral stone walls and small windows giving maximum privacy while keeping the house cool. The interior courtyard, the *kiwanda*, is the focus of all daytime activities and gives daylight and good ventilation to the house.

The entrance porch, or *daka*, is both part of the street and part of the house at the same time. The *wikio* is a part of the house bridging the street to connect two buildings. Lamu houses have very elabo-

Lamu from the Swahili House Museum.

rate carved doors and the limited span of the original structural timber led to the division of the house into a series of long, narrow galleries or *misana*, with beautiful carved decorations in the form of friezes and niches. One feature of stone houses is the contrast between the plain external walls and the elaborate ornamentation and subtle spaces of its interior, but, sadly, for most visitors, the interiors remain politely off-limits.

The shop buildings were built by the Indian merchants, mainly from Gujerat, who settled in Lamu in the 19th

century. The shop is at street level and often has a *baraza* or stone bench outside, while the living quarters are upstairs. Some of the buildings have a balcony.

Verandah houses are found along the sea front and were built by wealthy merchants at the turn of the century, and a particularly beautiful example is

The Swahili House Museum offers a view of the interior of a Swahili house.

the excellent little **Lamu Museum** which is well worth a visit. The museum used to be the home of the British District Commissioner. Interestingly, the first of Britain's consuls to the town was Captain Jack Haggard, whose brother, the writer Rider Haggard, wrote ***Allan Quatermain*** while visiting his brother in Lamu.

Many of the 26 mosques in Lamu were built or rebuilt during the 18th and 19th centuries. A traditional Swahili house has been refurbished and has opened as the **Swahili House Museum** offering an insight into traditional Swahili decor. You can explore the interior of the house and then climb onto the roof for a good view over the little streets of Lamu.

The donkey sanctuary tends to the island's population of helpful animals.

INTERNATIONAL DONKEY PROTECTION TRUST
REG. CHARITY NO 271410 SIDMOUTH, DEVON, ENGLAND
LAMU DONKEY SANCTUARY P.O. BOX 264
FEEDING, WATERING CENTRE SICK DONKEYS TREATED
ADMINISTRATOR
ENQUIRIES MANAGER ABDALLA HADI RIFAI MRS. E.D SVENDSEN MBE

Enjoying Shela Village waterfront.

The construction of **Lamu fort** was started in 1810 by the Sultan of Paté. In 1821 it was finished and occupied by the Omanis and from 1910 to 1984 the building was used as a prison. In 1985 restoration work started on the fort which will eventually be converted into a social and cultural center. The central courtyard will be used for social gatherings and special events like traditional weddings, festivals, films and meetings.

On the waterfront is a **donkey sanctuary**, run by a British charity, which cares for sick and injured animals. The

Dhows

The dhow is an essential means of transport.

Most visitors will take a trip on a dhow, typically a *mashua*, either as a sort of water taxi between Shela and Lamu, or as a half-day trip across to visit the Takwa ruins on Manda Island. Longer trips further afield to the other islands in the archipelago require a fair amount of planning and most importantly, time. The tides cannot be controlled, the dhow can run aground on a sand bank, so you must always factor in extra days if you are setting off on a long dhow trip.

One of the most characteristic and romantic sights in Lamu is that of a fleet of wooden dhows sailing along the shore with their slanting, triangular sails, known technically as a *lateen*, and often with a protective eye painted on the brightly painted hulls. Although the number of dhows has declined over the years in the face of competition from more efficient means of transport, there are still many tied up along the Lamu waterfront for they remain very much the local means of transport.

The large vessels are called *jahazi*, they are ocean going and they are planked rather than dug-out. Because they must be able to cope with rough conditions, including coral reefs and rocks, the *jahazi* is rugged, and often has two *lateen* sails. To reduce the amount of water splashing into the boat, woven coconut mats are fixed to their sides. If a *jahazi* has an inboard water, it becomes a *mtaboti*. Smaller dhows are known by the general name of *mashua* and are narrower, with only one sail.

Dhows vary in size and comfort but they are usually wooden, with only rudimentary seating, and if the winds pick up or the boat springs a leak, you will be expected to pitch in with the crew and help. Most dhow captains are very friendly and are, naturally, very knowledgeable about the islands, and you can learn much from them about the way of life of the islanders, about politics, the state of the economy and the latest fishing catch.

A two-hour sail from Lamu town, in the village of Matondoni, there are boat yards where dhows are built but if you wish to visit and, more especially, photograph the boats, you must ask permission first and be prepared to pay something to the boat yard owner.

charity, the International Donkey Protection Trust, sends out teams of vets regularly to check the health of all the island's donkey population, as well as organize competitions and awards for the best kept animal.

Villages on Lamu Island

After exploring Lamu town, you can take a 45-minute walk along the beach to the only other settlement of any size

Dhows are built in the village of Matondoni.

on the island, the pretty village of **Shela**. The village consists of a cluster of whitewashed stone houses, some remarkably elegant and luxurious looking, a Friday Mosque, built in 1829, and, totally unexpected in such a remote place, one of the best hotels in the world, the Peponi Hotel. Once you round the headland after Peponi's, there is nothing but sand dunes and beaches. Around the other side of the island from Lamu town is a tiny village called **Matondoni**. Dhows are built here and it is a good place to visit on a dhow trip.

In recent years, the main export from Lamu to the Persian Gulf was mangrove poles for scaffolding. The cutting of poles in the swamps is the major occupation of the local people. The cutting season was from January to April to prepare for the arrival of the dhows during the southwest monsoon. Now, steamships come all year around. At present, however, the cutting of mangroves is being increasingly controlled to avoid over-cutting.

Lamu's biggest event is the annual celebration of the Prophet's birthday, known as "**Maulidi al Nebi**", when thousands of pilgrims flock to the town, from all over Kenya as well as from abroad, for several days of prayers, dancing, ritual sword fights and singing. It is a fascinating time to be in Lamu but do be prepared for the crowds which are otherwise conspicuously absent from the island.

Island City States

A pleasant sail across the creek is **Manda Island**, home to the Takwa ruins, and if you are in the mood for a more adventurous trip, then head for the even more remote island of **Paté**. It takes about two hours in a motor launch to sail to the village of **Mtangawanda**, from where you walk for an hour through thick bush before arriving at **Paté town**. The little town today still shows some vestiges of its former glory as a 13th-century city state but it is a much sleepier place than Lamu. There are narrow streets and unplastered houses, but the best way to get a feel for the ancient state of Paté is to visit the extensive **Nabahani ruins**, just outside the village.

This settlement was founded by a group of Arab settlers called the Nabahani, who wielded considerable influence over the other coastal city

A Muslim farm community on Paté island, a remote island accessible only by boat.

states before seeing their fortunes decline. When the Portuguese arrived in the region in the early 16th century, Paté had a brief economic revival, mainly due to the island's silk industry. By the mid-17th century, the local people revolted against the Portuguese and especially against their taxes, and the Europeans left the island which briefly regained some of its former importance. Unfortunately for the island, its harbor was gradually silting up and Paté had to use Lamu's port, which led, inevitably, to tensions and disputes, and the two islands fought frequently. The year 1812 saw the death-knell of Paté for its army was convincingly defeated at Shela.

The channel between Paté and **Siyu** has also silted up making it virtually impassable for boats, so the best way to visit the 15th-century settlement of Siyu is on foot, from Paté. Between the 17th and 19th centuries, Siyu was a center for Islamic scholarship and craftsmanship but today it is little more than a village with scant evidence of its former glory. When the island was occupied by the Sultan of Zanzibar's troops in 1847, a huge fort was constructed which still stands outside the village and which is in a good state of repair. Siyu was formerly renowned for its carved doors with inlays of shell.

South of Siyu are the ruins of another ancient city state, **Shanga**, whose history dates back 1,200 years. The ruins were not seriously excavated until 1980, but archeologists have managed

Manda island, a favorite nesting place for birds.

to piece together something of the history of the settlement which was in its heyday a busy port.

If you feel like even more exploring, you can take a dhow at high tide, or walk for two hours across the island to the village of **Faza**, yet another former city state. Today, there are few ruins left to indicate that Faza was once a busy little kingdom, but the villagers are friendly, and as Faza is now the district headquarters for Paté island, the village is surprisingly busy. As with all trips to these remote little islands, you should always check timings and, most importantly, the tides. You may find that you can sail into Faza, but that if you leave at low tide, you will have to walk across the sand banks to regain your dhow, moored out at sea.

The island of **Kiwayu** is at the northern most tip of the Lamu archipelago, and is part of the Kiunga Marine National Reserve. You can only reach Kiwayu by dhow and as it takes three days to do the return trip from Lamu, it is a trip which needs a certain amount of planning, and, most importantly, supplies. There are good coral reefs to the east of the island.

Since these islands have only the simplest of infrastructures, if you are planning a trip there and especially if you are planning to sleep over, follow the advice of your dhow captain as to supplies – and remember to pack lots of mosquito repellent, for the island mosquitoes are nothing short of vicious.

5Y-GOV

Sports & Recreation

Just say "Kenya and sports" and certain images spring immediately to mind: the runner Kip Keino winning gold medals for his newly independent country in the All Africa Games, in the Commonwealth Games and then in the 1968 Mexico Olympic Games. Then inevitably other images would follow: the Safari Rally, and, in the days before visitors came armed only with cameras to shoot, big game hunters stalking the Maasai Mara for elephants and lions.

The balloon safari offers another way of observing wildlife.

Sport is not only for the visitors, of course. Kenyans are enthusiastic sportsmen and athletics, in particular, has been one of Kenya's success stories. The names and record times of their athletes in the few years since independence read like a roll-call of the world's best athletic achievements. Over the years, the Commonwealth Games, the Olympic Games and, increasingly, the marathon races the world over, have all given the coun-

Going on a safari now often means taking shots with a camera or video camera.

try clutches of medals. **Boxing** is another sport where Kenyans have won many medals for their country. **Football**, on the other hand, despite its wide following has not so far produced any really top class players yet.

Kenya, with its wide open spaces, its wealth of wildlife, its excellent coral reefs and its long beaches, offers a wide range of possibilities for sports. The land of **big game hunting** has slightly altered and enlarged its vocation. People now come to see the stunning wildlife rather than to shoot it for wall trophies. For those wanting to see the wildlife from a completely different perspective, a **balloon safari** is the answer. You see the game from above, you float at will over the plains and you land for an open-air champagne breakfast. A bal loon safari does not come cheap, fa from it in fact, but it is a truly uniqu occasion in a country already full c wonderful experiences.

Today's visitor to Kenya has a wid range of sports to tempt him or her awa from the game parks but there is choice to make : either they can practis their familiar, favorite sports from hom such as tennis or swimming or golf, c they can decide to try out sports that ar not so accessible back home such a windsurfing, diving, white-water raf ing or climbing a mountain. Those wit the time and the stamina can probabl have a go at both.

The familiar options first. The cour try has many excellent golf courses, an

Today's tented camp would be the envy of the explorers of yesteryear.

Jairobi alone has three – the **Railway** **:ourse**, the **Royal Nairobi**, and the **Iuthaiga Golf Club**. Each March, the enyan Open is played over the champonship Muthaiga course. Do rememer, though, when playing at the Kisumu olf course, to keep an eye open for rocodiles and hippos, though the club oes have its own local rule, just in case: If a ball comes to rest in dangerous roximity to a hippopotamus or a crocoile, another ball may be dropped at a afe distance...without penalty." Many otels and lodges, even out on safari, ave **swimming pools** and the large oastal hotels often have **tennis courts**.

Horse-racing enthusiasts or even asual visitors who want to see more of airobi life should go to the **Ngong Road Racecourse** where races are held most Sundays of the year.

Fishing is a popular recreation for many of Kenya's visitors and there is a wide choice of locations. **Lake Naivasha** contains large amounts of black bass and tilapia, the much more remote **Lake Turkana** offers Nile perch, tilapia and tiger fish, while in the Gura and Chania Rivers in the A**berdares**, large trout can be found. Tiny **Rusinga Island** in Lake Victoria offers excellent big game fishing. Some visitors to the island fly in from the Maasai Mara for the day, lured by the promise of a day's big game fishing. Nile perch are abundant, record-sized catches abound, and even though no one will actually guarantee the size of your catch, fish of 100 pounds are a

Hot Air Ballooning

Flames shoot up into the balloon heating the air inside.

It had all seemed quite straightforward during the pre-flight briefing with the pilot. After describing the way balloons operate and how the flights are manned, the pilot had said that the wind conditions appeared favorable but that if they were too strong in the morning the flight would have to be cancelled. He reminded everyone to dress up warm, to bring lots of film for the camera, and, just as the meeting was closing, he added, "Don't forget to bring a hat." For the sun, you presume.

Now it is 5.00 in the morning in the Maasai Mara. It is still dark but inside the lodge, one solitary light is on, and a small group of sleepy people stand around, drinking a cup of coffee. There is the sound of a jeep pulling up outside, a cheery "Good morning, everybody. Come on, let's go! " and you climb in, shake hands with your balloon pilot and set off to the launching area. Just before you leave, the pilot asks, "Did you all remember to bring a hat ?"

It is still dark when you arrive but it is a scene of activity already. The balloon is stretched out on the ground, the padded basket or gondola, which will be your base for the next hour, lies on its side and the crew are busy getting the gas burners ready.

The pre-dawn air is chilly, but the sky is beginning to get light as the crew begins to inflate the balloon. First, cold air from a fan is blown inside the balloon, and then, once it is half inflated, the crew ignites the gas burners. There is a loud, rushing sound, and flames shoot up into the balloon. As the air inside heats up, slowly the balloon rights itself until it is vertical and is being held down only by the crew, just long enough for the passengers to scramble aboard the wicker gondola. The pilot gives one last glance to check that all is in order, the crew releases the gondola and very slowly you drift up into the air and off over the Maasai Mara.

In the Balloon Basket

The gondola is divided into sections which are well-padded and with handles, one for the pilot and two for the passengers. When the pilot turns on the gas, there is a loud hissing noise and it is hot. Suddenly you realize why he had suggested hats – to protect you from the heat from the gas burners, and not from the sun.

As the balloon drifts along, with the ligh

fairly regular feature (see chapter on Western Kenya). Along the coast, fishing trips can be organized either on an individual level by arranging to go out with a local fisherman or by joining an organized big game fishing boat – there is a well-run operation from the little town of **Shimoni**, south of Mombasa towards the Tanzanian border. In **Lamu** fishing trips on a dhow can easily b getting stronger by the minute, you pass over a Maasai *boma* or village, its design clearly visible and its encircling protective bushes of thorns looking like a pattern on the ground. Then the serious wildlife spotting begins: giraffe, elephant, a long line of wildebeest moving in single file. A quick movement in the clump of trees over which you are floating and the pilot says excitedly, "Did you see that? Leopard." Just a glimpse, but leopard it was.

The noise from the gas burners alternates with total silence as the balloon drifts along, following the air currents. Dawn is the optimal time for balloon flights since the hot air inside the balloon is lighter than the cool air of the early morning. The hotter the air in the balloon, the quicker it rises. The cooler the air, the quicker it descends. The pilot can thus control the altitude of the balloon by controlling the temperature of the air in the balloon, but what he cannot control is the direction in which you fly. You simply drift along as the morning winds decide. Should the winds exceed 25 kmh (15 mph) the balloon flights are cancelled, but this morning there is only a gentle breeze pushing you slowly along and down below you can see the support vehicles following you. As no one yet has any idea of where the balloon will come down, the crew (and your breakfast) must follow, as you lead.

Everyone is engrossed in the stunning panorama, watching their own shadow as it is profiled by the sun. The few trees below make beautiful abstract patterns against the dusty land. More giraffe, wildebeest, another herd of elephants, impala, gazelles and all too soon, the pilot says "I think we'll land over there." Over there is a flat, empty expanse of land.

"Why don't you all sit down, and hold onto the straps," he suggests, having already outlined the procedure to follow should the balloon tilt over on landing. It does nothing of the kind, of course, simply bouncing once or twice before the ground crew grabs hold of it to steady the gondola. Out you all scramble and suddenly you are in the middle of a hive of activity.

Tables have been set out, food has appeared from nowhere and a smiling cook, complete with his white chef's hat, is standing at his portable stove, asking "How do you like your eggs?" Juice, coffee, and, well, why not, a glass of champagne. After all, it is not every morning that you fly over the Maasai Mara in a balloon and then have breakfast on the open plains. No one even quibbles that the champagne is actually fizzy white wine – the "Mimosas" of "champagne" and orange juice taste wonderful!

As you sit there, the sky by now a deep blue overhead, figures appear on the horizon seemingly out of nowhere. Maasai tribesmen and women march briskly towards your open air restaurant and sit solemnly in a circle, a polite distance away. More and more Maasai arrive until the tables are encircled. They have come to see the spectacle and also to try and sell the champagne breakfast crowd souvenirs. The balloon pilot makes a bee-line for one old Maasai man, and with the help of one of his ground crew, opens negotiations for a Maasai spear. A cup of coffee later and the price has been fixed. But the pilot realizes he has forgotten his wallet. No problem, smiles the old Maasai man, he will come to watch the balloon show tomorrow morning and collect his payment.

Reluctantly, everyone climbs into the jeeps for the scenic game drive along the banks of the Mara river, back to the lodge. It seems strange to be earth-bound again, but, then you look at your watch, see that it is still early in the morning and you realize that there is a whole day waiting ahead of you.

arranged and Peponi's Hotel also rent tackle as well as boats. For the competitive souls, the country hosts a number of major fishing competitions during the winter and early spring. (See chapter on Culture and Festivals.)

The coast offers a range of watersports, some of which can be easily arranged through your hotel such as **windsurfing** and **snorkeling**. Condi-

Crowds watching a horse race at the Ngong Road Racecourse.

Sportsman
Sportsman
No JOCKEY DR.H.WT
NJUGUNA
GODANA
GITAHI
ANDRADE
JOCKEY
Since 1922
KBL Brings people together

Snorkeling with the diving club in Diani Beach.

tions for windsurfing are ideal since the coral reef protects the water. Before being allowed to go **scuba diving**, you need to hold a permit which you really should have obtained before your trip to Kenya. However, if you decide that you want to go ahead and learn on your holiday, enquire at your hotel for a good diving instructor. The line of coral reefs that runs parallel along much of Kenya's beaches offers good diving opportunities and a wide range of fish can be seen. Currently, **Malindi** and **Watamu** are the most organized centers for diving, usually from a boat.

White-water rafting is still a new sport in Kenya and the seasonal nature of some of its rivers does not help the sport, but the Athi-Galan River has some very challenging rapids and waterfalls.

One of the highlights of the Kenyan sporting calendar is the **Safari Rally**, which is a 4,500-kilometer (2,700-mile) race through the Kenyan plains along Kenya's rough roads, bumping along in a jeep or a mini-van with clouds of red dust everywhere, and never quite knowing when a herd of elephants might amble into view to slow you down. The race takes place around Easter time each year and attracts drivers from all over the world.

The Safari Rally started life in 1953 to celebrate Queen Elizabeth II's coronation. The event was put up by Kenya, Uganda and Tanzania. Initially, it was open only to amateurs, no service crews were allowed and no prizes were given

The coast inevitably offers a variety of watersports.

Mountain Climbing and Hill Walking

Kenya's mountains offer challenging climbing, and, with a certain amount of planning and organization, you can enjoy the thrill of seeing Kenya from a different angle.

The principal mountains which offer worthwhile climbing possibilities are Mount Kenya, Mount Elgon, the Aberdares and the Cherangani Hills, all of which are also covered in their respective travel chapters.

Since Mount Kenya is the biggest and the best because it is the most challenging, its various trails are covered in detail here. The advice as to logistics, guides, equipment and supplies naturally applies to any mountain climbing expedition. A brief list of the principal mountains and their heights is given at the end of this box.

Although ordinary running shoes are adequate at lower altitudes, good walking shoes make definite sense and for higher altitudes, boots are essential. Wear layers of clothing which are not only more efficient at keeping your body warmth in, but they allow you to strip off layers should you get too hot. If you are going up to higher altitudes, you will need proper thermal underwear, hat, gloves, and jacket. An extensive first-aid kit, a torch, a knife, (the Swiss Army knife is ideal) and a lighter are all essential. Always carry enough food and water with you, and if you are intending to camp, check with your guides and porters before setting off as to what foodstuffs and what equipment – tents, bedding, cooking utensils – are required. Always have a sunhat, sunglasses and sun lotion. Try and obtain all the maps you need in Nairobi before leaving.

Healthwise, you have to bear in mind that not only do you need medication for any potential cuts, bruises, blisters and stings but also for altitude sickness. The thin air, especially at the summit of Mount Kenya, can cause high altitude headaches and insomnia, so make sure that you include pain killers and sleeping tablets. There is no need to be alarm about climbing Mount Kenya – many people do it every season – but neither is it the same as setting off for a Sunday afternoon stroll. If you ascend too quickly, you could (but not necessarily) be affected by altitude sickness. Climb slowly, stopping to acclimatize, and should you feel unwell, descend immediately. Remember that your body needs much more liquid the higher you climb, so always take ample supplies of water.

Mount Kenya

There are various trails that lead up to the summit of Kenya's highest mountain, some of which are difficult and will require you to hire guides, whereas the three principal trails are well marked and are briefly described below. You will have to pay to enter the National Park and at the park headquarters they will be able to advise you as to the weather conditions and the desirability of taking guides and porters. Alternatively, contact the main lodges who often organize climbing expeditions. There are huts on the mountain but you need to book them in advance.

The **Naro Moru trail** is the most popular and requires a minimum of four days climbing. For all information, contact the Naro Moru River Lodge. The final day's climbing takes you across a snow-covered glacier.

The **Sirimon trail** requires at least five days and it is the least frequented of the trails.

The **Chogoria trail** is the easiest of the three, and also the most picturesque, with some superb views. You will require at least three days.

Mount Elgon

The highest peak, Wagagai 4,321 m or 14,173 ft is actually just across the border in Uganda for the mountain straddles the border between the two countries. The highest peak on the Kenyan side is Koitoboss. Mount Elgon is wet for much of the year so you will need good waterproof

By 1957, it had been granted international status but soon the political difficulties of driving through Uganda and Tanzania changed the character of the clothing as well as warm clothes for the cold nights.

The Aberdares

The country's third highest mountain range offers several possibilities for climbers, walkers and trekkers.

Satima 3,999 meters or 13,120 feet – strenuous, high-altitude walking
Table Mountain 3,971 meters or 12,438 feet
The Kinangop 3,906 meters or 12,816 feet
The Elephant 3,590 meters or 11,780 feet
Kipipiri 3,349 meters or 10,987 feet

Maasailand and the south
Subogo 2,683 meters or 8,802 feet
Ngong 2461 meters or 8,074 feet
Chyulu 2,438 meters or 7,996 feet – hill walking, take adequate water
Susua 2,357 meters or 7,732 feet – hot, take adequate water with you
Nzuai 1,830 meters or 6,003 feet
Oloolkisaili 1,760 meters or 5,774 feet – take plenty of water, and wear boots

The Matthews Range
Warges 2,688 meters or 8,820 feet – a guide is essential
Losiolo 2,470 meters or 8,104 feet
Matthews Peak 2,375 meters or 7,792 feet – good walking, cool, pleasant
Ol Doinyo Lenkiyo 2,286 meters or 7,505 feet – remote
Matthews South Peak 2,285 meters or 7,497 feet – a guide is recommended
Lololokwe 1,853 meters or 6,080 feet

The Mau Escarpment
Melili 3,098 meters or 10,165 feet
Loldiani 3,011 meters or 9,878 feet
Buru 2,854 meters or 9,365 feet
Tinderet 2,640 meters or 8,663 feet

The Ndoto Range

Alimision 2,637 meters or 8,650 feet – challenging

Baio 1,751 meters or 5,746 feet – challenging, and a guide is recommended

The North

Given the remoteness and sparse population of the north of Kenya, before setting out on any trip there, be it driving or a more adventurous climb, ask about the conditions there, follow all advice that the local authorities offer and try and always travel in convoys to guard against being stranded, should a breakdown occur. It is essential to take all supplies with you in the north – petrol, food and water.

Nyiru 2,829 meters or 9,283 feet – challenging
Kulal 2,285 meters or 7,498 feet – very challenging
Supuko 2,067 meters or 6,780 feet – difficult ridge walking
Forole 2,007 meters or 6,584 feet – on the Ethiopian border
Jabisa 1,544 meters or 5.065 feet – very hot
Porr 668 meters or 2,191 feet – suitable for hill walking

Taita Hills
Vuria 2,209 meters or 7,248 feet
Kasigau 1,641 meters or 5,383 feet

The Tugan Hills
Kapkut 2,800 meters or 9,185 feet
Saimo 2,501 meters or 8,207 feet
Tiati 2,351 meters or 7,713 feet – hot, rugged climb
Kibimjor 2,347 meters or 7,699 feet
Marop 2,306 meters or 7,567 feet

Safari Rally. Now it is a uniquely Kenyan affair and better cars and the increasing number of participants have made it into a major event.

A fishing trip on a dhow is often successful.

Shopping

Shopping for a reminder of a holiday is always one of the pleasures of any trip, and after a satisfying safari where you may well have had an intensive, in-depth, crash course in East African wildlife, a day or so shopping in Nairobi or Mombasa can be great fun. In all honesty it must be said that Kenya is not one of the world's great shopping destinations. It is definitely not Hong Kong or Singapore but there are still some good things on offer, many of them with an appropriate wildlife theme.

The market in the Old Town of Mombasa selling a variety of crafts and cloths.

Some of the Kenyan-made **clothing** is lovely, especially casual clothes like tee-shirts and shorts, many of which, not surprisingly, are decorated with animal or bird motifs. No one likes to be thought of as an impulsive buyer but in Kenya, if you do see a tee-shirt or a pair of bermuda shorts or a sun hat that you particularly like, for example in the boutique of a lodge where you are staying, buy it there and then. Chances

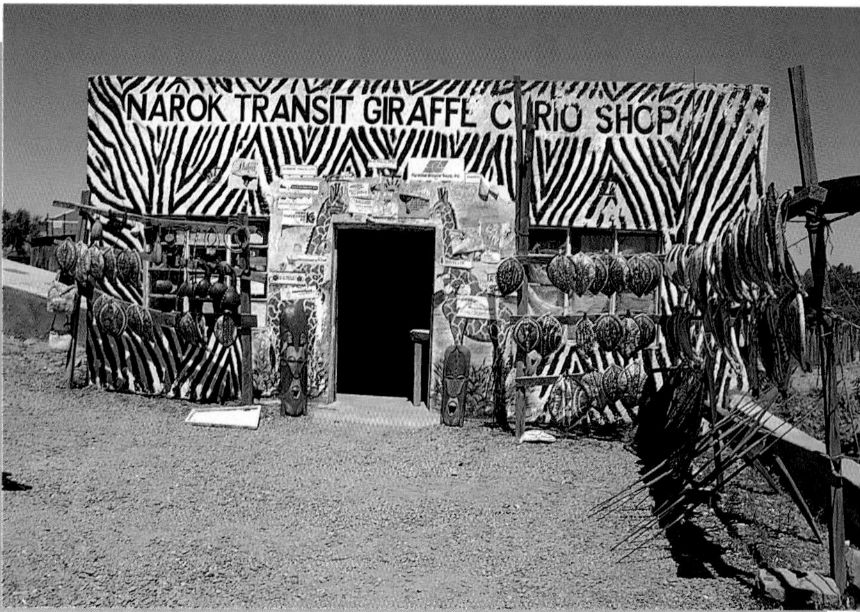

A shop in Narok.

are, when you reach Nairobi or Mombasa, you will not find it again. Good **safari clothes** and **sunhats** are available in Nairobi, in authentic khaki colors. **Safari boots** are also a good buy in Nairobi but if you intend doing a lot of walking during your safari, make sure that you break your new shoes in first, otherwise you will have aching feet for much of your trip. The best place to buy safari boots is from Bata in Nairobi.

Authentic Kenyan clothing, like **kikois** and **kangas** make a good buy and are good for casual beach wear as well as making nice, light-to-carry presents. Unfortunately the same cannot be said of one of Kenya's specialties, Ki**sii soapstone** carvings. There are small carved animals available, of course, but

A display of handicrafts in Mombasa.

Maasai bead necklaces.

:he large, absolutely gorgeous pale pink hippos and elephants are, well, frankly speaking, very heavy. Irresistible, but extremely heavy. So the solution is to have them shipped home which can be easily arranged. Other lovely objects in Kisii soapstone are chess sets, some of which are real works of art.

Local Handicraft

Carved wooden animals are another popular and good buy and they range in size from toy animals, ideal for children, to huge, stylized giraffes – another candidate requiring shipping as there is not a suitcase in the world into which these carvings would fit. You can buy

Maasai shields of bold design.

Preparing for a Safari

Looking for game.

Everyone knows how to dress for a safari: a khaki safari jacket with lots of professional looking little pockets and flaps, a matching pair of trousers, stout boots, heavy socks and, of course, a hat – either a hard-brimmed, colonial-looking hat, or a large-brimmed cloth one, preferably with more intriguing little pockets stitched onto it. The reality is, however, that the outfit described is absolutely fine for the set of an "Out of Africa" type film but is totally over the top for a Kenyan safari, 1990s style. You are going to look at wild animals, not dressing for an exotic theme party.

Unless you are embarking on a safari that involves a great deal of walking or riding (and that means on a camel, and not in a jeep), the plain truth is that most of the above outfit, no matter how stylish, is totally redundant. For the majority of Kenyan safaris, you actually do very little walking at all since most of the reserves and game parks insist that you remain in your vehicle. So the stout shoes and the comfortable socks can probably be dispensed with unless, of course, you seriously intend to try and walk, in which case, pack them. But remember one thing about walking in the reserves: if it is allowed, and do check with your lodge for details, you will always have to go with a Ranger. Never set off for a walk on your own.

Before we go any further with the packing list, a word first about luggage. You will spend a lot of time in dusty jeeps traveling from one game park to another, so you should have solid luggage that fastens tightly against the all pervasive dust. Since some lodges like The Ar[k] encourage you to take nothing more than an overnight bag, it makes sense to pack a smaller bag for any overnight trips when you can safely leave the bulk of your luggage at your base camp. Soft luggage makes the best sense for traveling in Kenya since it can be fitted into the back of a jeep with more ease. Remember t[o] take padlocks and keys. For the day time, when you go out for your game drives, a small sturdy bag or rucksack is a good idea. Sturdy, because it will get the most bouncing of all your luggage and will be exposed to dust too. The padded camera bag or rucksack is ideal not only for protecting your camera gear during the drives, but you will also be able to fit in some of the "extras" you will want to take along for the day: paper tissues, perhaps a pack of moist towelettes, your wildlife reference books, your binoculars, and all that extra film you will need.

Once the luggage has been selected, what will you pack in it for your safari? Well, first things first, there is no need to "dress up" on safari. No one dresses for dinner, so other than a smart outfit for the hotels and restaurants in Nairobi and Mombasa, out in the bush you will need only loose, cool, comfortable clothing. Light-weight cotton trousers and shorts, tee-shirts and cotton shirts, comfortable shoes, and, for the early morning drives and the evening, a warm sweater and an anorak. If you are planning any bush walking, however leisurely, do make sure that your shoes are comfortable and "broken in", and under no circumstances should you wear sandals in the bush – unless you wish to be scratched and, possibly, stung or bitten by something. Trousers rather than shorts and long-sleeved shirts are the most sensible combination for they protect you from too much sun and also from mosquitoes in the evenings. With all that ever-present red Kenyan dust around, you will get grimy but laundry can be done overnight in most camps and lodges so there is no need to weigh your bags down with too many changes of outfit – save your luggage space for a wonderful Kisii soapstone carving instead !

Do bear one thing in mind: if you are also combining your safari with a stint on the beach at Mombasa, you will need to pack more conservative clothing for the coast is essentially a Muslim dominated area. Beach wear will be fine for the Mombasa beaches but definitely not for exploring the old town or for a trip to Lamu. Away from the beaches, women should make sure that their shoulders are covered and that they wear skirts that reach the knees at least, and men should avoid wearing shorts.

A Comprehensive List

What else should be on your packing list ? A swimming costume, for those rare moments when you find that there is no game drive, no wildlife checklist to be updated and no diary to be written. A good sunhat that will shade your neck as well as your face and good sunglasses. A small torch is useful, as is an all-purpose knife, such as the Swiss Army knife. Bring any prescription medicines with you for out in the bush there will be no chemist available, and also a small first-aid kit for any cuts and bruises. Do not forget suntan lotion and after sun products, a good moisturising cream and a lip moisturising stick for windy and dusty rides will take their toll on your skin and lips. Sad to say, a mosquito repellent is a must and also whatever malaria tablets your doctor at home has prescribed – remember to start the course before leaving for Kenya, and, imperatively, to complete it on your return home.

Bring a sufficient amount of reading material to tide you through your flights and those occasional evenings when you find you have enough energy left to read after your 6.00 a.m. start. Binoculars are invaluable. Photography enthusiasts should make sure that they pack far

...Preparing for a Safari

more film than they expect to use, for you will definitely take more than you think, as well as spare batteries for the camera and for your flash-gun, plus a camera cleaning kit – Kenyan dust is all pervasive, as a glance at your clothes at the end of the day will prove.

If you are intending to do any camping, then your packing list will have to be more extensive including at least a sleeping bag, a mosquito net, and perhaps even your own tent. Check with your camping safari company before leaving as to what will be provided and what equipment you may need to bring with you.

The majority of visitors to Kenya opt for an organized safari but for those who prefer to drive themselves, there are some extra things to bear in mind. After deciding on the kind of vehicle you wish to rent, bearing in mind the rough roads and the weather, it is imperative to check that the vehicle you have rented is in tip-top condition, that its tyres are good and that you have all you need in the way of spare tyres, extra tubes, a jack and a tool kit. Also take along an extra jerry-can for spare petrol. If you intend driving into the very remote Northern Frontier District of the country, usually known by its initials as the NFD, do be prepared. Petrol and water are both very scarce there so make sure that you have adequate supplies and that you know where garages are, and their telephone numbers. You might need to telephone ahead for extra supplies, in case of a problem.

Most visitors will arrive first in Nairobi and a day there at the beginning of your safari is a very good idea. As well as giving you time to recover from your jet-lag, you can also stock up on various things for your safari. Maps, especially if you are driving yourself, are one thing you should aim to buy in Nairobi, as well as reading material for your trip: all the bookshops stock the Kenya-based novels of Karen Blixen and Beryl Markham among others, which are the perfect companions on your safari. You can find most standard kind of film in Nairobi – Kodacolor, Fujicolor, as well as some limited stock of Ektachrome and Fujichrome, but the professional photographer should bring all of his or her film. Kodachrome is unavailable and since stocks of other slide film are limited, you could find yourself unlucky.

If you want to go ahead and kit yourself out in full safari regalia, there are any number of expensive shops in Nairobi selling equally expensive safari jackets, hats with leopard-spotted bands and even carved wooden jewelry to match the outfit. But, bearing in mind that most of this gear is for the fashion conscious, it is better to go to a less flashy outfitter where the prices are more reasonable and where there is a wide choice of styles. Some of the safari jackets and waistcoats do make traveling sense for photographers who can put film and filters and lens caps in all the assorted little pockets. The best known safari outfitter is **Colpro** in Kimathi Street, which, as they proudly claim about themselves, is open "eight days a week." They have a particularly wide choice of sunhats, including, of course, the leopard-spotted print variety.

A final word for safari packing. Just be thankful that you are not setting off a century ago when a Victorian lady, according to Agnes and Cecily Herbert, would wear "knickerbockers, gaiters, stout English shooting boots and khaki safari jackets, the wide pockets busy with string, knives and other handy aids."

cute wooden bowls with the figure of an animal leaning over to "drink" from it as well as wooden bookends, wooden cocktail sticks, wooden napkin rings, all with a wildlife motif.

In a different league altogether are the beautiful makonde carvings made from ebony, a heavy wood. These elegant, soothing-looking carvings are often of a very high standard. Enquire around and investigate prices, artists and quality before you invest. A good makonde sculpture is not a souvenir. It is a work of art.

Colorful kiondos for sale.

Another kind of purchase where you should shop around for prices and quality before buying, is for **African artifacts** such as shields, spears, and any other tribal objects, including the gorgeous **beaded jewelry** and elaborate bead-work collars. As you drive through Kenya, at almost every stop for petrol or cold drinks, you will be inundated with shields and spears for sale. If you are in the market for a really good shield to be used as a decorative piece in your home, then road-side purchases should best be avoided. However, if you are simply looking for a present to make a little boy back home happy, then go ahead and buy from one of these stalls, remember to bargain hard, and you will be able to pick up a nice hide shield for a very reasonable price.

Baskets, or **kiondos**, woven from sisal fibers are a good buy and are also a useful present. As you wander around Nairobi, you will see many stalls selling kiondos for they are used by all the Kenyans, so it makes sense to buy from where the local people buy. In the center of Nairobi, around the hotels and the main shopping area, you will be offered **"elephant's hair" bracelets** for sale. Don't be fooled for one minute. What you are being offered, at exorbitant prices, are either reed grass which has been blackened with polish, or thin slivers of cow horn.

One of the most interesting shops in Nairobi and an absolute "must" for all visitors, is the **African Heritage Store.**

The Bombolulu Workshop supplies a good selection of handicraft.

The store, which was founded in December 1972, specializes in pan-African art and craft and so is the perfect place to see not only Kenyan crafts but also those from all over the continent. There are sumptuous displays of jewelry, fabrics and ready-made clothing and although the fixed prices are a little on the high side, you know that you are buying good quality products.

Besides the large gallery which showcases artists' work and the ever-expanding original range of designs in jewelry, crafts and clothing, there is also a branch of **Spinners Web** in the store which sells hand-woven articles from all parts of the country. In addition, there is also jewelry and clothing from **Bombolulu**, a workshop which draws its craftsmen from people who have been severely injured in accidents as part of their rehabilitation. Bombolulu was also started at about the same time as African Heritage (see chapter on Handicrafts). A women's co-operative called **Kazuri** also sells its attractive jewelry through the African Heritage shop. For those women who love beads or for those who simply cannot decide which color they prefer, in the African Heritage store, you can buy separate strings of beads, plus a clasp and then you can go ahead and make your own necklaces.

The in-house **African Heritage jewelry collection** combines contemporary designs, often juxtaposing them with ancient beads and other items of

African personal adornment. Gold and lost wax sculptures from the Ivory Coast or Ghana, silver from Ethiopia, polished cow horn from Madagascar, beads chipped from the thick shell of coconut from Nigeria, or even ostrich eggshells from Kenya: from such old exotic elements, along with other African and international designs, modern compositions are created.

Since there is also a small garden where crafts people may be seen at work everyday and where coffee and tea is served to visitors, all in all this shop is an ideal place to sit and relax in and decide how you can fit all your shopping into your suitcase.

Entertainment

After a hard day's shopping, pounding the streets of Nairobi looking for Kisii soapstone statues and safari clothes, what better way to relax than a night out ? Nairobi is about the only place on your Kenyan holiday where you will really have the chance to go out and hit the night spots, so make the most of it. Well, just stop and think for a moment: in the middle of the Maasai Mara or half way up Mount Kenya, where exactly do you go if you feel like going out? So, enjoy Nairobi's nightlife because once out on safari, with all those dawn starts to your day, you will be too tired even to contemplate partying.

Let us deal with the quieter options first. Opposite the Norfolk Hotel is the **National Theater** which often has good plays in English. Check in the papers for concerts and other plays, some of which are presented in hotels. For cinemas, also check the local papers.

Otherwise, the city's nightlife essentially revolves around restaurants, bars and discos – all of which go in and out of fashion, and business, with amazing speed. Certain "institutions" survive, however, such as the **Simba Saloon**, attached to the equally famous Carnivore restaurant (see box story p.354). The Simba Saloon is definitely one of the best night spots in town and has a disco on Wednesdays, Fridays, Saturdays and Sundays. It is usually packed which makes it a good place to get to meet the real Nairobi residents. The last Friday night of every month is "African Night" where African music is featured rather than the international disco fare.

For live African music, try the **African Heritage Café** where live bands usually play on weekend afternoons. Ask around at your hotel for the best "in" places for music and entertainment. And, just as in any city in the world, if you are heading off to bars, be sensible. Avoid the less frequented areas of town and do not go out dripping with jewelry and cameras.

In a more traditional city like **Mombasa**, with its strong Islamic ethos, your nightlife will be very much centered around the string of hotels along the beaches, most of which have excellent bars and discos.

Cuisine

Even the most adventurous of travelers might hesitate to taste some of Kenya's local tribal specialties. The Maasai diet consists largely of fermented milk which may be mixed with blood taken from the jugular vein of a cow or a bullock. Blood is mixed with the urine of cattle to ferment it to form a stimulant. Many other tribes, such as the Samburu, also mix milk and blood, and the Samburu also add tree bark and plant roots to their soup. (See chapter on People.)

Peponi's Hotel in Shela Village offers excellent seafood.

Set against this unpalatable sounding tribal food, Kenyan food is otherwise, basically simple, cheap, and to western and Asian palates, rather plain. Less wealthy Kenyans eat a diet which is high in starchy food. It may not be the healthiest way to eat but it does fill you up quickly. Starch comes in three main ways in Kenya – potatoes, rice and *ugali*, a kind of porridge which is the staple in many tribal diets. *Ugali* is made from maize milled into flour and then boiled into what can only be described as a stiff porridge,

FOR THE SPECIAL OCCASION
A SEA FOOD FONDUE WITH CHIPS
AND SALAD
A MEAL FIT FOR A
KING - 150/-
RICH LOBSTER SOUP
A WHOLE SILVER FISH CHARCOAL
GRILLED WITH EXOTIC SPICES
CHIPS
FOR FILLET STEAKS - POULTRY
LOBSTER - CRAB AND FISH
SEE OUR ALA CARTE MENUE
ON THE RECEPTION

Seafood is particularly good along the coast.

which is eaten as an accompaniment to a beef or chicken stew. To eat *ugali* properly, you should roll it into a little ball which you hold in your right hand and then use that to scoop up the meat stew or fish stew, or vegetables that are traditionally eaten with it.

Another popular Kenyan dish is *irio*, which has the advantage of being both filling and cheap. *Irio* is made from green peas which are first soaked overnight and then added to maize kernels and potatoes which are then all cooked together until the maize is soft, and served salted and mashed. You eat *irio* in very much the same way as *ugali*, with a meat stew.

Vegetarians and the health conscious will be slightly shocked at the amount of meat that Kenyans eat. If you want to summarize Kenyan cuisine it is meat and yet more meat. *Nyama Choma* or roast meat is very popular as are meat stews. Beef, mutton, zebra, crocodile – you name it, and the Kenyans will probably eat it. Not for nothing is one of Nairobi's most popular restaurants called "The Carnivore".

Fish is excellent in Kenya, especially on the coast where you can also eat good shell fish. One of the most famous dishes on the coast is called **prawns pili pili** which consists of prawns cooked in an explosive sauce, made from some or all of the following ingredients: butter, chillies, garlic, lime juice, coconut, coriander and paprika. Among the best **freshwater fish** are tilapia, Nile perch and trout. Nile perch is particularly versatile, and its firm texture lends itself to many different styles of cooking

The successive waves of foreigners who came to conquer, settle and develop the country, depending on how you view history, also had an influence on the dietary habits of the local Kenyans. Coastal Swahili food draws much of its inspiration from **Arab** cuisine and the Arabs introduced the habit of eating rice and the early use of spices. When the **Portuguese** came, they brought with them foods that they themselves had only recently discovered in their new territory of Brazil – such things as maiz and bananas, chillies, peppers, pineap ples, sweet potatoes and manioc. Man of these foods are now established sta ples in the Kenyan diet. When the **Bri**

Tucking in at The Carnivore, where you cannot do otherwise.

ish came, although not ranked among the world's greatest gourmets, they did bring with them new strains of cattle, sheep and goats and they planted coffee. They were also responsible for many of the desserts that are still to be found on any self-respecting Kenyan sweet trolley: sherry trifle, blancmange, jelly, and just about anything with custard. English nursery food is alive and well and living in lots of Kenyan five-star hotels.

When the British came and decided to build their railway, their much maligned "Lunatic Express", they brought over from **India** thousands of indentured laborers. It is these Punjabis and Gujeratis, of all the overseas visitors, who had the most lasting impact on Kenyan food. Indian restaurants abound in the country, many of them excellent, and almost every hotel buffet will include several Indian dishes. Twentieth-century eating habits have led to pizzas, hamburgers and fried chicken making their appearance in the major cities.

During your stay in Kenya, especially out on safari, you will eat well. Amazingly, given the logistics of providing huge **buffets** in the middle of the bush three times a day, your lodge will lay on vast amounts of food for you. These kind of buffets tend to be of the fairly bland "International Cuisine" variety with sadly, very little in the way of Kenyan specialties on offer.

Breakfast consists of all the usual items found in an English-style breakfast such as eggs of all kinds, sausages and various cold meats, bread and lots of fresh fruit, plus, of course, tea and coffee, both of which are grown in the country. **Lunch** and **dinner** are usually huge, lavish buffet spreads with soup, salad, lots of meat, sometimes fish, a wide choice of vegetables, potatoes and rice or pasta. Desserts are usually sweet and filling, and there is always some fruit on offer.

All of this food is good, there is usually far too much to eat and it is an even more impressive spread when you remember that you are kilometers from anywhere, surrounded by savannah grasslands and wild animals. Given all these constraints, it is perhaps carrying gastronomic criticism a little too far to say that the food is bland. You will eat copiously on your safari, you will eat

Kenyan Wines

Say the word "vineyard" and you instantly think of an elegant 18th-century French château, surrounded by rows and rows of neat vines, or perhaps the vineyards of the rugged Italian hills basking in the late afternoon sun, or the sunny vineyards of Australia and California. But the African Equator? Welcome to the **Lake Naivasha Vineyard**.

The Lake Naivasha Vineyard is situated, as the name implies, on the shores of Lake Naivasha, in Kenya's Rift Valley, and is a little over ten years old now. A Kenyan farmer called John D'Olier and his American wife started their vineyard in 1982 with grapes originally imported from Californian vines. The Kenyan farmer imported one ton of cuttings from various vineyards in California, choosing stocks he had researched to be most suitable for the climate and the growing conditions of his farm. The attractions of the Lake Naivasha area for grape growing are many: the sandy soil, the hot days and cold nights which produce fruit at just the right acid/sugar content for premium quality wines, the dry climate which helps eliminate fungus problems and the availability of irrigation.

Despite these advantages, the first harvest was not without its teething troubles, some of them decidedly unique in the world of wines and vines. During the three years prior to 1985, when the first vintage was harvested, when the vines were maturing in the volcanic soils of the Lake Naivasha basin, they were subjected to all sorts of hazards and survived admirably.

One major problem was the abundant local fauna. The first predators who used to arrive at night, to feed on the young shoots emerging from the cuttings, were the rabbit-sized dik-dik antelopes who found the sweet leaves irresistible. While giraffes did not actually eat the vines, they did present a problem, for they stalked through the vineyards, damaging the vines as they took their pick of the delicate leaves of the acacia thorn trees that are one of Naivasha's landmarks. Night visits from hippos coming up from the lake were also a problem, to put it mildly, and of course, the thousands upon thousands of exotically colored birds that make Naivasha home, were, and still are, a constant threat to the crop.

However, despite all the dire predictions and the nocturnal visits from the local wildlife, the volume of wine produced each season by Lake Naivasha vineyards has continued to grow by leaps and bounds. From the initial modest production of 3,000 bottles in 1985, the winery ultimately aims to produce an anticipated 10,000 cases, or 120,000 bottles, which represents approximately 10 percent of Kenya's domestic demand for wine.

Kenya Wine Agencies Ltd in Nairobi, imports wine from all over the world, in addition to producing wines from the country's abundant supply of papaya. The organization has been involved from the outset in assisting the Naivasha operation and now handles all the bottling and distribution for the Lake Naivasha Vineyards.

In addition to wine grapes, of which there are 10 varieties, the vineyards also contain several kinds of table grapes, the most popular of which is the "Flame Seedless Variety".

During the harvest, which takes place in March, the grapes are picked in the early hours of the morning, usually between 6.00 and 10.00, so that they are at their coldest and freshest. They are taken immediately to the winery where they are crushed and transferred to 1,000 gallon tanks.

As far as the future is concerned, there are plans to make Kenyan "bubbly" using the *méthode champenoise* and the Colombard grapes.

well, but sad to say, your meals will not be memorable ones.

On the drinks' front, Kenyan **beer** is excellent and widely available. One of the pleasures of safari life, after a shower to rinse off all that red dust, is to sit down in the evening, slightly sunburned and pleasantly tired, and have a glass of ice cold Tusker or White Cap. Wine drinkers can choose among the good **Lak**

Out in the bush, the meals are copious.

Naivasha wines or a local wine, made from papayas, which is quite frankly an acquired taste.

Since restaurants are currently opening up in Nairobi at the rate of about two a month and existing places are closing down at the rate of one a month, compiling any kind of definitive list of recommended restaurants in the capital is not an easy task. But the more famous places survive and thrive, and some or all of them should be a part of your visit to Nairobi. There are some eating places in Nairobi that must not

The bar at the Norfolk Hotel, a meeting place for everyone.

be missed, as much for their atmosphere as for their food. Lunch on the verandah of the **Norfolk Hotel** offers you good food and serious people watching. The always-packed outdoor café of the **Thorn Tree Café** in the New Stanley Hotel is a fun place to stop for a refreshing drink or afternoon tea. Travelers and backpackers stop by to read the famous bulletin board which is fixed to

a real thorn tree growing in the courtyard, the local Nairobi residents drop by on the way to or from the office and sightseers sit reading up on the sights to be seen. Undoubtedly the best restaurant to eat seafood in Nairobi is **The Tamarind**, which is decorated in an Arab-Moorish style, and where most importantly, there is a superb choice of fish and shellfish. Ask what is the catch of the day and you may find yourself enjoying wonderful oysters, flown in that morning from Malindi.

One of the obvious places to eat

The Carnivore Restaurant

The gigantic roasting pit where the restaurant's selection of more than 10 kinds o meats are cooked.

Two words of warning. First, go on a starvation diet before you go to Nairobi's popular restaurant, "The Carnivore", and second, if you are a vegetarian, don't worry, for despite the name, the restaurant does serve non-carnivorous meals.

The Carnivore restaurant is situated 4 km (13 miles) from the city center, and was built on what was formerly Nairobi's only golf range. It opened in September 1980.The main restau rant of the Carnivore is on three levels with a outside eating area.

The first thing that greets you on arrival is very large charcoal roasting-pit where a batte of chefs attend to the meats that are spit roas ing there. Whole joints of meat are roasted o traditional Maasai swords and the chefs co

authentic African food is at the excellent shop-cum-gallery the **African Heritage Store**, which has a small restaurant attached (see chapter on Shopping). If you are intending to spend any time in Kenya, try and find a small booklet called the "Eating Out Guide". It lists over 200 restaurants, is regularly updated, and so if you have a sudde craving for Austrian food or Ethiopia or Spanish food, you will know where t find it. As far as quick snacking goes, a over Nairobi you will see roadside ve dors of charcoal-roasted corn on the co which Kenyans love.

Although out in the bush you nev

stantly turn and baste the meat. Once it is ready, the entire roast, as well as the sword, is removed from the pit, and a waiter then takes it from table to table, carving off as much of the delectable meat as the diner wants straight onto a very hot, cast-iron plate.

There are usually more than 10 meats on offer at any one time including game meat, and the menu will include some of the following : amb, pork, venison, beef, spare ribs, sausages, kidneys and crocodile. Try and go easy on the wonderful sausages and spare ribs, and save place for some of the more exotic fare on offer - crocodile, which has a lovely texture, delicious zebra and the slightly chewier hartebeest. In case you wonder about the appearance of these meats on the menu, given the country's strict rules about game hunting, rest assured. The restaurant has a license to sell these meats which come from special farms and not from the wild. Salads, sauces and side dishes accompany the succession of meats that arrive. Try the house cocktail, a Brazilian drink called "Dawa", which is delicious and deadly. If you have any space left, there is dessert.

The Carnivore which is open for lunch and dinner every day of the week is justifiably famous for its copious, excellent quality fixed price meals. It is very popular with both locals and visitors alike so make sure you reserve your table before arriving. It can serve 380 people. There is also an attached Simba Saloon which serves snacks, take-away food, drinks and daily specials and which can seat 400 people. The saloon is also the venue for a very popular disco and live music at weekends.

dress for dinner, some of the restaurants and hotels in Nairobi are formal and you will need to remember to wear your jacket and, possibly, tie, and ladies will need something smarter than their safari trousers and tee shirts. One of the most formal places in Kenya must be the **Mount Kenya Safari Club** where

Menu at a roadside café.

jackets and tie are obligatory for the excellent, very formal seven-course dinner. When you travel to such a remote, timeless place as the little island of Lamu, you do not expect a gourmet treat in store which makes eating at **Peponi's Hotel** a wonderful surprise. The seafood is excellent, especially the crabs, and the open-air lunch time grills and pizzas very good.

Kenya has one very special gastronomic treat to offer, the traditional champagne breakfast that follows a dawn balloon flight. So what if the champagne is actually only sparkling white wine when you are surrounded by the vast open plains, after an hour drifting over them in a hot-air balloon, the eggs and coffee taste absolutely wonderful.

TRAVEL TIPS

BUSINESS HOURS

From 08.00 - 17.00 from Monday to Saturday and from 08.30 - 13.00 on Saturdays. Sunday is a holiday. In Mombasa, offices often open earlier and close for a couple of hours in the middle of the day.

CLIMATE AND TEMPERATURE

Generally the country is warm and along the coast it is also very humid. You will need warm clothes for early mornings and evenings and in the hilly areas. It rains from October to December (the short rains) and from March to early June (the long rains).

CULTURE AND CUSTOMS

Kenyans are very friendly, outgoing people and very polite. Everyone shakes hands on meeting. In Muslim areas, such as Mombasa Old Town and Lamu, be circumspect – no holding hands, kissing or other demonstrative behavior in public. Also, do not drink in public in Muslim areas.

CUSTOMS

Customs formalities are minimal and you can import camera and film, temporarily, duty free. Check with your nearest Kenyan Embassy or High Commission regarding the rules for video equipment.

The import of fire-arms is prohibited.

DOMESTIC TRAVEL

There are regular inter-city buses but you should always book in advance.

Kenya Airways has domestic services.

ELECTRICITY

240 volts

FESTIVALS

The main events of the year are the Safari Rally at Easter, the autumn agricultural shows and the Maulidi festival in Lamu. For more details, see the chapter on Festivals.

GETTING THERE

By air

There are two main points of entry for the air traveler, Nairobi and Mombasa, both of which are well connected with flights to and from the rest of the world.

By sea

Fewer people sail into Mombasa these days but some cruise ships do make calls.

By road

You can drive into Kenya from Somalia, Ethiopia, Sudan, Uganda and Tanzania. There are customs check posts on the main roads.

By rail

You can arrive in Kenya by train from Tanzania, via Taveta and from Uganda via Malaba. Customs formalities must be done at both these stations.

HEALTH

All visitors require a yellow fever vaccination certificate and if you are coming from an area where cholera exists, you should bring proof of valid inoculation.

Malaria is endemic so do take the relevant precautions, remembering to start before your trip and imperatively, to continue the course after your return home. Check with your local doctor.

HOLIDAYS

January 1 - New Year's Day
Good Friday
Easter Monday
May 1 - Labor Day
June 1 - Madaraka Day

October 10 - Nyayo Day
October 20 - Kenyatta Day
December 12 - Jamhuri - Uhuru Day
December 25 - Christmas Day
December 26 - Boxing Day

MEDIA – RADIO AND TELEVISION

Both radio and television broadcast in English and Kiswahili. The Kenyans are avid newspaper readers and are very well informed about current affairs and politics. Newspapers are in English and Kiswahili.

MEDICAL SERVICES, HOSPITALS, DOCTORS, PHARMACIES

The major hospitals are listed in the Directory section. Chemists abound in Kenya and each town has a duty chemist who operates on weekends and at night.

MONEY/CURRENCY

The Kenyan shilling, though you will find many hotel prices are shown in US$. The import and export of the Kenyan shilling is prohibited.

Declare all foreign currency on arrival in the country.

ON FOOT

Only in the main cities – for obvious reasons ! No one goes for a stroll through a game park. Some game parks, though, do have escorted walks with rangers who usually carry guns, so you can safely take one of those.

PASSPORTS AND VISAS

All visitors require a valid passport. All visitors also require a visa **except** the nationals of the following countries : British subjects, Bahamas, Bangladesh, Belize, Botswana, Brunei, Canada, Cyprus, Denmark, Ethiopia, Fiji, Finland, Gambia, Germany, Ghana, Grenada, Ireland, Italy, Jamaica, Kiribati, Lesotho, Malawi, Malaysia, Maldives, Malta, Mauritius, Nauru, Norway, Papua New Guinea, Samoa, San Marino, Seychelles, Sierra Leone, Singapore, Solomon Islands, Spain, St. Lucia, St. Vincent, Swaziland, Sweden, Tanzania, Tonga, Trinidad, Tobago, Turkey, Tuvalu, Uganda, Uruguay, Vanuatu, Zambia, Zimbabwe.

However, since visa requirements do change, always double-check with the Kenyan Embassy or High Commission in your own country.

PHOTOGRAPHY

Kenya is the photographer's paradise with all that wildlife posing beautifully next to your jeep. You will need a long lens, preferably a tripod or some form of support, and lots of patience. You have to wait for the animals to come to you since vice versa is out of the question. Take much more film than you think you are going to use since you will quickly become shutter-happy and there will also be a certain wastage for animals do not always make perfect, immobile models. The best shooting light is early in the morning and just before sunset, when the game is also the most active.

Do not try photographing women in Lamu – the local people can get pretty aggressive if you do.

Never take pictures of the Maasai or other tribal people without permission. Ask your driver for his opinion for many Kenyans do not like being photographed and in the more "touristy" areas, they may expect to be paid for the picture. Fix the rate before starting to shoot.

POSTAL SERVICES

Post offices are numerous and you can also post letters from most major hotels. Post restante is free.

PRIVATE TRANSPORT

You can easily hire a car either on a self-drive basis or with a driver. If you intend going anywhere off the beaten track, take a 4WD and make sure you have a spare wheel, tool kit and ample supplies of food, water and petrol. Before heading off to really remote areas like the north and the northeast of the country, seek local advice : security is sometimes a problem and you are often required to drive in a convoy.

PUBLIC TRANSPORT – TRAIN, BUS, TAXI

The main train services link up Nairobi to Mombasa, and Nairobi with Kisumu, and all the stations en route.

The main means of local transport in Nairobi and Mombasa is the *matatu,* which are privately owned brightly painted mini buses, packed like sardine cans and driven by speed freaks. Best avoided unless you really want the local color.

Taxis are easily found in the towns but always fix the price before you set off.

TELEPHONE

Very good telephone links all over the country even in remote lodges and islands. To simplify life for visitors, most hotel chains have centralized reservations offices in Nairobi.

TIME ZONES

GMT + 3 hours

TIPPING

A service charge is usually included in the price in the better hotels and restaurants.

TOURS

Any of the many travel agents in Nairobi and Mombasa will be able to arrange short local sightseeing tours or longer safari trips.

WEIGHTS AND MEASURES

The metric system is used in Kenya.

WHAT TO WEAR

Comfortable cotton clothes for safari though the whole panoply of safari jackets and solar "topis" can be avoided. Sunhat and sunglasses. Warm jacket and sweater for the early morning game drives – it can be chilly at dawn. If you are intending to do any trekking or climbing, then you will need lots of warm clothes, strong boots or shoes, and wet-weather protective clothing. When selecting beach wear for Mombasa, do remember that Mombasa and Lamu are Muslim areas, so skimpy clothes should be avoided. Smart clothes are not really required on safari, however, do pack a jacket and tie if you intend going to the very formal Mount Kenya Safari Club.

DIRECTORY

ACCOMMODATION

Hotel rates vary according to the season so there may well be slight variations from these rates. Most hotels work on the "Bed & Breakfast" system though on safari the rates given are for full board. In the middle of Maasai Mara, there is nowhere else to eat except at your lodge ! However, some lodges do offer half board, so check first if you feel that you are not going to require three hearty meals a day.

The rates given below are, as far as possible, accurate as at 15 December 1993. Unless otherwise stated, they are for a standard double room usually on a B & B (bed and breakfast) basis and are in US$. Where the rates are quoted in Kenyan shillings, this is shown as Ksh.

Other than Nairobi and Mombasa where there are "walk in" clients, most of the safari lodges handle their reservations either through their own Nairobi booking office, or, more usually, through travel agents.

THE ABERDARES

The Aberdare Country Club
Tel: Nyeri 0171-55620
Reservations also via Lonrho Hotels Nairobi office
Tel: 216940
Twin room, full board US$ 102

The Ark
Tel: Nyeri 0171-55620
Reservations also via Lonrho Hotels Nairobi office
Tel: 216940
Twin room, full board US$ 122, excluding national park fees

Treetops
Reservations via Block Hotels Nairobi
Tel: 335807
Full board, double room, US$ 100. This does not include the national park entrance fees.

AMBOSELI

Amboseli Serena Lodge
Tel: Amboseli 18
Twin, Full Board US$ 150
Reservations via Serena Hotels Nairobi office
Tel: 711077

LAKE BARINGO

Lake Baringo Club
Reservations via Block Hotels Nairobi
Tel: 335807
Standard double half board US$ 62

LAKE NAIVASHA

Lake Naivasha Country Club
Reservations via Block Hotels Nairobi
Tel: 335807
Standard double half board US$ 68

LAMU ISLAND

Lamu Village

Petley's Inn
Kenyatta Road
Tel: 0121-48107
Double room, B & B Ksh 1500.00

Shela Village

The Island Hotel
P.O.Box 179
Tel: 0121-3290
Double room, B & B US$ 62

Kijani House
P.O.Box 266
Tel: 0121-33374/33235
Fax: 0121-33237
Single B & B US$ 65, full board US$ 90
The hotel is closed in May and June

Peponi Hotel
P.O.Box 24
Tel: 0121-33029
Fax: 0121-33154
Single B & B US$ 130, full board US$ 150
The hotel is closed in May and June

MAASAI MARA

Keekorok
Reservations via Block Hotels Nairobi
Tel: 335807
Twin room, full board US$ 82
Twin tent, full board US$ 70

Kichwa Tembo Luxury Tented Camp
Reservations via Windsor Ho-tels Nairobi
Tel: 219784, 217497/9, 336805
Double tent, full board, three game drives & transfer from air-strip US$ 242

Mara Safari Club
Reservations via Lonrho Hotels Nairobi office
Tel: 216940
Twin room, full board and three game drives per day US$ 217

Mara Serena Lodge
Twin, Full Board US$ 150
Reservations via Serena Hotels Nairobi office
Tel: 711077

Sarova Mara
Double room, full board
US$ 170
Reservations via Sarova Hotels Nairobi, Central Reservations office
Tel: 333248/49/50/51

Siana Springs Luxury Tented Camp
Reservations via Windsor Ho-tels Nairobi
Tel: 219784, 217497/9, 336805
Double tent, full board, three game drives & transfer from air-strip US$ 242

MOMBASA
Africana Sea Lodge,
Diani Beach, P.O.Box 84616
Tel: 0127-2622
Reservations also possible through Alliance Hotels Nairobi office
Tel: 337501/8, 221049, 330357
Twin room, B & B US$ 70

Golden Beach Hotel
Reservations via African Tours & Hotels, Nairobi office
Tel: 336858
Twin room, half board US$ 142

The Indian Ocean Beach Club
Diani
Reservations via Block Hotels Nairobi
Tel: 335807
Deluxe club double B & B
US$ 140

Jadini Beach Hotel
Diani Beach, P.O.Box 84616
Tel : 0127-2121/5, 2622
Reservations also possible through Alliance Hotels Nairobi office
Tel: 337501/8, 221049, 330357
Twin room, B & B US$ 75

Mombasa Beach Hotel
Reservations via African Tours & Hotels, Nairobi office
Tel: 336858
Twin room, half board US$ 142

Nyali Beach Hotel
Reservations via Block Hotels Nairobi
Tel: 335807
Standard double B & B US$ 86

Safari Beach Hotel
Diani Beach, P.O.Box 90690
Tel: 0127-2726
Reservations also possible through Alliance Hotels Nairobi office
Tel: 337501/8, 221049, 330357
Twin room, B & B US$ 90

Serena Beach Hotel
P.O.Box 90352
Tel: 11-485721/2/3/4
Standard double room, B & B
US$ 100

Tradewinds Hotel
Diani Beach
Tel: 2016, 2116
Reservations via African Tours & Hotels, Nairobi office
Tel: 336858
Twin room, full board US$ 120

Whitesands
P.O.Box 90173
Tel: 011-485926/7/8/9, 485763
Double room, half board Ksh 5,550.00
Reservations also possible via Sarova Hotels Nairobi, Central Reservations office
Tel: 333248/49/50/51

NAIROBI
Fairview Hotel
Bishops Road
Tel: 723211
Single room with buffet break-fast from US$ 36

Hotel Ambassadeur
P.O. Box 30399
Tel : 336803
Double room US$ 45
Reservations also possible via Sarova Hotels Nairobi, Central Reservations office
Tel: 333248/49/50/51

Jacaranda Hotel
Reservations via Block Hotels Nairobi
Tel: 335807
Standard double B & B US$ 69

Nairobi Hilton
All reservations through Nairobi office
Tel: 334000
Double room US$ 130 - 180

Nairobi Serena Hotel
P.O.Box 46302
Tel: 725111
Twin room US$ 146

New Stanley Hotel
P.O.Box 30680
Tel: 333233/4/5/6, 217294/5
Double room Ksh 3,370.00
Reservations also possible via Sarova Hotels Nairobi, Central Reservations office
Tel: 333248/49/50/51

The Norfolk Hotel
P.O.Box 40064
Tel : 335422
Twin room US$ 175

Reservations via Lonrho Hotels Nairobi office
Tel: 216940

Panafric Hotel
Kenyatta Avenue, P.O. Box 30486
Tel: 720822
Double room B & B Ksh 2,400.00
Reservations also possible via Sarova Hotels Nairobi, Central Reservations office
Tel: 333248/49/50/51

Safari Park Hotel
P.O.Box 45038
Tel: 802493
Double room US$ 130

The Windsor Golf & Country Club
Reservations via Windsor Hotels Nairobi
Tel: 219784, 217497/9, 336805
Twin room US$ 142

NAKURU
Sarova Lion Hill
Reservations via Sarova Hotels Nairobi, Central Reservations office
Tel: 333248/49/50/51
Double room Ksh 4,350.00

Sundowner Lodge
P.O.Box 561
Tel: 037-211204/214216
Double B & B US$ 33

NANYUKI
Mount Kenya Safari Club
Twin room, full board US$ 244
Reservations via Lonrho Hotels Nairobi office
Tel: 216940

Mountain Rock Hotel
P.O.Box 333
Nanyuki
Tel: 0176-62625, 62098/9
Standard room, double occupancy B & B Ksh 700.00

Ol Pejeta
Reservations also via Lonrho Hotels Nairobi office
Tel: 216940
Twin room, full board, inclusive of reserve fees US$ 100

Sweetwaters Tented Camp
P.O.Box 763, Nanyuki
Tel: 55620
Reservations also via Lonrho Hotels Nairobi office
Tel: 216940
Twin tent, full board, inclusive of reserve fees US$ 90

NARO MORU
Naro Moru River Lodge
P.O.Box 18
Naro Moru
Tel: 0176-62023
Reservations also possible through Alliance Hotels Nairobi office
Tel: 337501/8, 221049, 330357

NYERI
Outspan
Reservations via Block Hotels Nairobi
Tel: 335807
Standard twin room B & B US$ 58

RUSINGA ISLAND
Rusinga Island Fishing Club
Reservations via Lonrho Hotels Nairobi office
Tel: 216940
Overnight excursion: return flight Mara-Rusinga-Mara, overnight, full board, morning's fishing, beer with lunch and wine with dinner, per person US$ 400

SAMBURU
Buffalo Springs Lodge
Reservations via African Tours & Hotels, Nairobi office
Tel: 336858
Twin room, half board US$ 114

Larsens
Reservations via Block Hotels Nairobi
Tel: 335807
Twin tent full board US$ 110

Samburu Game Lodge
Reservations via Block Hotels Nairobi
Tel: 335807
Double, full board US$ 92

Samburu Serena Lodge
Twin, Full Board US$ 120
Reservations via Serena Hotel Nairobi office
Tel: 711077

Sarova Shaba
Reservations via Sarova Hotel Nairobi, Central Reservation office
Tel: 333248/49/50/51
Double room, full board US$ 160

SHIMBA HILLS
Shimba
Reservations via Block Hotel Nairobi
Tel: 335807
Standard double B & B US$ 8

TAITA HILLS
Hilton Safari Camp
All reservations through Nairol office
Tel: 334000
Double room US$ 286

Hilton Salt Lick Safari Lodge
All reservations through Nairol office
Tel: 334000
Twin, full board US$ 286

Hilton Taita Hills Safari Lodge
All reservations through Nairol office
Tel: 334000
Twin, full board US$ 224.50

TSAVO
Kilaguni Lodge
Reservations via African Tou & Hotels, Nairobi office

el: 336858
win room, full board US$ 148

/oi Safari Lodge
Reservations via African Tours
& Hotels, Nairobi office
el: 336858
win room, full board US$ 148

AIRLINES

NAIROBI

AEROFLOT
Corner House
P.O. Box 44375
Mama Ngina Street
el: 220746.

AIR BOTSWANA
Hilton Hotel
Mama Ngina Street
el: 33 16 48

AIR CANADA
onrho House
tandard Street
.O. Box 30601
el: 218776/7

IR FRANCE
nternational House, 5th floor
Mama Ngina Street
el: 216954

IR INDIA
evan Bharati House
arambee Avenue
O. Box 43006
el: 334788/340925

IR MADAGASCAR
ilton House
ama Ngina Street
el: 225286/226494

IR MALAWI
ilton Hotel Arcade
ama Ngina Street
el: 33 36 83

IR MAURITIUS
nion Towers
oi Avenue
O. Box 45270
el: 221006

AIR TANZANIA
Chester House
Koinange Street
Tel: 336224/33637

AIR ZAIRE
Arrow Motors House
Monrovia Street
Tel: 222271

AIR ZIMBABWE
Chester House
Koinange Street
P.O. Box 41127
Tel: 339522

ALITALIA
Hilton
Mama Ngina Street
P.O. Box 72651
Tel: 224361-3

AMERICAN AIRLINES
I P S Building
Executive Towers
Kimathi Street
Tel: 23 04 45/6

BRITISH AIRWAYS
International House
Mama Ngina Street
Tel: 334400/822555

CAMEROON AIRLINES
Rehani House
Kenyatta Avenue
Tel: 337788/224743

CATHAY PACIFIC
Lonrho House
Standard Street
Tel : 23 02 35/6

EGYPTAIR
Hilton Hotel
Tel: 226821-2

EL AL (ISRAEL AIRLINES)
Sweepstake House
Mama Ngina Street
Tel: 228123/330935

ETHIOPIAN AIRLINES
Anniversary Towers
University Way
Tel: 330837/214519

GULF AIR
P.O.Box 44417
Tel: 822399

IBERIA
Hilton Hotel
Mama Ngina Street
Tel: 33 16 48/33 86 58

JAPAN AIRLINES
International House
Mama Ngina Street
Tel: 220591

KLM
Fedha Towers
Tel: 332673/4/7

KENYA AIRWAYS
P.O. Box 19002
Tel: 229291

LUFTHANSA
P.O. Box 30320
Tel: 335819/335846

NIGERIA AIRWAYS
Hilton Hotel
Tel: 336555

OLYMPIC AIRWAYS
Hilton Hotel
Tel: 338026

PIA
ICEA Building
Kenyatta Avenue
Tel: 219176/333900-1

ROYAL SWAZI
Reinsurance Plaza
Taifa Road
P.O. Box 58716
Tel: 210670

SABENA
International House
Mama Ngina Street
Tel: 222185/332608

SAUDIA
Anniversary Towers
University Way
Tel: 334270/335612

SOUTH AFRICAN AIRWAYS
Lonrho House
Standard Street
Tel : 22 96 63/22 74 86-8

SUDAN AIRWAYS
UTC Building
General Kago Street
Tel: 225129/221326

SWISSAIR
Corner House
Kimathi Street
Tel: 340231

UGANDA AIRLINES
Uganda House
Kenyatta Avenue
P.O. Box 59732
Tel: 221354/228668

VARIG
Lonrho House
Standard Street
Tel: 220961/337097

ZAMBIA AIRWAYS
Lonrho House
Kaunda Street
P.O. Box 42479
Tel: 332052/221007

BANKS

There are 24-hour banking facilities at Kenya's two international airports at Nairobi and Mombasa.

Standard banking hours are 09.00 to 14.00 Monday to Friday with some banks open for two hours on Saturday mornings.

In Mombasa, the banking hours are 09.00 to 15.30 Monday to Friday and from 09.00 to 11.30 on Saturday mornings.

CINEMAS

There are cinemas in Nairobi and Mombasa, often showing English language films. Check the local papers for times.

FOREIGN DIPLOMATIC MISSIONS

MOMBASA

Denmark
P.O. Box 99543
Tel: 316051

Finland
P.O. Box 99543
Tel: 20501/20229

France
P.O. Box 90262
Tel: 21141/25380

Germany
P.O. Box 90262
Tel: 24938/39

India
P.O. Box 90614
Tel: 24433/311051

Italy
P.O. Box 84958
Tel: 311532/26955

Netherlands
P.O. Box 90230
Tel: 311434-5

Norway
P.O. Box 83058
Tel: 485494/471771

Switzerland
P.O. Box 85722
Tel: 316684-5

United States of America
P.O. Box 88079
Tel: 31510

NAIROBI

Algeria
Matungulu House
North Mamlaka Road
Tel: 724663

Argentina
No address given
Tel: 582791

Australia
Development House
Moi Avenue
P.O. box 30360
Tel: 334666/334672

Austria
City House
Wabera Street
P.O. Box 30560
Tel: 228281-2

Bangladesh High Commission
Maisonette no. 5
Rose Avenue
Tel: 729012

Belgium
Limuru Road
Muthaiga
Tel : 74 15 64

Brazil
Jeevan Bharati Building
Harambee Avenue
Tel: 337722-3

British High Commission
Bruce House
Standard Street
Tel: 335944

Bulgaria
P.O. Box 44778
Tel: 561200/567308

Burundi
Development House
Moi Avenue
Tel: 728340

Canadian High Commission
Comcraft House
Haile Selassie Avenue
Tel: 214804

Chile
International House
Mama Ngina Street
Tel: 337987/337934

:mbassy of the People's Republic of China
Voodlands Road
Tel: 722559

Colombia
'.O. Box 48494
Tel: 765927

Consulate General of Costa Rica
No address given
Tel : 88 26 46

Cyprus High Commission
:agle House
Kimathi Street
'.O. Box 30739
Tel: 220881

Czech Republic
mbassy House
Coronation Avenue
Tel : 22 34 47

Denmark
HFCK Building
Corner Kenyatta Avenue
'.O. Box 40412
el: 331088/331098

Djibouti
.O. Box 59528
el: 521774

gypt
Harambee Plaza
Haile Selassie Avenue
el: 211560

thiopia
tate House Avenue
el: 722091

inland
nternational House, 2nd floor
Mama Ngina Street
el: 336717/334777-8

rance
mbassy House, 2nd floor
arambee Avenue
el: 339783-4

Gabon
Othaya Road
Lavington
P.O. Box 42551
Tel: 569429

Federal Republic of Germany
Embassy House
Harambee Avenue
Tel: 221316

Greece
IPS Building
Kimathi Street
Tel: 340722/340744

Holy See (The Vatican)
Mnyani Road
P.O. Box 14326
Tel: 48468/48583/48370

Hungary
Agip House
Haile Selassie Avenue
Tel : 22 05 37

Consulate General of Iceland
No address given
Tel : 52 14 87

India
Jeevan Bharati Building
Harambee Avenue
P.O. Box 30074
Tel: 24500/22566-7

Indonesia
Utalii House
Uhuru Highway
Tel: 340721

Embassy of Iran
Anniversary Tower
University Way
Tel : 21 43 14

Iraq
P.O. Box 49213
Tel: 580262

Ireland
Maendeleo House
Monrovia Street
P.O. Box 30659
Tel: 26771-4

Consulate of Ireland
Westlands
Tel : 44 23 38

Embassy of Israel
Bishops Road
Tel : 72 40 21/22

Embassy of Italy
International Life House
Mama Ngina Street
Tel : 22 78 43

Japan
ICEA Building
Kenyatta Avenue
Tel: 332955-9

Korea (South)
Kencom House
Moi Avenue
Tel: 333581-3

Kuwait
No address given
Tel: 760893

Lebanon
Maendeleo House
Monrovia Street
P.O. Box 55303
Tel: 23708

Lesotho
International House, 4th floor
Mama Ngina Street
Tel: 224876

Liberia
Bruce House
Standard Street
P.O. Box 30546
Tel: 22604-5

Libya
Jamhiriya House
Loita Street
P.O. Box 60149
Tel: 29884/29857

Luxembourg
International House

Mama Ngina Street
P.O. Box 30610
Tel: 26183/24318

Madagascar
Koinange Street
P.O. Box 30793
Tel: 26494

Malawi
Bruce House, 6th floor
Standard Street
Tel: 221174

Malaysia
Eagle House
Kimathi Street
P.O. Box 48916
Tel: 29724-5

Mauritius
Union Towers
P.O. Box 45270
Tel: 330215

Mexico
Kibagare Way
Loresho Ridge
P.O. Box 41139
Tel: 582850/582579

Morocco
Diamond Trust Building
Moi Avenue
P.O. Box 61098
Tel: 222361/222264

Embassy of Mozambique
No address given
Tel : 58 18 57

Netherlands
P.O. Box 41537
Tel: 581125

Nigeria
Lenana Road
Hurlingham
Tel: 564116

Norway
Rehani House, 7th floor
Koinange Street
Tel: 22933

Oman
Matundu Road
Muthaiga
P.O. Box 43458
Tel: 65674/93/94

Peru
Enterprise Road
P.O. Box 59446
Tel: 554317/555744

Philippines
State House Road
P.O. Box 47941
Tel: 725897/721791

Poland
Ngong Road
Tel: 727701

Portugal
Reinsurance Plaza
Taifa Road
Tel: 337862

Romania
Norfolk Towers
Kijabe Street
P.O. Box 48412
Tel: 27515

Russia
Lenana Road
Tel : 72 87 00

Rwanda
International House, 12th floor,
Mama Ngina Street
Tel : 33 14 12

Saudi Arabia
Muthaiga Road
P.O. Box 58297
Tel: 762781-4

Somalia
International House
Mama Ngina Street
P.O. Box 30769
Tel: 224301/580165

Spain
Bruce House
Standard Street
P.O. Box 45503
Tel: 336330/335711/222150

Sri Lanka
No address given
Tel: 27577-78/726784

Sudan
Minet Building
Mamlaka Road
Tel: 720883/720889/53

Swaziland
International House, 7th floor
Mama Ngina Street
P.O. Box 41887
Tel: 227736

Sweden
International House
Westlands
Tel: 449072

Switzerland
International House
Mama Ngina Street
P.O. Box 30752
Tel: 28735-6

Tanzania
Continental House, 4th floor
Uhuru Highway
P.O. Box 47790
Tel: 331150

Thailand
Rose Avenue
P.O. Box 58349
Tel: 714276

Uganda
2nd floor, Baring Arcade
Kenyatta Avenue
Tel: 330899

United States of America
Moi Avenue
P.O. Box 30137
Tel: 441909

Venezuela
International House, 3rd floor
Mama Ngina Street
Tel: 332300/340167/34

Yemen (People's Democratic Republic)
No address given
Tel: 564379/564517

Yugoslavia
State House Road
P.O. Box 30504
Tel: 720670/723392

Zaire
Electricity House, 12th floor
Harambee Avenue
Tel: 229771-2/334539

High Commission of the Republic of Zambia
Nyerere Road
Tel: 718494

Zimbabwe
Minet ICDC House
Mamlaka Road
P.O. Box 30806
Tel: 721045/49/71

HOSPITALS

Aga Khan Hospital
Corner of 3rd Parklands Avenue
and Limuru Road
Nairobi
Tel: 742531

Aga Khan Hospital
Vanga Road
Mombasa
Tel: 312953

Nairobi Hospital
Arwings Kodhek Road
Tel: 722160 - 6

In an emergency, dial 999

KENYA TOURIST OFFICES

FRANCE
? Rue Volney
Paris 75002
Tel: 260-66-88

GERMANY
000 Frankfurt
A Main 1
Hosch-Strasse 53
Tel: 282551/282552

HONG KONG
1309 Liu Chong Hing
Bank Building
24 Des Voeux Road
Central
P.O. Box 5280
Tel: 236053-4

JAPAN
Yurakucho Building
1-10 Yurakucho Chome
Chiyoda-ku
Tokyo
Tel: 2143595

SWEDEN
Birger Jarlsgatan 37
2TR
P.O. Box 7692
Stockholm 11145
Tel: 218300/04/09

SWITZERLAND
Bleicherweg 30
P.O. Box 770
8039 Zurich
Tel: 01-202-22-43/44/46

UNITED KINGDOM
25/25 New Bond Street
London W14 9HD
Tel: 071-355-3144

UNITED STATES OF AMERICA
424 Madison Avenue
New York
NY 10017
Tel: 486 1300

Suite 111-12 Doheny Plaza
9100 Wiltshire Boulevard
Beverly Hills
California 90121
Tel: 274 6635

KENYAN MISSIONS ABROAD

AUSTRALIA
P.O. Box 1990
Canberra
ACT 2600
Tel: 474788

BELGIUM
1-5 Avenue de la Joyeuse Entrée
1040 Brussels
Tel: 2303065/2303100

CANADA
Gillin Building
141 Laurier Avenue
West Ottawa
Ontario KIP 5J3
Tel: 613563

CHINA
No. 4 Xi Liu Jie
San Li Tun
Beijing
Tel: 523381

ETHIOPIA
P.O. Box 3301
Addis Ababa
Tel: 180033/1810136

EGYPT
20 Boulos Hanna Street
Dokki
P.O. Box 362
Cairo
Tel: 704455-6

FRANCE
3 Rue Cimaros
75016 Paris
Tel: 45 53 35 00

FEDERL REPUBLIC OF GERMANY
Villichgasse 17
5300 Bonn-Bad
Godesberg 2
Micael Plaza
Tel: 353066/356041

INDIA
66 Vasant Marg
Vasant Vihar
New Delhi
Tel: 672280/672053

ITALY
Via Del Circo Massimo
Rome 00153
Tel: 5781192/5780995

JAPAN
24-20 Nishi-Azobu
3 Chome, Minato Ku
Tokyo 794006

THE NETHERLANDS
The Hague
Tel: 636175

NIGERIA
52 Queen's Drive
Ikiyi
P.O. Box 6464
Lagos
Tel: 682768/685531

PAKISTAN
8 Street 88
P.O. Box 2097
Islamabad
Tel: 823819

RWANDA
P.O. Box 1215
Kigali
Tel: 2774

SAUDI ARABIA
Baladia Street
P.O. Box 6347
Jeddah
Tel: 6656718/6601885

SOMALIA
P.O. Box 618
Mogadishu
Tel: 80857/80858

SUDAN
Opposite Dolly Hotel
P.O. Box 8242
Khartoum
Tel: 940386

SWEDEN
2TR Birger
Jarilsgatan 37
71145
Stockholm
Tel: 218399/04/09

SWITZERLAND
80 Rue de Lausanne
1202 Geneva
Tel: 327272/327038

TANZANIA
NIC Investment House
Samora Avenue
P.O. Box 5231
Dar-es-Salaam
Tel: 31526

UGANDA
60 Kira Road
P.O. Box 5220
Kampala
Tel: 231861/233146

UNITED ARAB EMIRATES
P.O. Box 3854
Abu Dhabi
Tel: 36630

UNITED KINGDOM
45 Portland Place
London WIN 4AS
Tel: 071-362371-5

UNION OF SOVIET SOCIALIST REPUBLICS
Bolshyaya Ordinka
Dom 70
Moscow
Tel: 2373462/2374702

UNITED STATES OF AMERICA
2249R Street NW
Washington DC 20008
Tel: 440215

UNITED STATES OF AMERICA
866 United Nations Plaza
New York 10017
Tel: 4214740

ZAIRE
5002 Avenue de 1 Ouganda
Zone de Gombe
P.O. Box 9667
Kinshasa
Tel: 30117

ZAMBIA
5207 United Nations Avenue
P.O. Box 50298
Lusaka
Tel: 212531/212361

ZIMBABWE
5 Park Lane
P.O. Box 4069
Harare
Tel: 790847

LIBRARIES

As well as the international libraries and cultural centers, such as the Alliance Française, the British Council, the Goethe Institute, etc., the main Kenyan libraries are :

Kenya National Archives
Moi Avenue
Nairobi
Tel: 28959, 28020

Kenya National Library Service
Ngong Road
Nairobi
Tel: 27871, 29186

National Library Service
Moi Avenue
Mombasa
Tel: 26380

MacMillan Library
Nairobi

MUSEUMS

Nairobi Museum
The Karen Blixen House
Fort Jesus, Mombasa
Lamu Museum
Kitale Museum
Meru Museum
Kisumu Museum
There are also sites and monuments operated by the National Museums of Kenya : Gede, Jumba la Mtwana, Siyu, Olorgesailie, Nakuru, Koobi Fora, and Maralal.
There is also the charming Railway Museum in Nairobi.

NIGHTSPOTS

Nightclubs and discotheques go rapidly in and out of fashion, so check in the papers and ask at your hotel since many Nairobi and Mombasa hotels have their own discos and bars.

PLACES OF WORSHIP

There are Christian churches of all denominations, mosques and Hindu temples all over the country, as well as some synagogues. Check the local paper for the times of services.

POST OFFICE

Post offices can be found in virtually every village.

TRAVEL AGENTS

Many visitors to Kenya will arrive with their safari already arranged but if you have not prebooked it from overseas, arranging it in Nairobi is the easiest thing in the world. There are literally dozens of travel agents, all highly efficient and geared totally to the safari business. You can walk into just about any travel agency, ask them to arrange a safari and return in a few hours to find it all fixed up for you.

Most travel agencies are in the town center, along Mama Ngina Street and Kimathi Street, very near the Hilton Hotel. Just avoid like the plague all the touts hanging around offering you cheap safaris.

PHOTO CREDITS

Rahul Akerker : 331
Biofoto/Schack Nielsen : 227 (top)
Biofoto/ Nikolaj Saharff : 227 (bottom)
Lee Foster : x, xi, Backcover (top right), xvi, 25, 70, 96, 124, 152/153, 158, 186, 188, 191 (bottom), 193, 217 (bottom), 222/223, 229 (bottom), 257 (top & bottom), 266 (bottom), 296, 349, 354
Cherie Glaser : Facing Travel Tip, 8/9, 24, 64, 73, 74 (left top & bottom), 86, 87, 92, 94/95, 100 (top), 101, 128 (top), 139 (top), 163 (top), 166, 246, 250, 251 (bottom), 339 (top & bottom), 352/353
Odyssey/Robert Frerck : 142
Odyssey/Wendy Stone : 40, 44/45, 52/53, 99, 111, 120, 129 (top), 134, 149, 162, 170/171, 192/193, 204, 208/209, 214/215, 217 (top), 218/219, 253, 260, 304/305, 320, 328/329, 330, 334/335, 336
Christine Pemberton : xii, xiii, 2/3, 10, 14, 16/17, 17, 18, 26, 31, 38, 39 (bottom), 41, 42/43, 47, 48, 54, 54/55, 56, 57, 63, 66, 74 (left), 75, 79, 85, 92/93, 112/113, 114, 116/117, 118, 126, 132/133, 138, 139 (bottom), 140, 141, 143, 144, 146, 152, 154/155, 155, 156, 157, 159, 160, 169, 174, 177, 180/181, 181, 184, 185 (top), 187 (bottom), 191 (top), 195, 196, 197 (bottom), 201, 207, 209, 210/211, 216, 220, 221, 224/225, 229 (top), 233, 238, 239, 241, 244, 245 (top & bottom), 247, 252, 254/255, 258, 263, 268, 270, 271, 272, 274/275, 275, 276, 277, 278, 279, 280, 282/283, 285 (top & bottom), 286, 288, 289, 290/291, 293, 294, 295
Ann Purcell : Backcover (bottom), 4, 34/35, 50, 58, 72, 83, 91, 98, 102/103, 108, 119 (top & bottom), 127, 129 (bottom), Backend, 167, 172, 173 (bottom), 182/183, 187 (top), 194, 197 (top), 198, 199, 230, 240/241, 251 (top), 343
Carl Purcell : xiv, xv (top & bottom), Frontend, Backcover (top left), 5, 6, 13, 19, 20, 22/23, 28, 29, 36, 39 (top), 46, 51, 60, 67, 78, 80/81, 90, 100 (bottom), 103, 104, 105, 106, 107, 110, 122, 123, 128 (bottom), 131 (top & bottom), 136, 137, 145, 161, 163 (bottom), 164, 168, 173 (top), 175, 176/177, 185 (bottom), 200, 203, 212, 213, 226, 234/235, 236/237, 240, 248, 256, 259 (top & bottom), 264, 265, 267, 269, 322, 351
Morten Strange : 266 (top)

INDEX

M

N

O